A WESTERN WORLD

"ALL DOGS ARE DOGS" DESIGNED BY HANNAH K. LEE

PUBLISHED BY KOYAMA PRESS
KOYAMAPRESS.COM

FIRST EDITION: MAY 2018

ISBN: 978-1-927668-48-1

PRINTED IN CHINA

KOYAMA PRESS GRATEFULLY ACKNOWLEDGES THE CANADA COUNCIL FOR THE ARTS AND ONTARIO ARTS COUNCIL FOR THEIR SUPPORT OF OUR PUBLISHING PROGRAM.

THE AUTHOR ADDITIONALLY ACKNOWLEDGES THE CANADA COUNCIL FOR THE ARTS FOR THEIR ASSISTANCE WITH THIS BOOK.

Canada Council for the Arts Conseil des arts du Canada

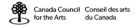

A WESTERN WORLD

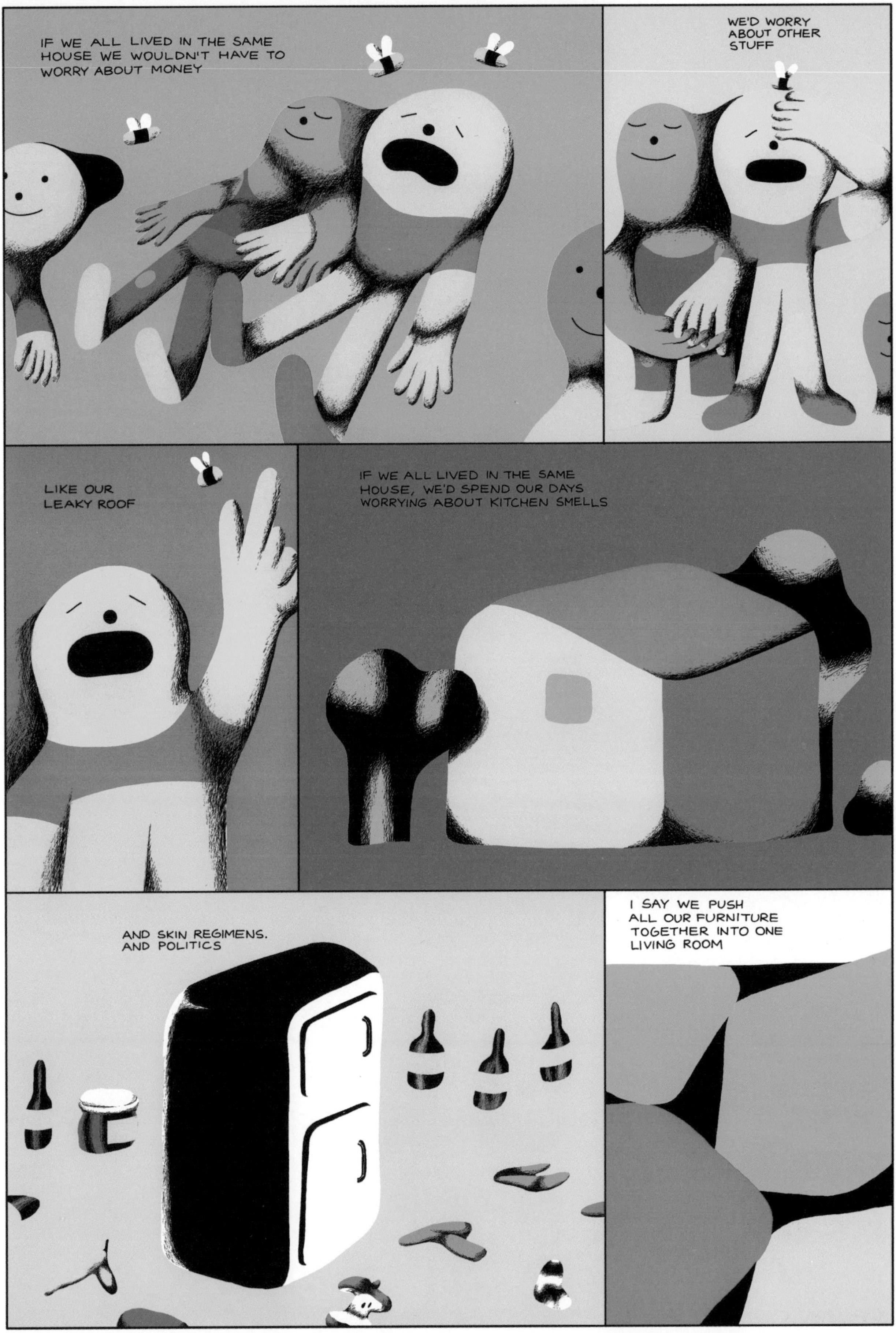
IF WE ALL LIVED IN THE SAME HOUSE WE WOULDN'T HAVE TO WORRY ABOUT MONEY
WE'D WORRY ABOUT OTHER STUFF
LIKE OUR LEAKY ROOF
IF WE ALL LIVED IN THE SAME HOUSE, WE'D SPEND OUR DAYS WORRYING ABOUT KITCHEN SMELLS
AND SKIN REGIMENS. AND POLITICS
I SAY WE PUSH ALL OUR FURNITURE TOGETHER INTO ONE LIVING ROOM

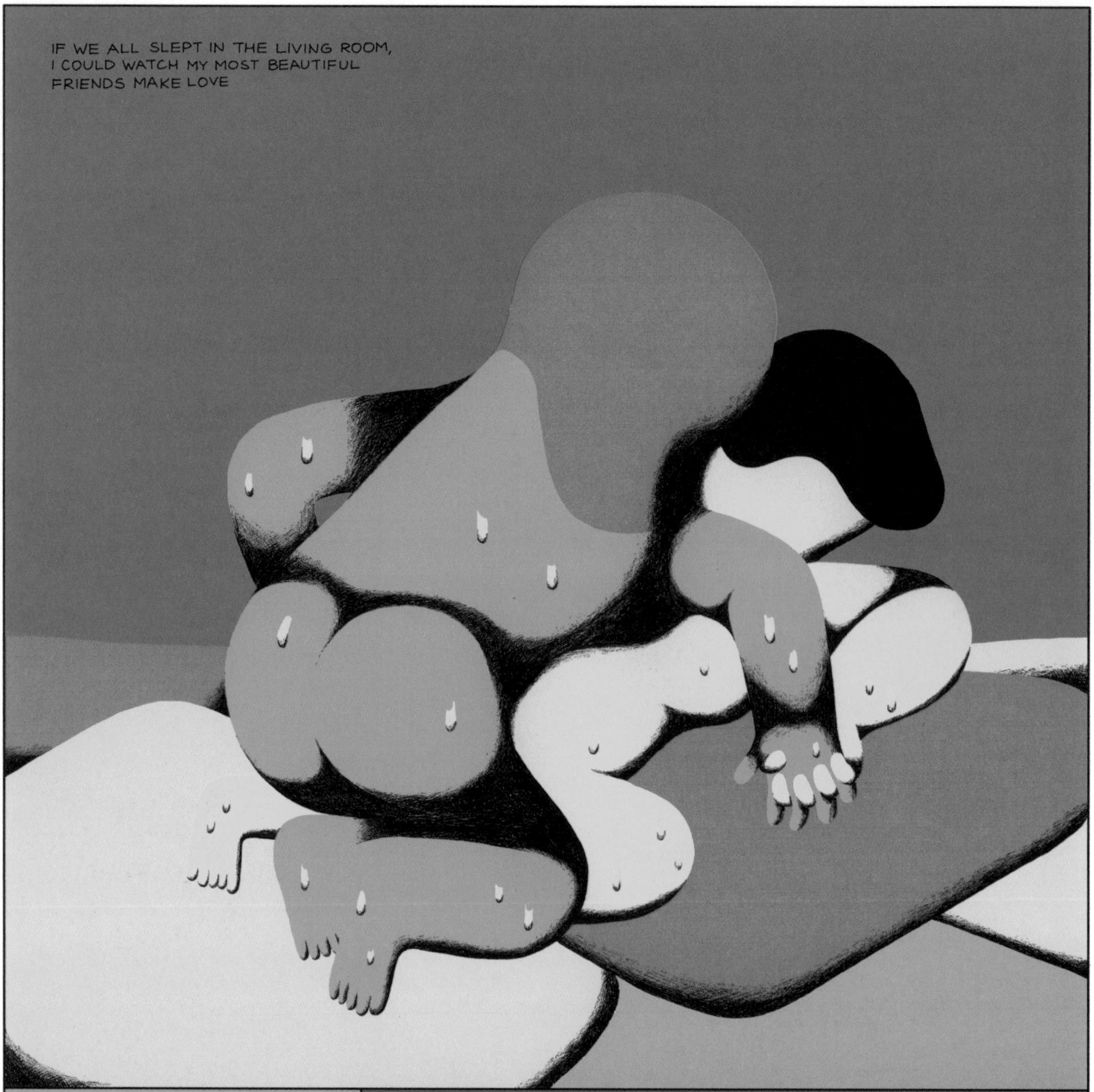
IF WE ALL SLEPT IN THE LIVING ROOM,
I COULD WATCH MY MOST BEAUTIFUL
FRIENDS MAKE LOVE

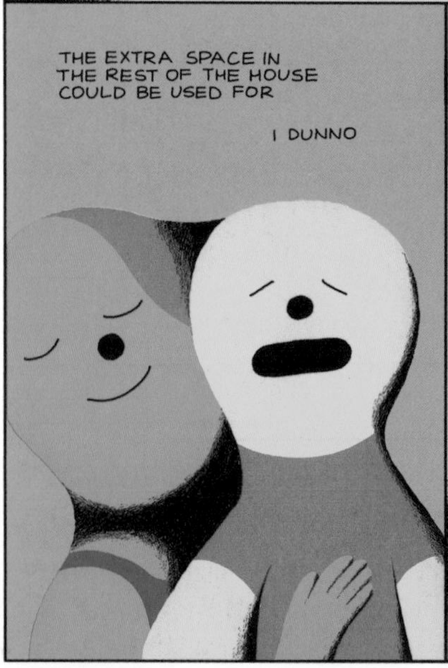
THE EXTRA SPACE IN
THE REST OF THE HOUSE
COULD BE USED FOR
I DUNNO

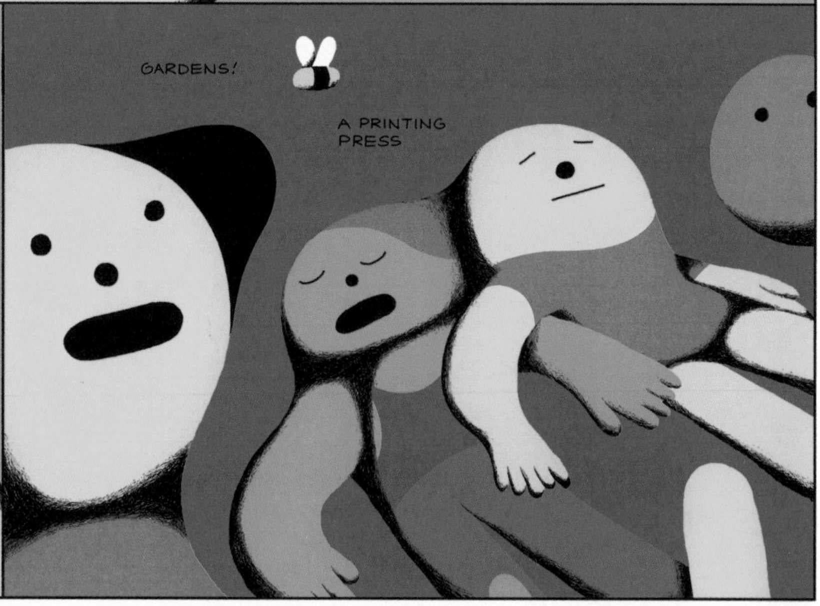
GARDENS!
A PRINTING
PRESS

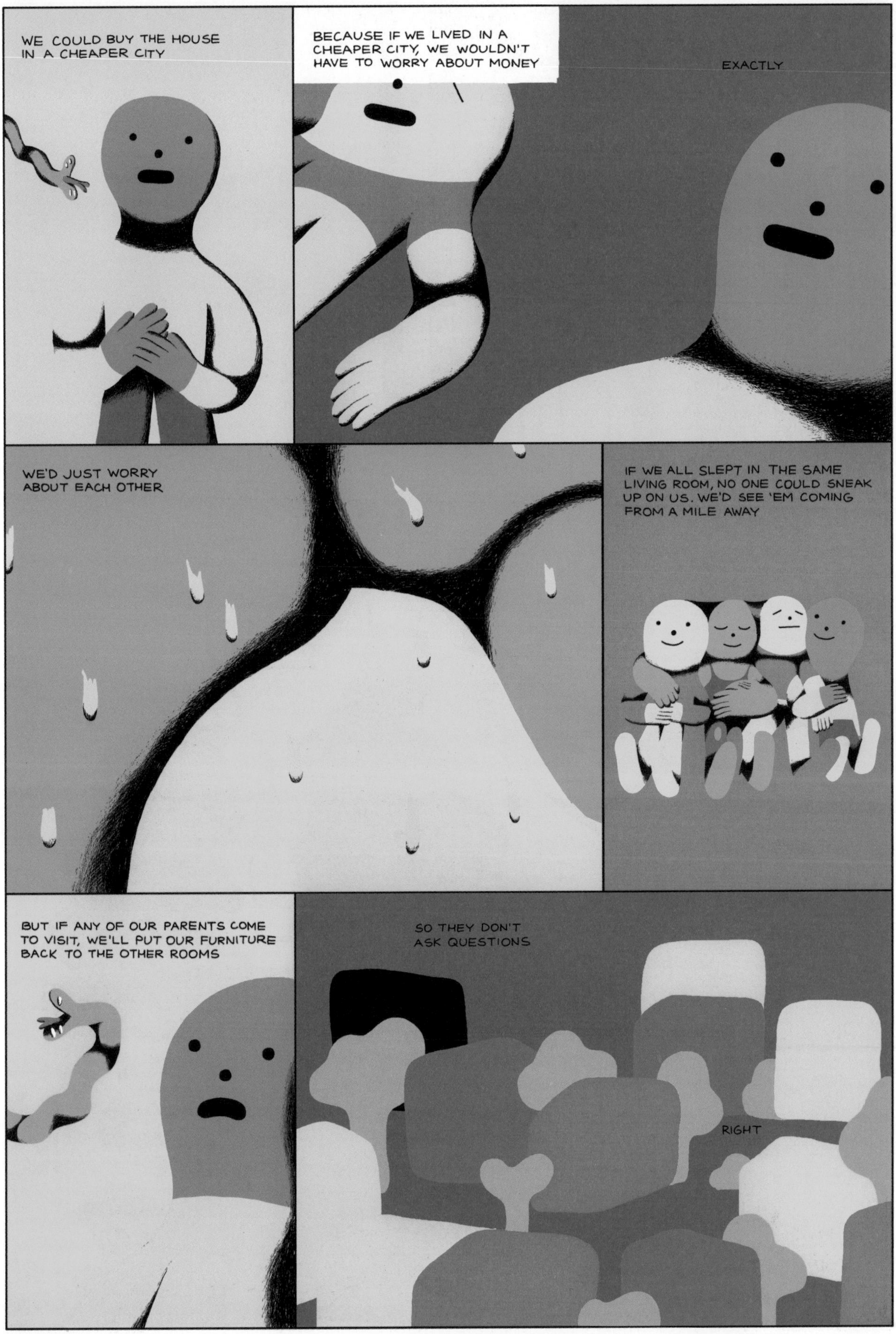
WE COULD BUY THE HOUSE IN A CHEAPER CITY
BECAUSE IF WE LIVED IN A CHEAPER CITY, WE WOULDN'T HAVE TO WORRY ABOUT MONEY
EXACTLY
WE'D JUST WORRY ABOUT EACH OTHER
IF WE ALL SLEPT IN THE SAME LIVING ROOM, NO ONE COULD SNEAK UP ON US. WE'D SEE 'EM COMING FROM A MILE AWAY
BUT IF ANY OF OUR PARENTS COME TO VISIT, WE'LL PUT OUR FURNITURE BACK TO THE OTHER ROOMS
SO THEY DON'T ASK QUESTIONS
RIGHT

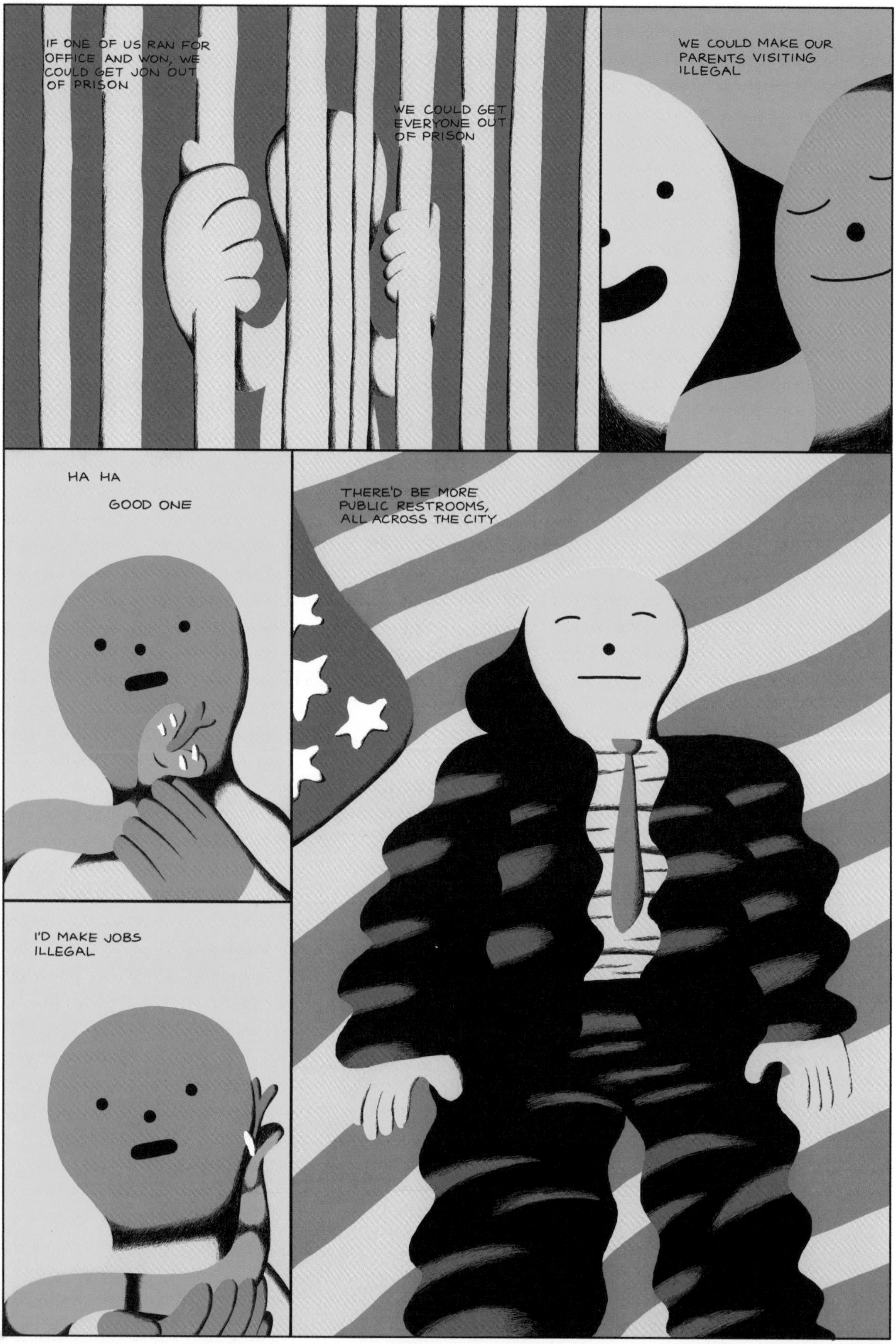
IF ONE OF US RAN FOR OFFICE AND WON, WE COULD GET JON OUT OF PRISON
WE COULD GET EVERYONE OUT OF PRISON
WE COULD MAKE OUR PARENTS VISITING ILLEGAL
HA HA
GOOD ONE
THERE'D BE MORE PUBLIC RESTROOMS, ALL ACROSS THE CITY
I'D MAKE JOBS ILLEGAL

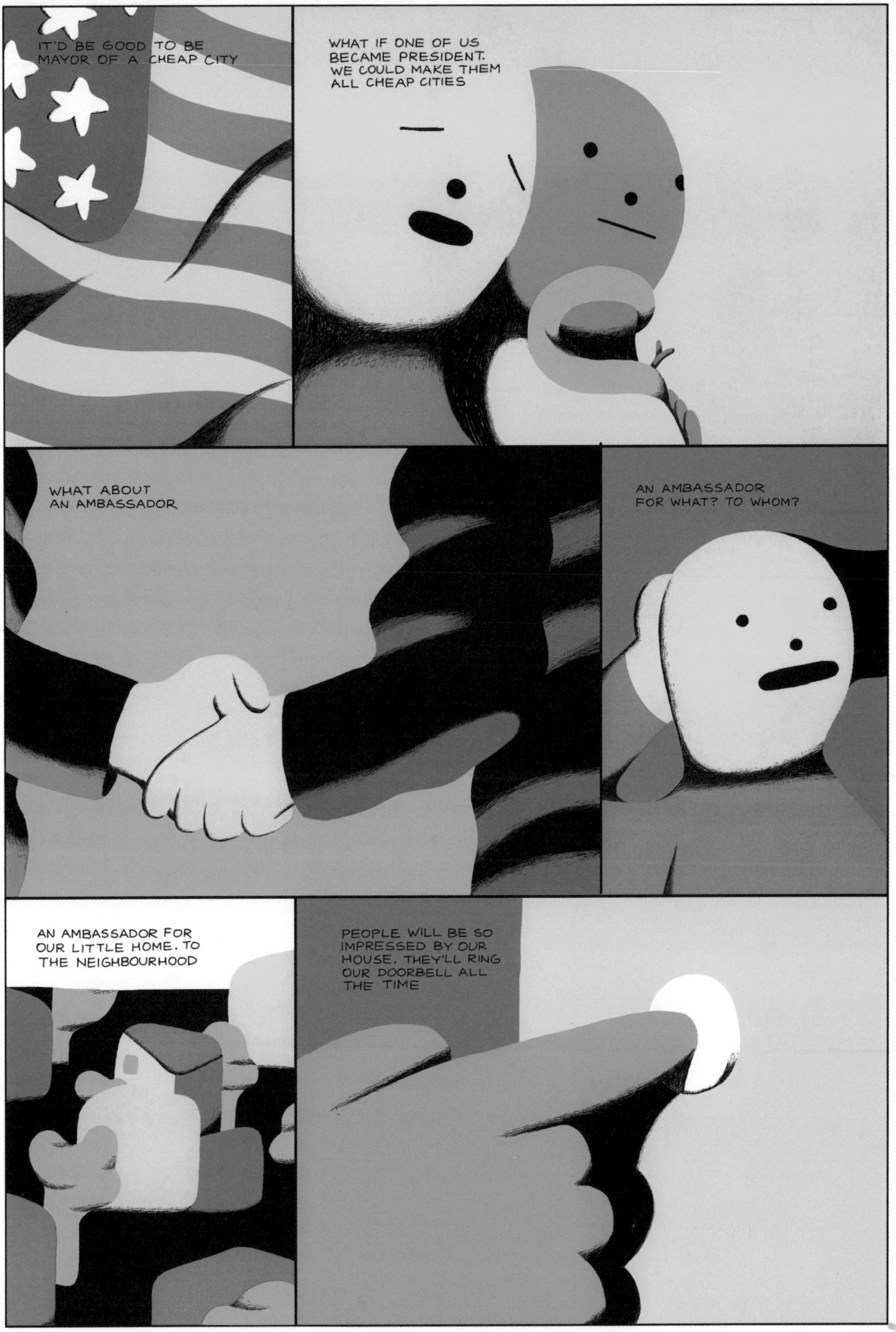
IT'D BE GOOD TO BE MAYOR OF A CHEAP CITY
WHAT IF ONE OF US BECAME PRESIDENT. WE COULD MAKE THEM ALL CHEAP CITIES
WHAT ABOUT AN AMBASSADOR
AN AMBASSADOR FOR WHAT? TO WHOM?
AN AMBASSADOR FOR OUR LITTLE HOME. TO THE NEIGHBOURHOOD
PEOPLE WILL BE SO IMPRESSED BY OUR HOUSE. THEY'LL RING OUR DOORBELL ALL THE TIME

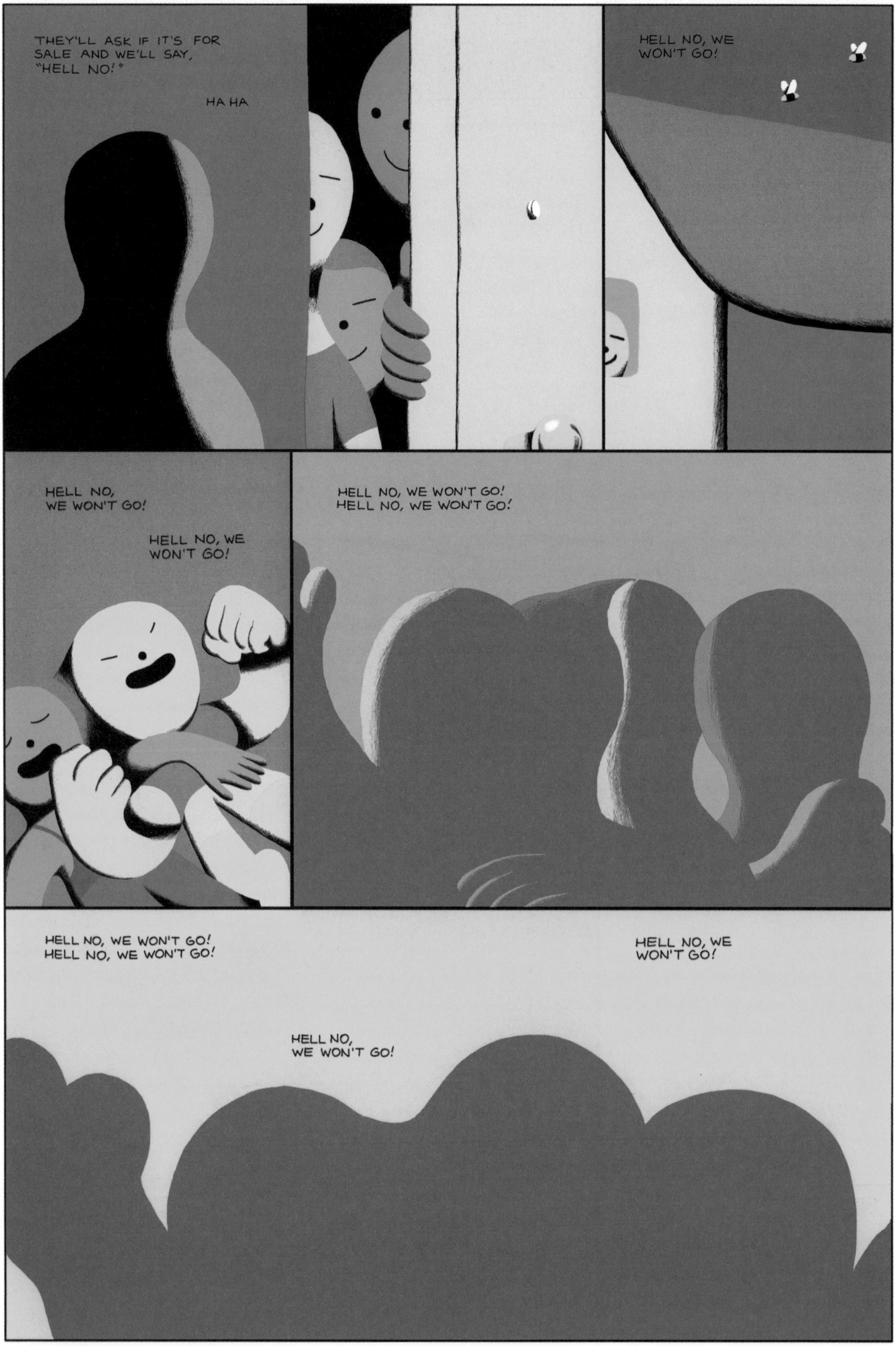
THEY'LL ASK IF IT'S FOR SALE AND WE'LL SAY, "HELL NO!"
HA HA
HELL NO, WE WON'T GO!
HELL NO, WE WON'T GO!
HELL NO, WE WON'T GO!
HELL NO, WE WON'T GO! HELL NO, WE WON'T GO!
HELL NO, WE WON'T GO! HELL NO, WE WON'T GO!
HELL NO, WE WON'T GO!
HELL NO, WE WON'T GO!

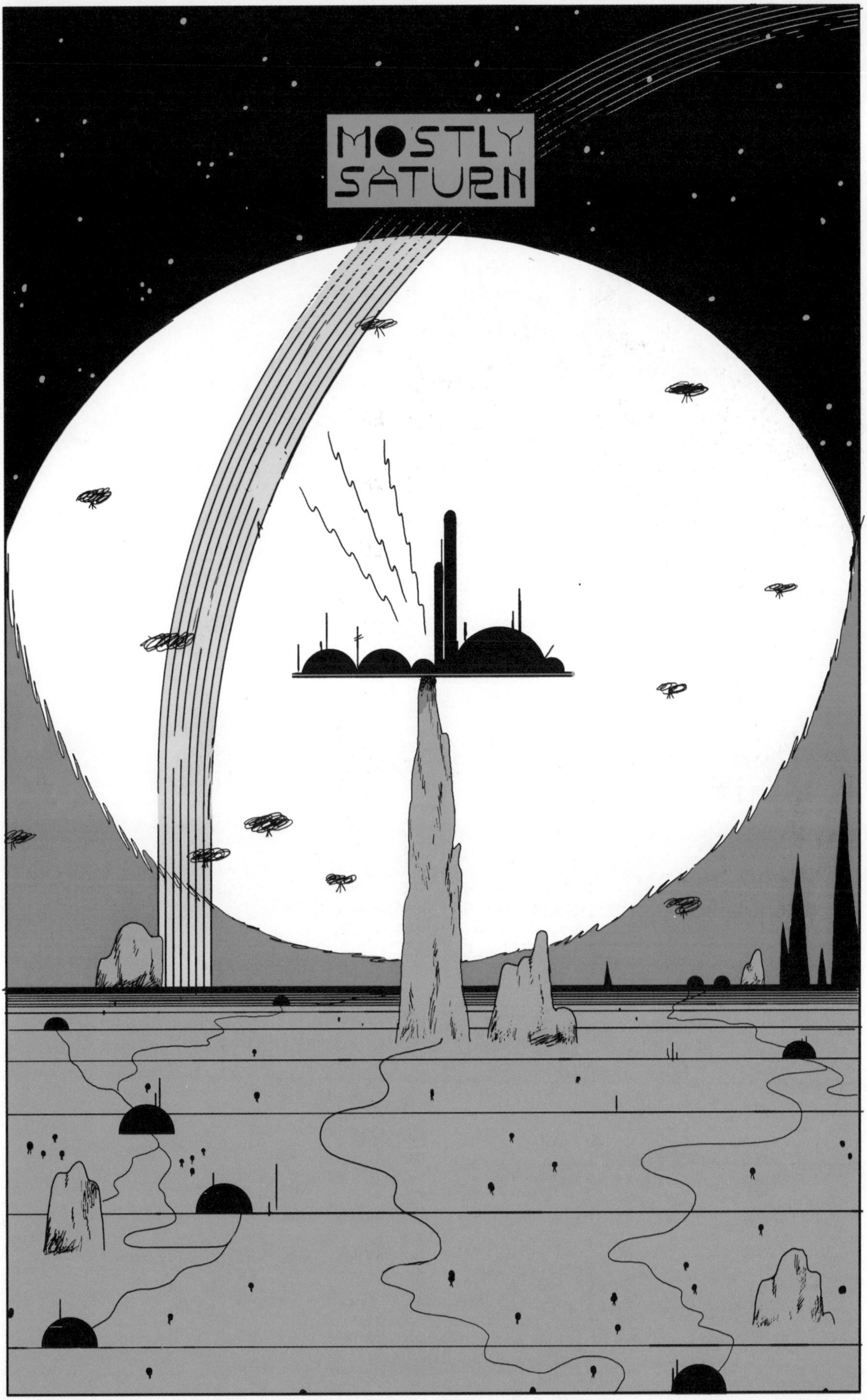
MOSTLY
SATURN

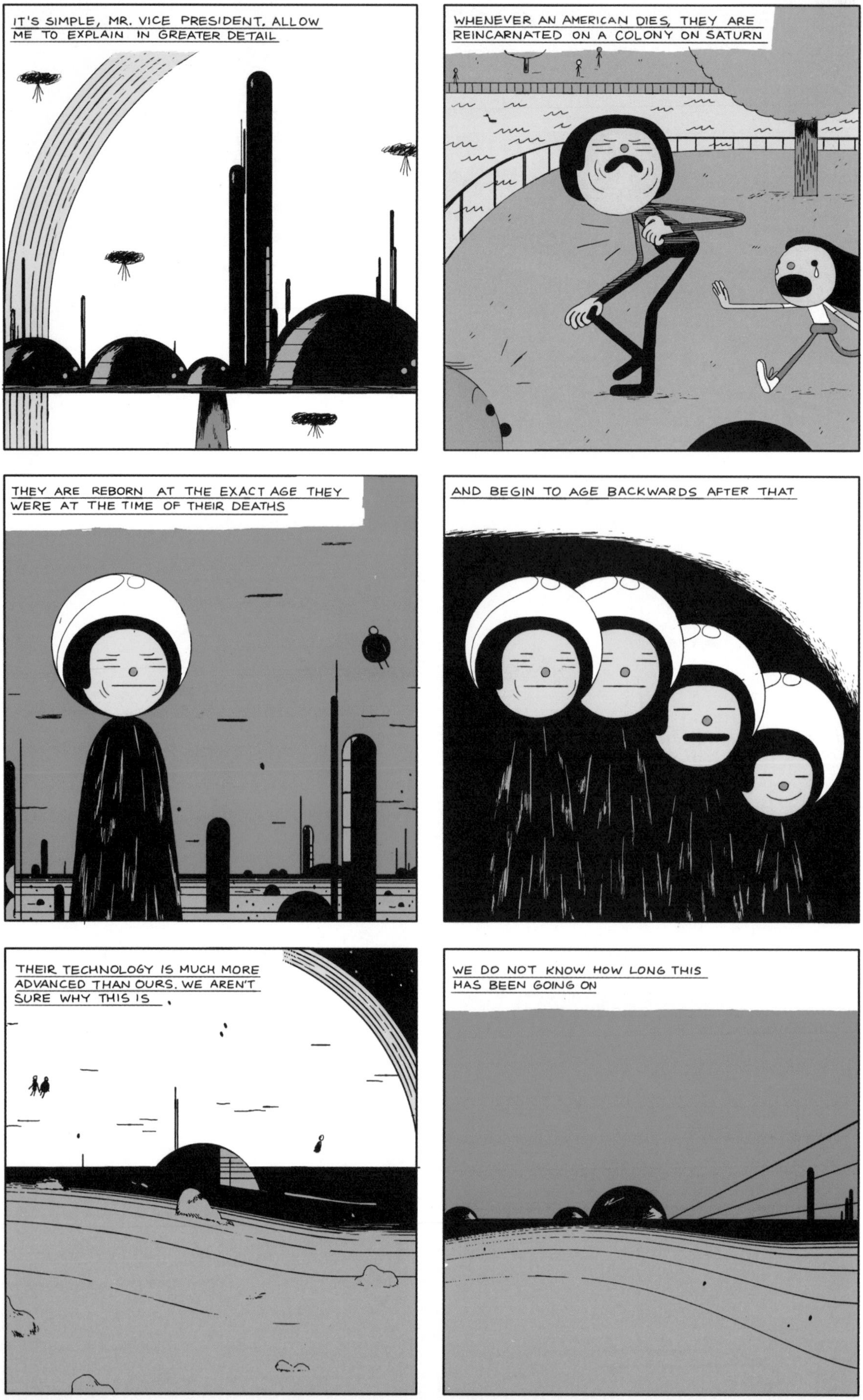
IT'S SIMPLE, MR. VICE PRESIDENT. ALLOW ME TO EXPLAIN IN GREATER DETAIL
WHENEVER AN AMERICAN DIES, THEY ARE REINCARNATED ON A COLONY ON SATURN
THEY ARE REBORN AT THE EXACT AGE THEY WERE AT THE TIME OF THEIR DEATHS
AND BEGIN TO AGE BACKWARDS AFTER THAT
THEIR TECHNOLOGY IS MUCH MORE ADVANCED THAN OURS. WE AREN'T SURE WHY THIS IS
WE DO NOT KNOW HOW LONG THIS HAS BEEN GOING ON

MAYBE THE COLONY WAS BUILT FOR THEM, MAYBE THEY BUILT IT THEMSELVES

AS FAR AS I CAN TELL FROM OUR SATELLITE FOOTAGE, THE REINCARNATION PROCESS WORKS LIKE THIS:

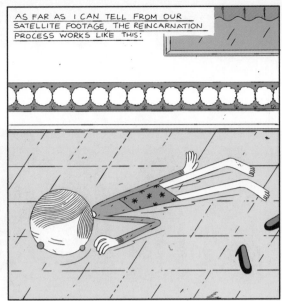

UPON A PERSON'S DEATH, A ROCK FROM SATURN'S RINGS PLUMMETS DOWN TO THE PLANET'S SURFACE

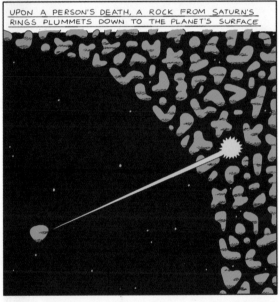

AND TAKES THE FORM OF THE DECEASED

THEY MATERIALIZE IN TRADITIONAL SATURN GARB - A FLOWING BLACK ROBE AND HELMET

THEY DON'T APPEAR TO BE DISORIENTED. THEY IMMEDIATELY INTEGRATE INTO THE COLONY

SINCE THE AGING PROCESS ON THE PLANET IS REVERSED, IT IS FREQUENTLY THE INFANT-BODIED WHO HAVE LIVED LONGEST

THERE ARE OBVIOUSLY MANY EXCEPTIONS TO THIS

STILL, IT SEEMS AS THOUGH THE COLONY HAS BUILT ITSELF AROUND THE SERVICE OF THE INFANT-BODIED

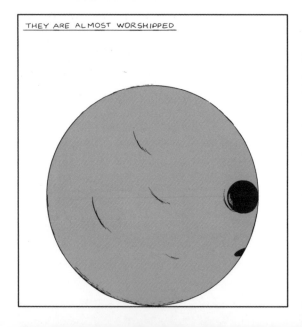

THEY ARE ALMOST WORSHIPPED

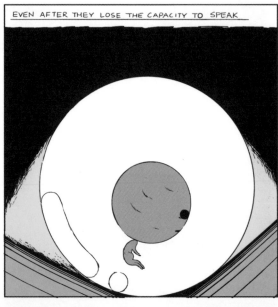

EVEN AFTER THEY LOSE THE CAPACITY TO SPEAK

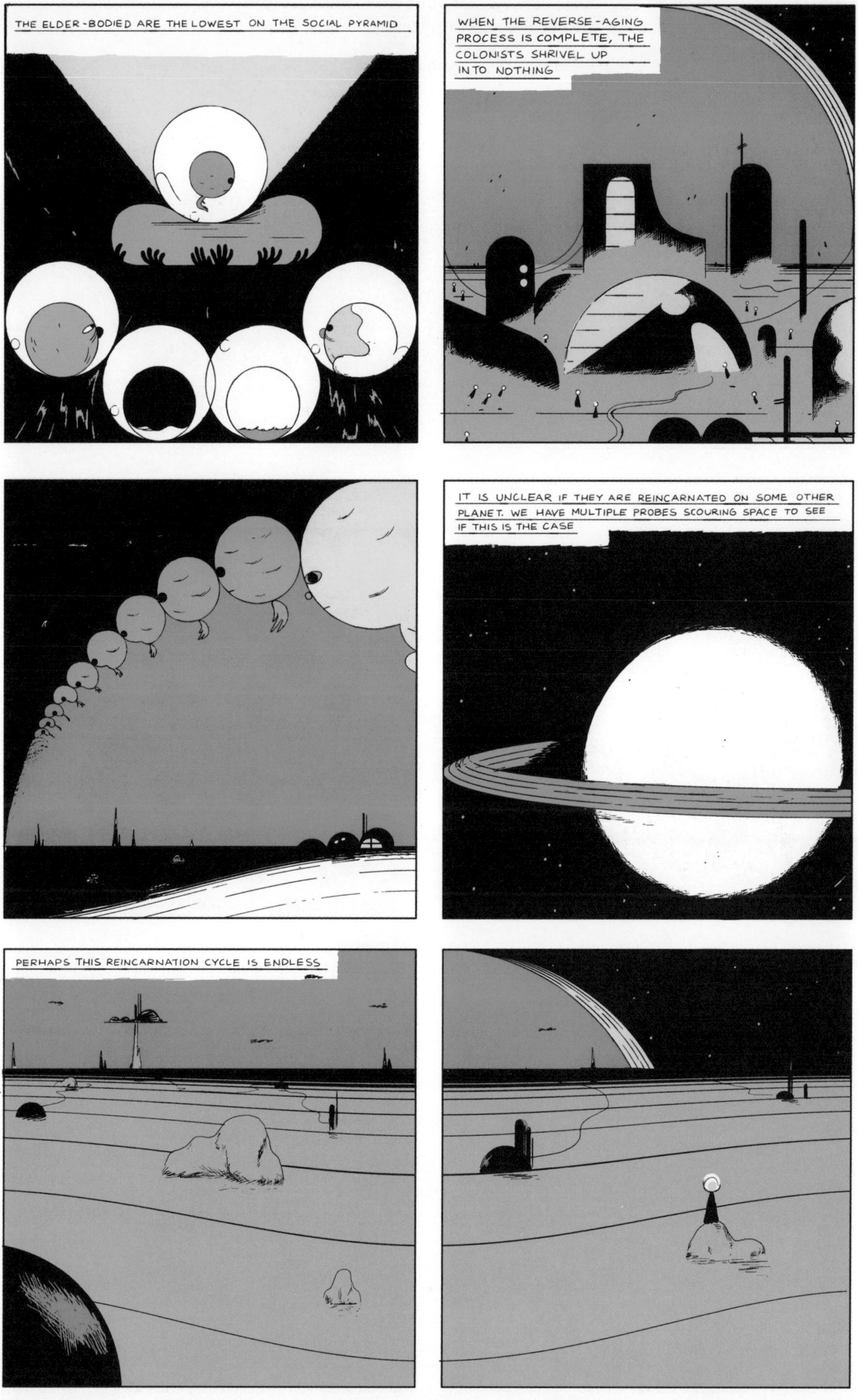

THE ELDER-BODIED ARE THE LOWEST ON THE SOCIAL PYRAMID
WHEN THE REVERSE-AGING PROCESS IS COMPLETE, THE COLONISTS SHRIVEL UP INTO NOTHING
IT IS UNCLEAR IF THEY ARE REINCARNATED ON SOME OTHER PLANET. WE HAVE MULTIPLE PROBES SCOURING SPACE TO SEE IF THIS IS THE CASE
PERHAPS THIS REINCARNATION CYCLE IS ENDLESS

THE QUALITY OF LIFE ON SATURN
IS MUCH HIGHER THAN IN AMERICA

THE COLONISTS SEEM TO LIVE
WITHOUT ILLNESS OR DISEASE

COLONISTS ENGAGE IN THRILLING ORGIES

THEY DEDICATE AN INCREDIBLE AMOUNT OF RESOURCES TO
CULTURAL PROGRAMS - THEATRE, DANCE, VISUAL ART, MUSIC

ARTIFICIAL WEATHER SYSTEMS HAVE MADE IT POSSIBLE
FOR THE COLONISTS TO FARM

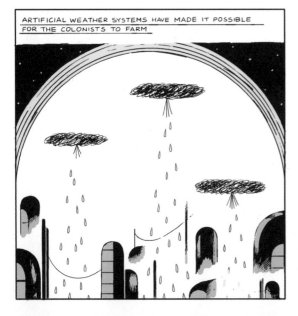

THEIR FOOD LOOKS VERY SOPHISTICATED

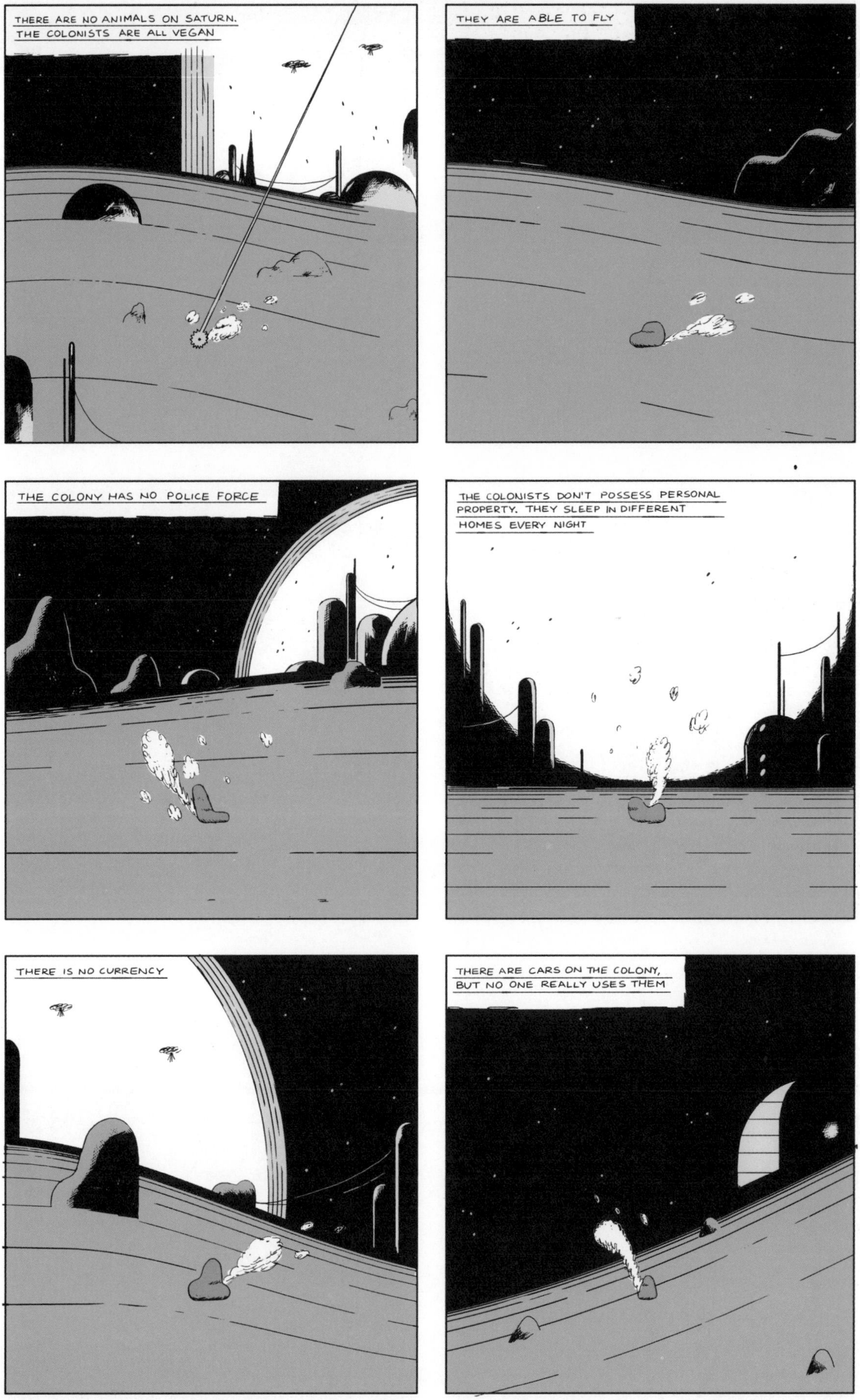
THERE ARE NO ANIMALS ON SATURN. THE COLONISTS ARE ALL VEGAN
THEY ARE ABLE TO FLY
THE COLONY HAS NO POLICE FORCE
THE COLONISTS DON'T POSSESS PERSONAL PROPERTY. THEY SLEEP IN DIFFERENT HOMES EVERY NIGHT
THERE IS NO CURRENCY
THERE ARE CARS ON THE COLONY, BUT NO ONE REALLY USES THEM

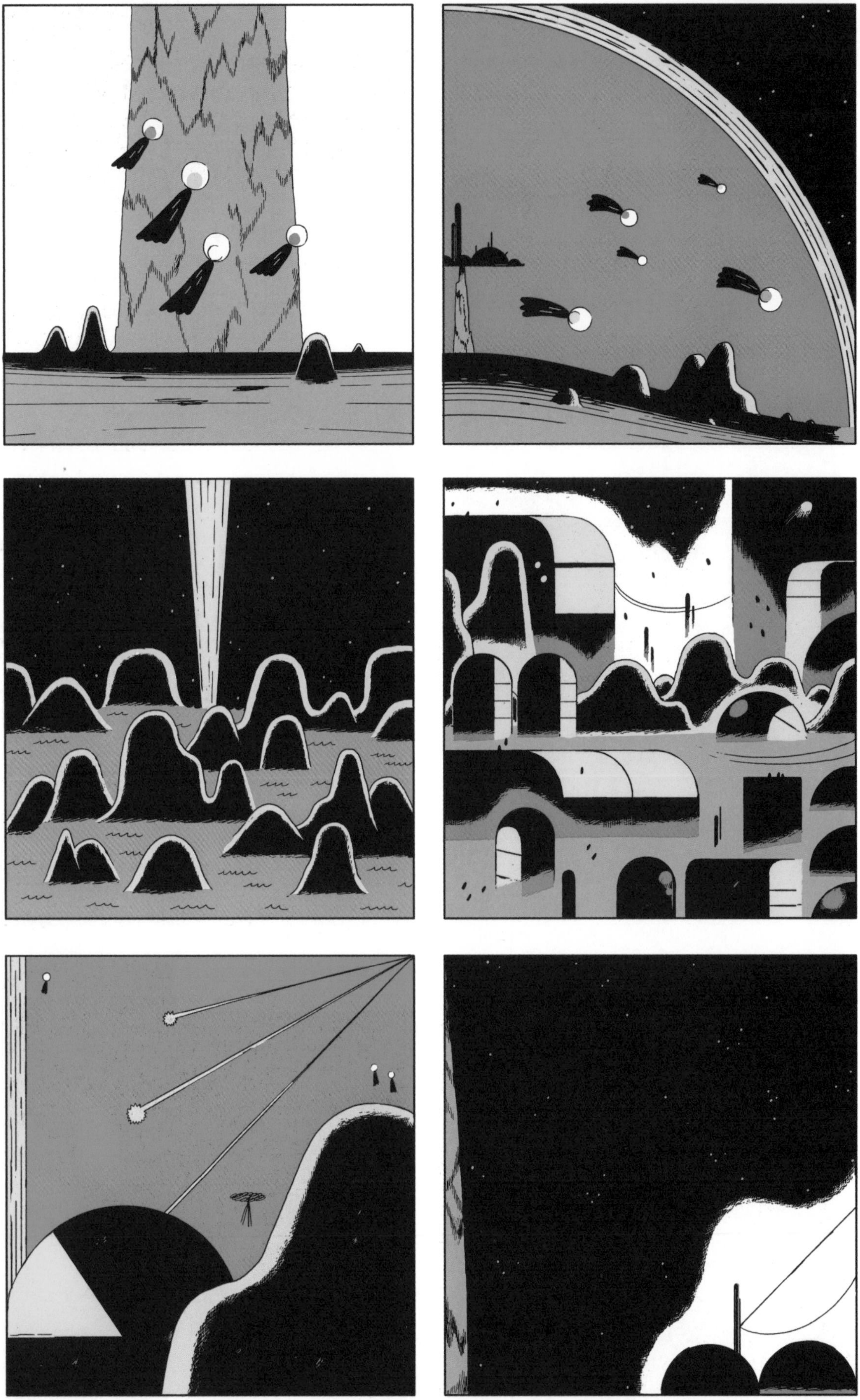

THIS INFORMATION MUST BE KEPT
SECRET FROM THE WORLD

WE FEAR LIFE ON SATURN MAY BE SEEN
AS OVERLY APPEALING TO AMERICANS

ONLY 33 MILITARY AND GOVERNMENT PERSONNEL
HAVE BEEN BRIEFED ON THE EXISTENCE OF THIS
COLONY. YOU ARE THE 34TH

AS OF RIGHT NOW, 9 OF THOSE INITIAL
33 HAVE KILLED THEMSELVES

PRESUMABLY SO THEY COULD
BE REINCARNATED ON SATURN

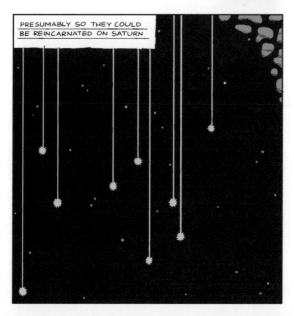

THIS IS WHY THE PRESIDENT IS DEAD

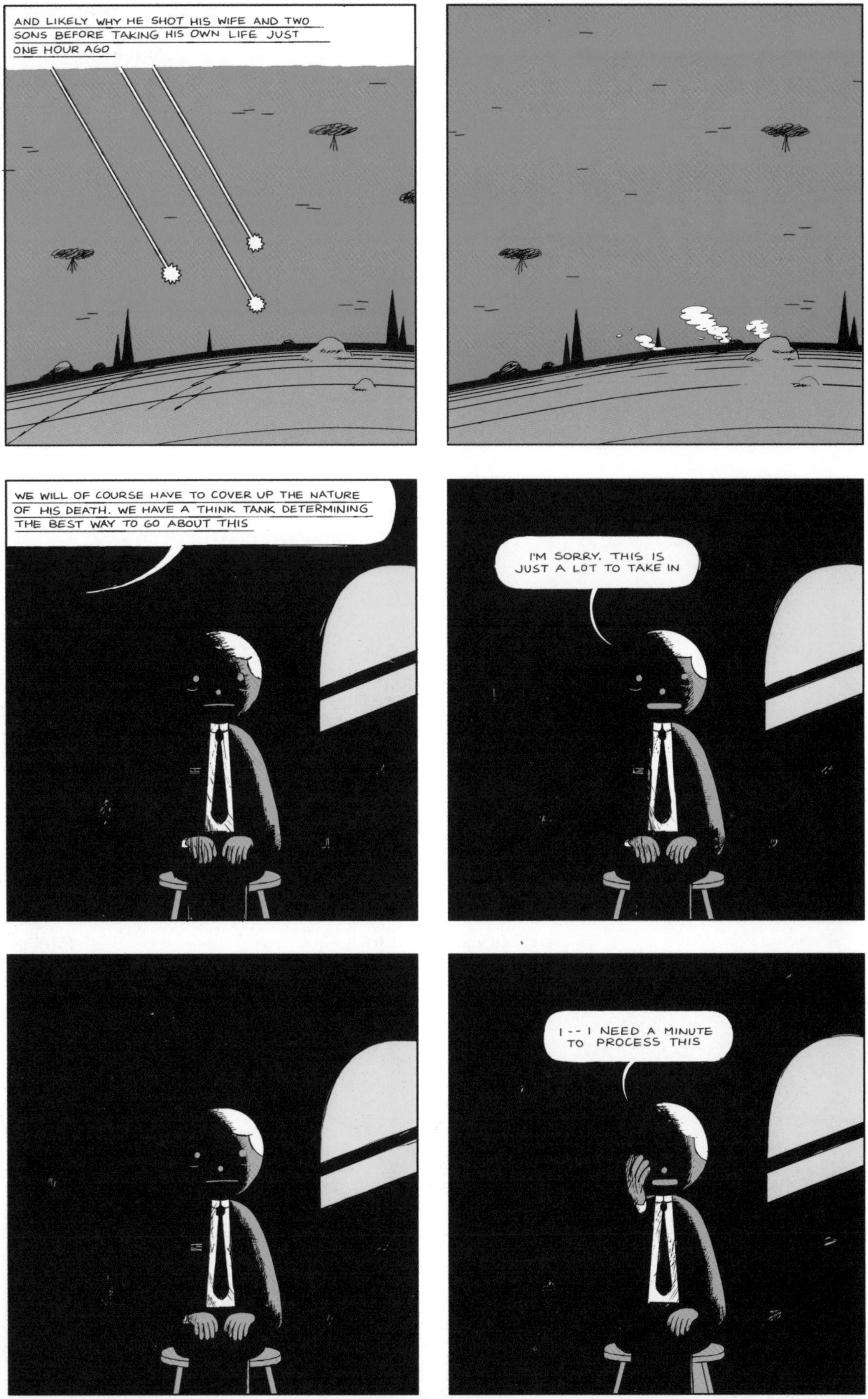
AND LIKELY WHY HE SHOT HIS WIFE AND TWO SONS BEFORE TAKING HIS OWN LIFE JUST ONE HOUR AGO
WE WILL OF COURSE HAVE TO COVER UP THE NATURE OF HIS DEATH. WE HAVE A THINK TANK DETERMINING THE BEST WAY TO GO ABOUT THIS
I'M SORRY. THIS IS JUST A LOT TO TAKE IN
I -- I NEED A MINUTE TO PROCESS THIS

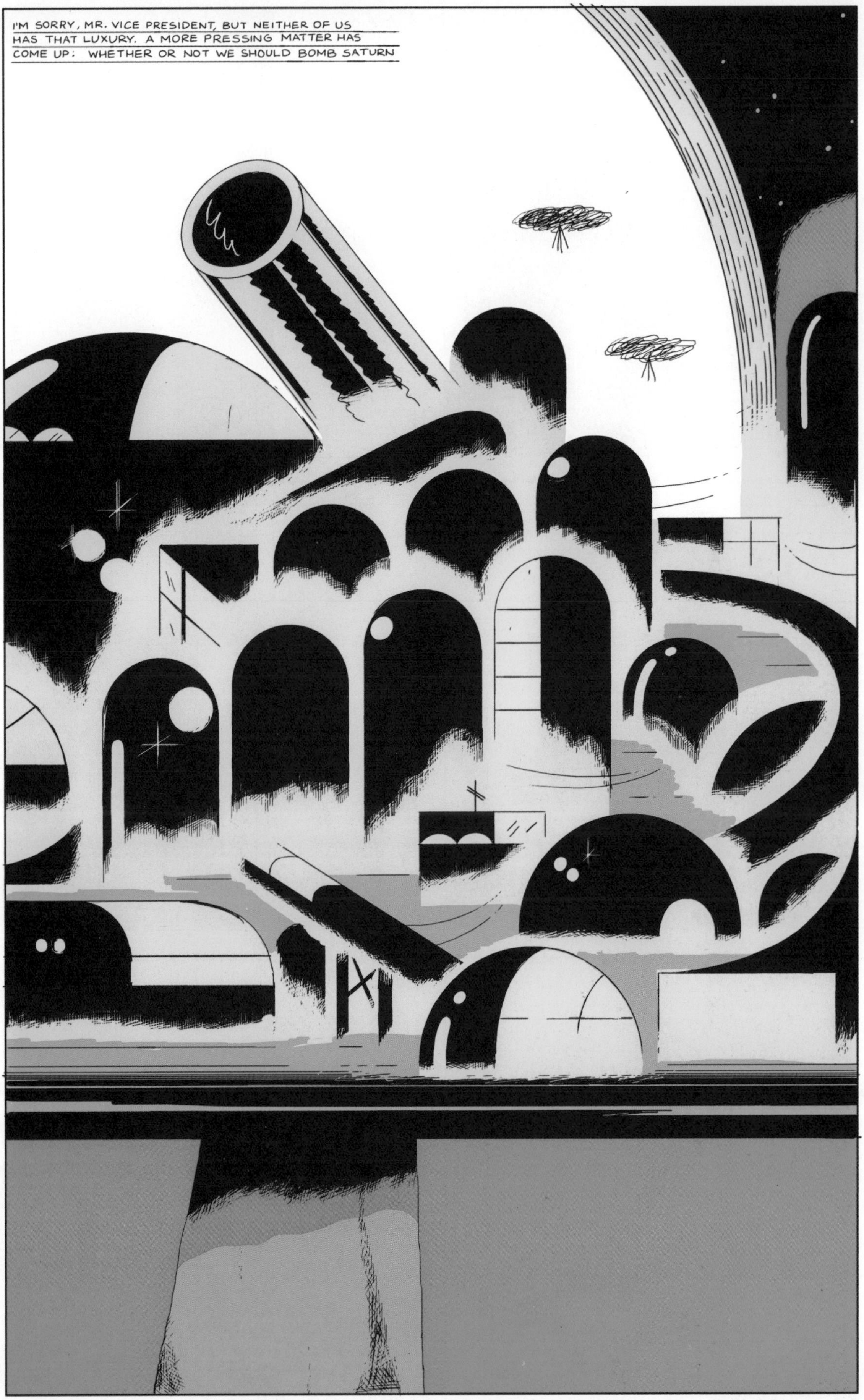
I'M SORRY, MR. VICE PRESIDENT, BUT NEITHER OF US HAS THAT LUXURY. A MORE PRESSING MATTER HAS COME UP: WHETHER OR NOT WE SHOULD BOMB SATURN

CONTRARY TO WHAT WE TOLD THE PUBLIC, THE TRAGEDIES IN CHICAGO AND TAMPA LAST MONTH WERE NOT ACTS OF DOMESTIC TERROR

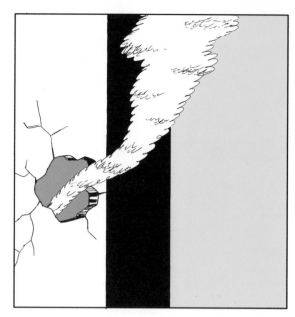

THEY WERE MISSILES

SENT FROM SATURN

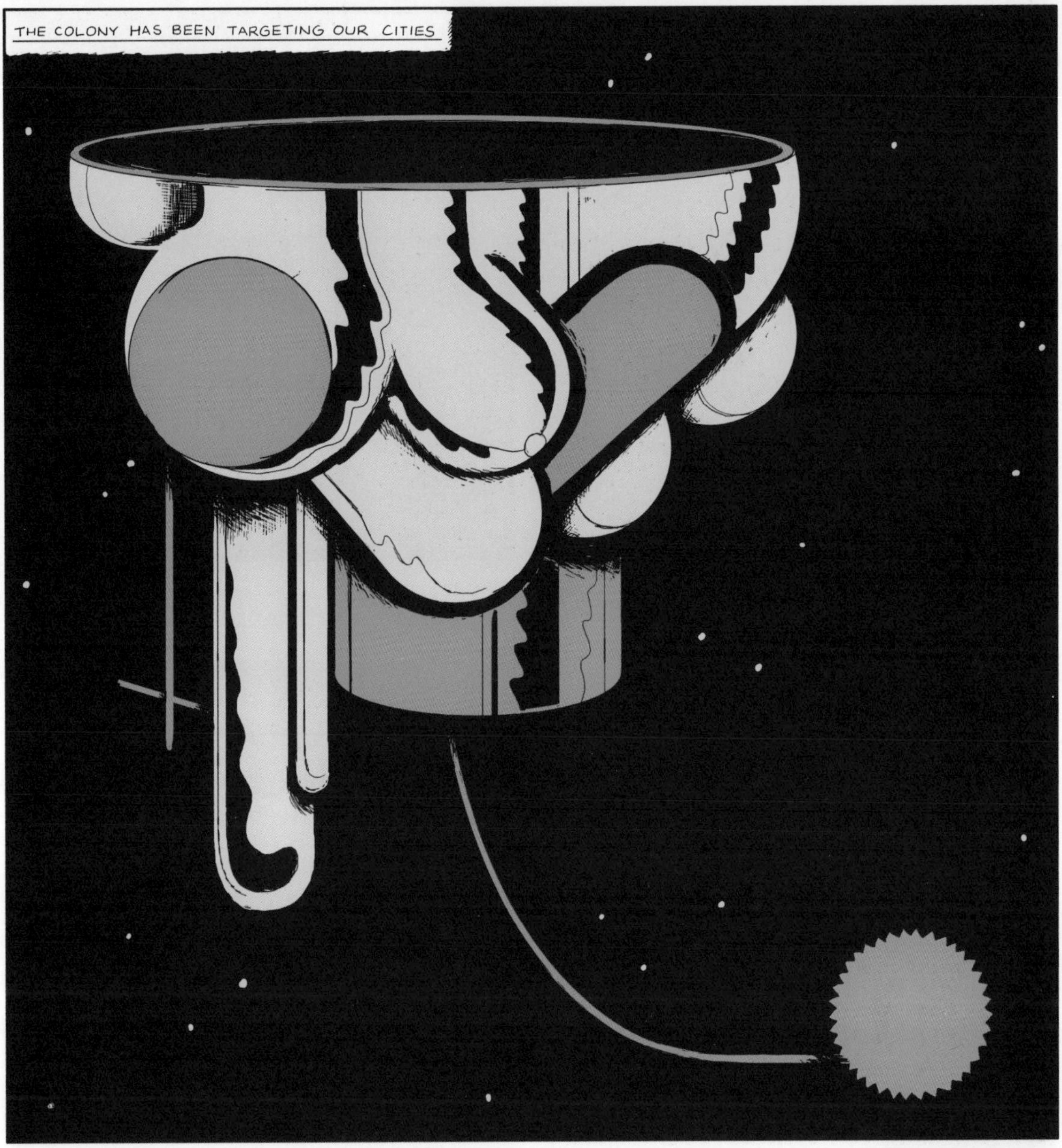
THE COLONY HAS BEEN TARGETING OUR CITIES

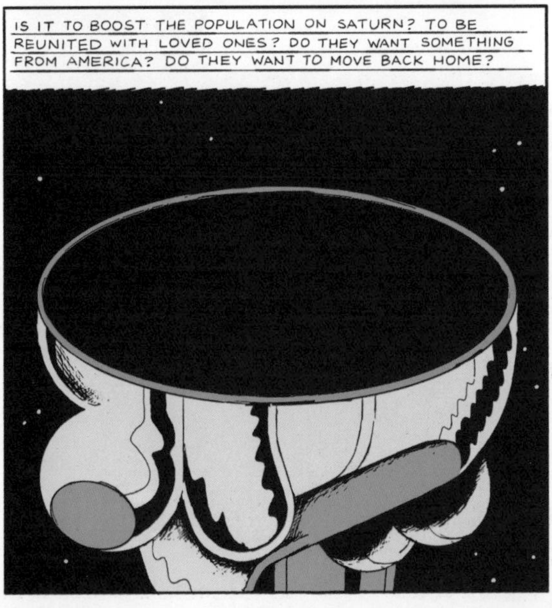
IS IT TO BOOST THE POPULATION ON SATURN? TO BE REUNITED WITH LOVED ONES? DO THEY WANT SOMETHING FROM AMERICA? DO THEY WANT TO MOVE BACK HOME?

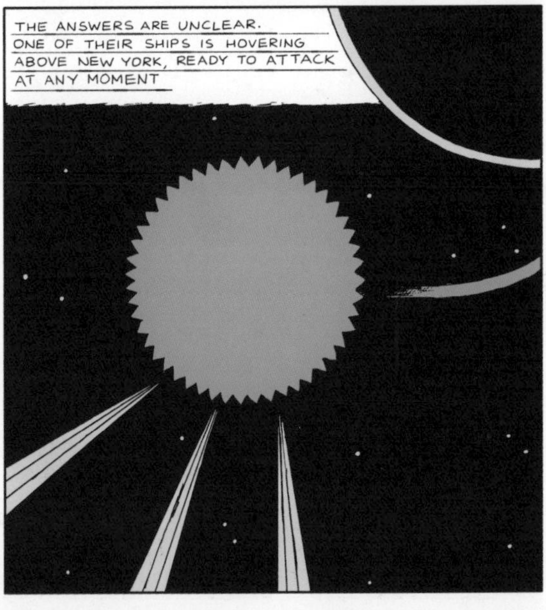
THE ANSWERS ARE UNCLEAR.
ONE OF THEIR SHIPS IS HOVERING ABOVE NEW YORK, READY TO ATTACK AT ANY MOMENT

THEY HAVE REBUFFED ALL COMMUNICATION ATTEMPTS

AMERICA IS IN CRISIS

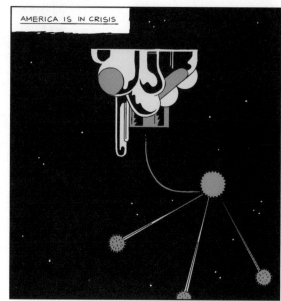

WE MUST ENGAGE IN A SECRET WAR. A SECRET WAR AGAINST SATURN

THE PENTAGON WANTS TO DESTROY THE ORBITING SHIP FIRST

HOWEVER, THEY ALSO SUGGEST WE LAUNCH A NUCLEAR STRIKE ON SATURN ITSELF

THEY BELIEVE OUR RETALIATION MUST BE SWIFT AND MERCILESS

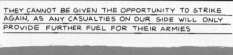

THEIR OBLITERATION MUST BE ABSOLUTE

THEY CANNOT BE GIVEN THE OPPORTUNITY TO STRIKE AGAIN, AS ANY CASUALTIES ON OUR SIDE WILL ONLY PROVIDE FURTHER FUEL FOR THEIR ARMIES

ROUGHLY 10 AMERICANS DIE PER MINUTE, JOINING THE RANKS OF ENEMY COLONISTS

MR. VICE PRESIDENT, WE ARE AWARE THAT YOUR DAUGHTER IS TERMINALLY ILL

SHE'S VERY SICK

BEFORE MAKING A DECISION, FIRST CONSIDER:

IF WE DESTROY THE SATURN COLONY, WE HAVE NO REASON TO BELIEVE AMERICANS WON'T CONTINUE TO BE REINCARNATED ON THE PLANET'S SURFACE

THEY WILL MATERIALIZE ON AN IRRADIATED NUCLEAR WASTELAND WITH LITTLE TO NO CHANCE OF SURVIVAL

EVERY FUTURE DEAD AMERICAN WILL BE DENIED AT LEAST ONE AFTERLIFE

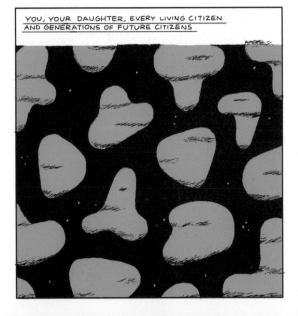

YOU, YOUR DAUGHTER, EVERY LIVING CITIZEN AND GENERATIONS OF FUTURE CITIZENS

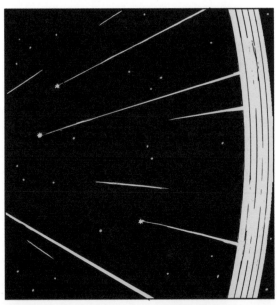

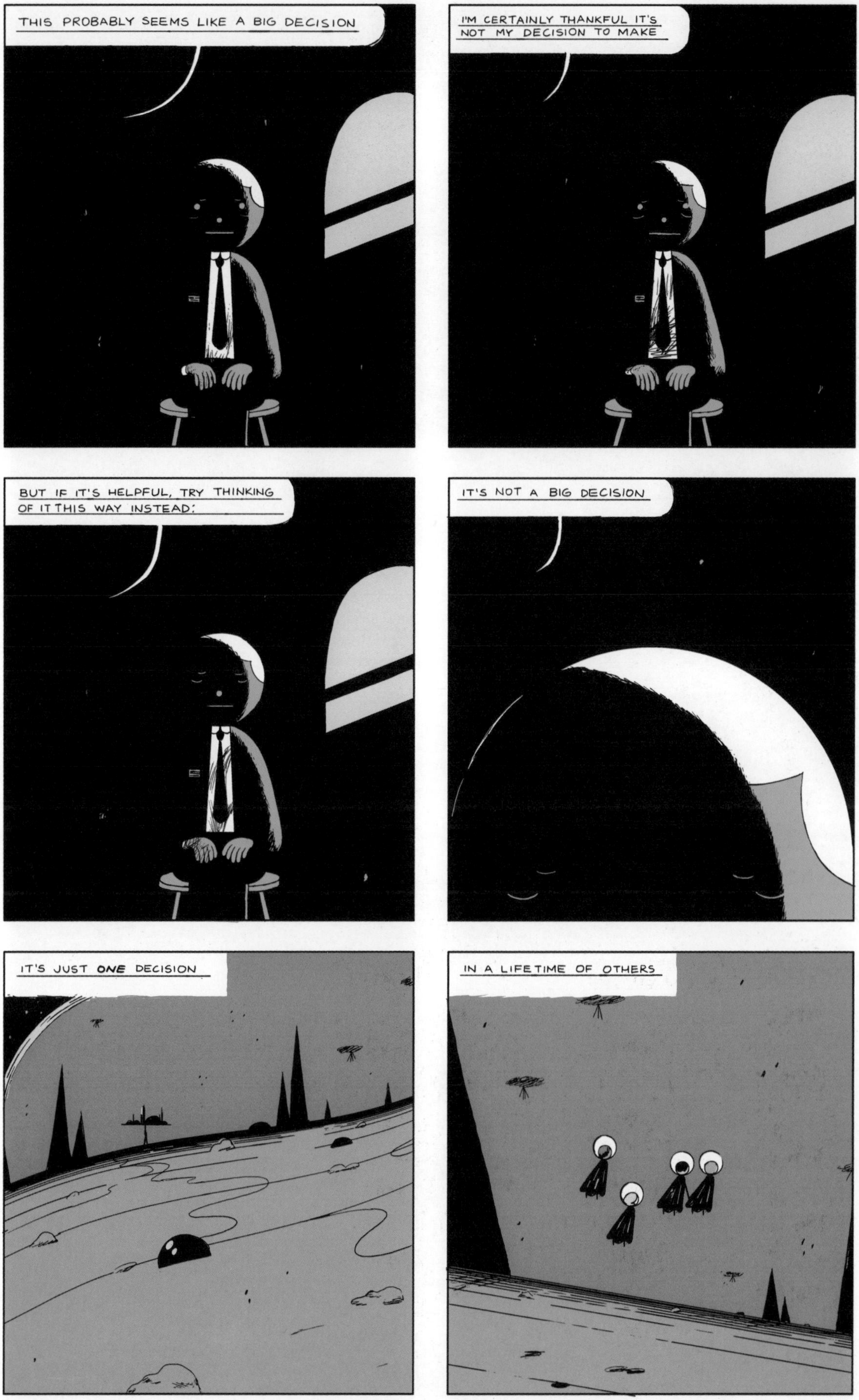
THIS PROBABLY SEEMS LIKE A BIG DECISION
I'M CERTAINLY THANKFUL IT'S NOT MY DECISION TO MAKE
BUT IF IT'S HELPFUL, TRY THINKING OF IT THIS WAY INSTEAD:
IT'S NOT A BIG DECISION
IT'S JUST ONE DECISION
IN A LIFETIME OF OTHERS

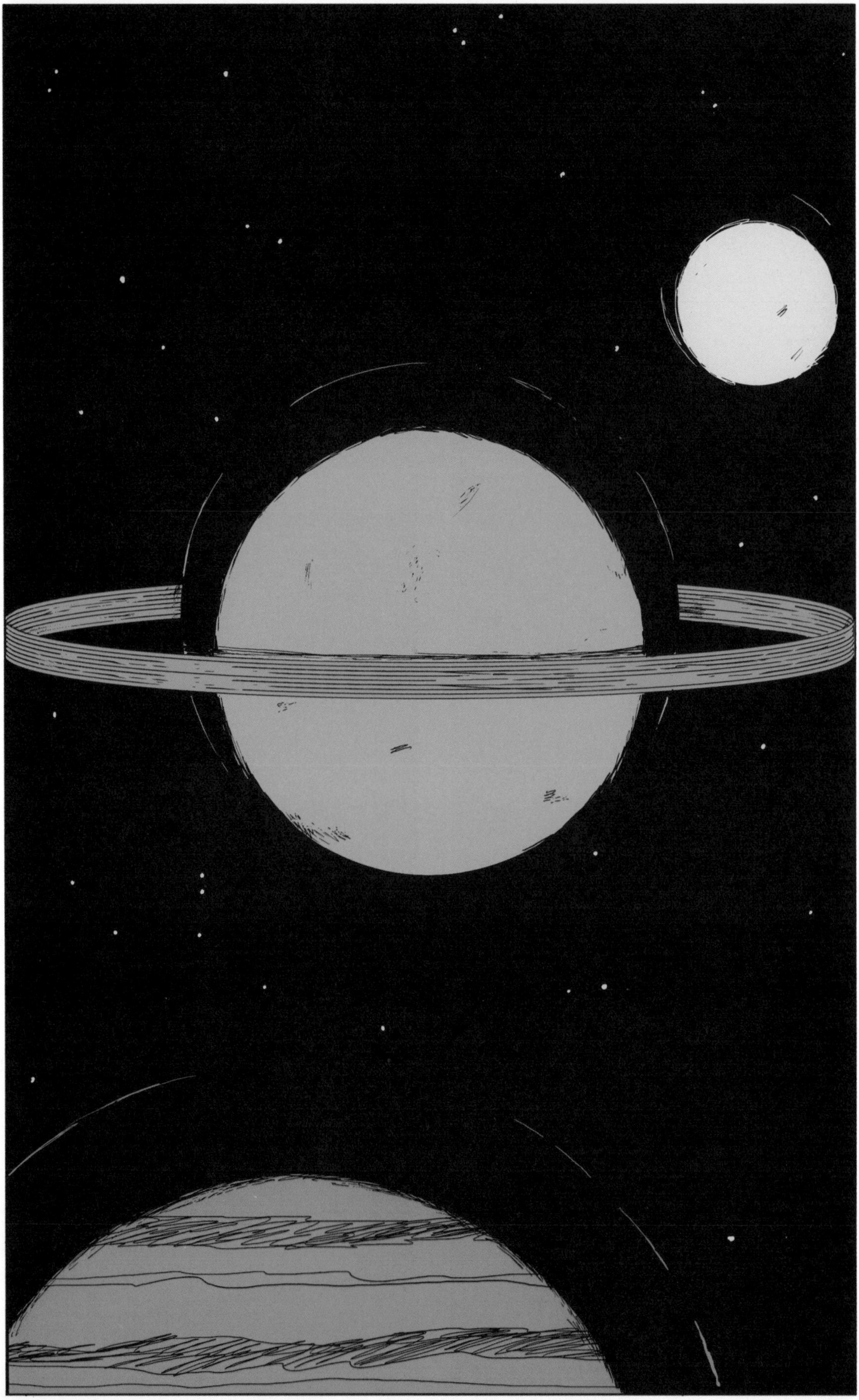

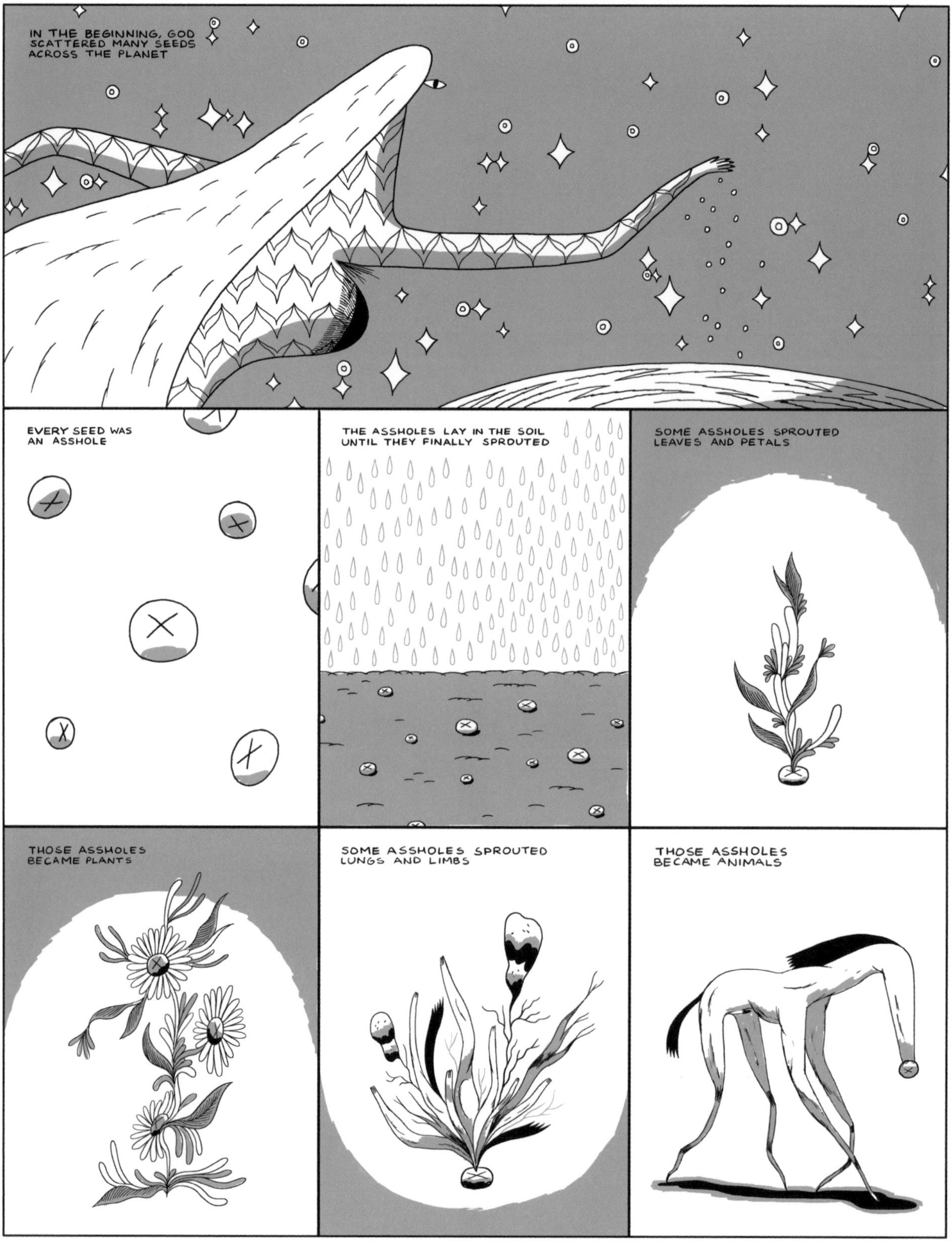
IN THE BEGINNING, GOD SCATTERED MANY SEEDS ACROSS THE PLANET
EVERY SEED WAS AN ASSHOLE
THE ASSHOLES LAY IN THE SOIL UNTIL THEY FINALLY SPROUTED
SOME ASSHOLES SPROUTED LEAVES AND PETALS
THOSE ASSHOLES BECAME PLANTS
SOME ASSHOLES SPROUTED LUNGS AND LIMBS
THOSE ASSHOLES BECAME ANIMALS

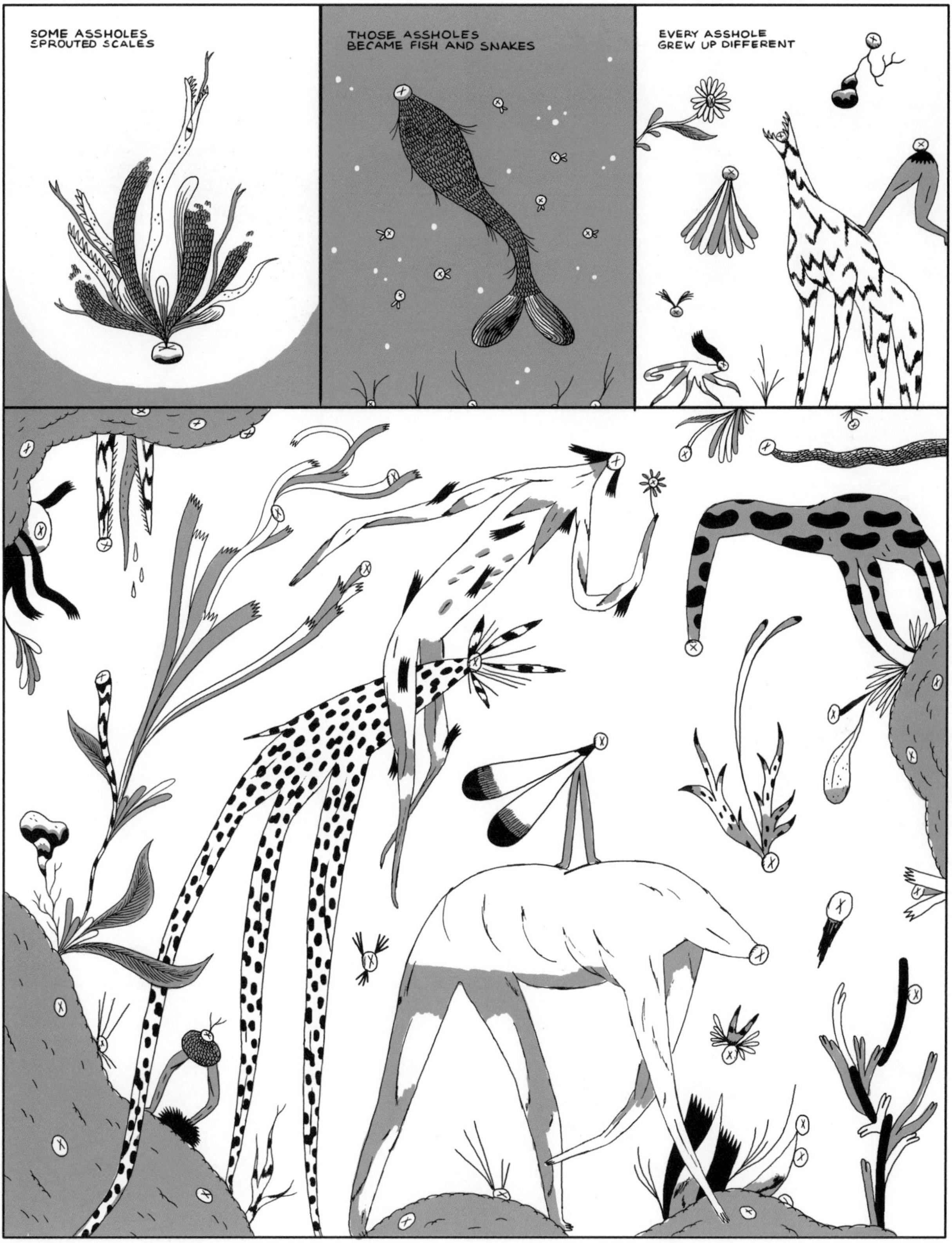
SOME ASSHOLES SPROUTED SCALES
THOSE ASSHOLES BECAME FISH AND SNAKES
EVERY ASSHOLE GREW UP DIFFERENT

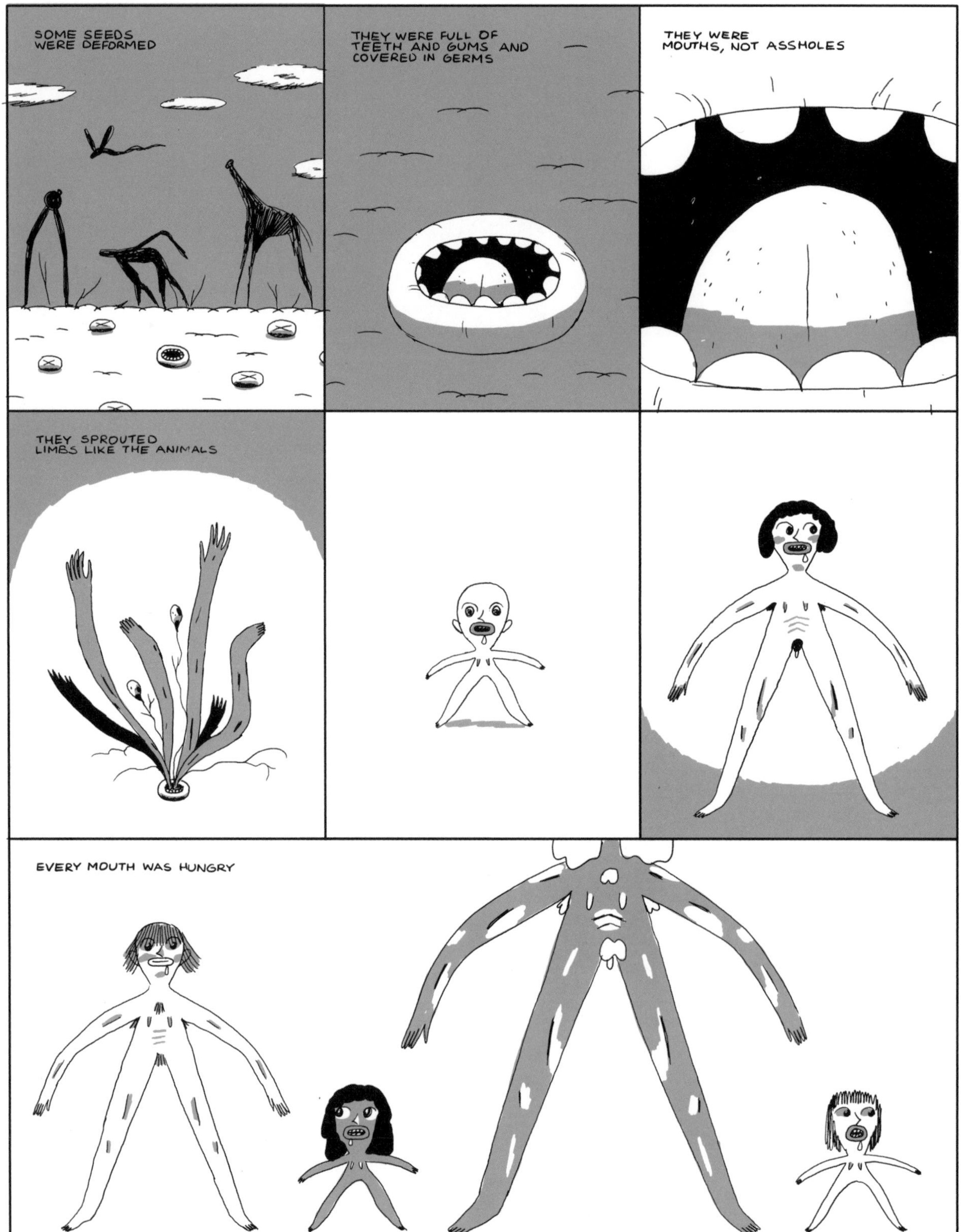
SOME SEEDS
WERE DEFORMED
THEY WERE FULL OF
TEETH AND GUMS AND
COVERED IN GERMS
THEY WERE
MOUTHS, NOT ASSHOLES
THEY SPROUTED
LIMBS LIKE THE ANIMALS
EVERY MOUTH WAS HUNGRY

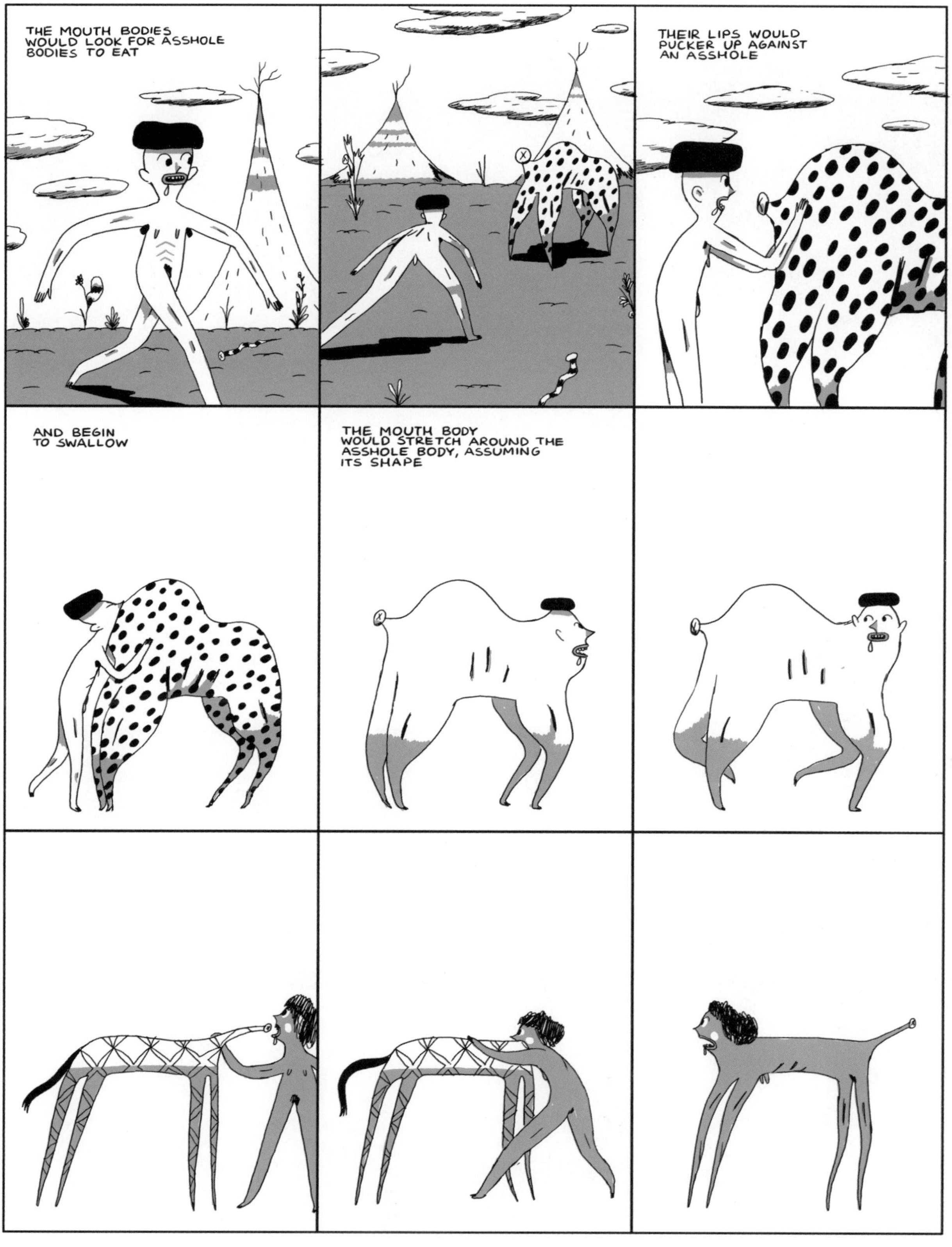
THE MOUTH BODIES WOULD LOOK FOR ASSHOLE BODIES TO EAT
THEIR LIPS WOULD PUCKER UP AGAINST AN ASSHOLE
AND BEGIN TO SWALLOW
THE MOUTH BODY WOULD STRETCH AROUND THE ASSHOLE BODY, ASSUMING ITS SHAPE

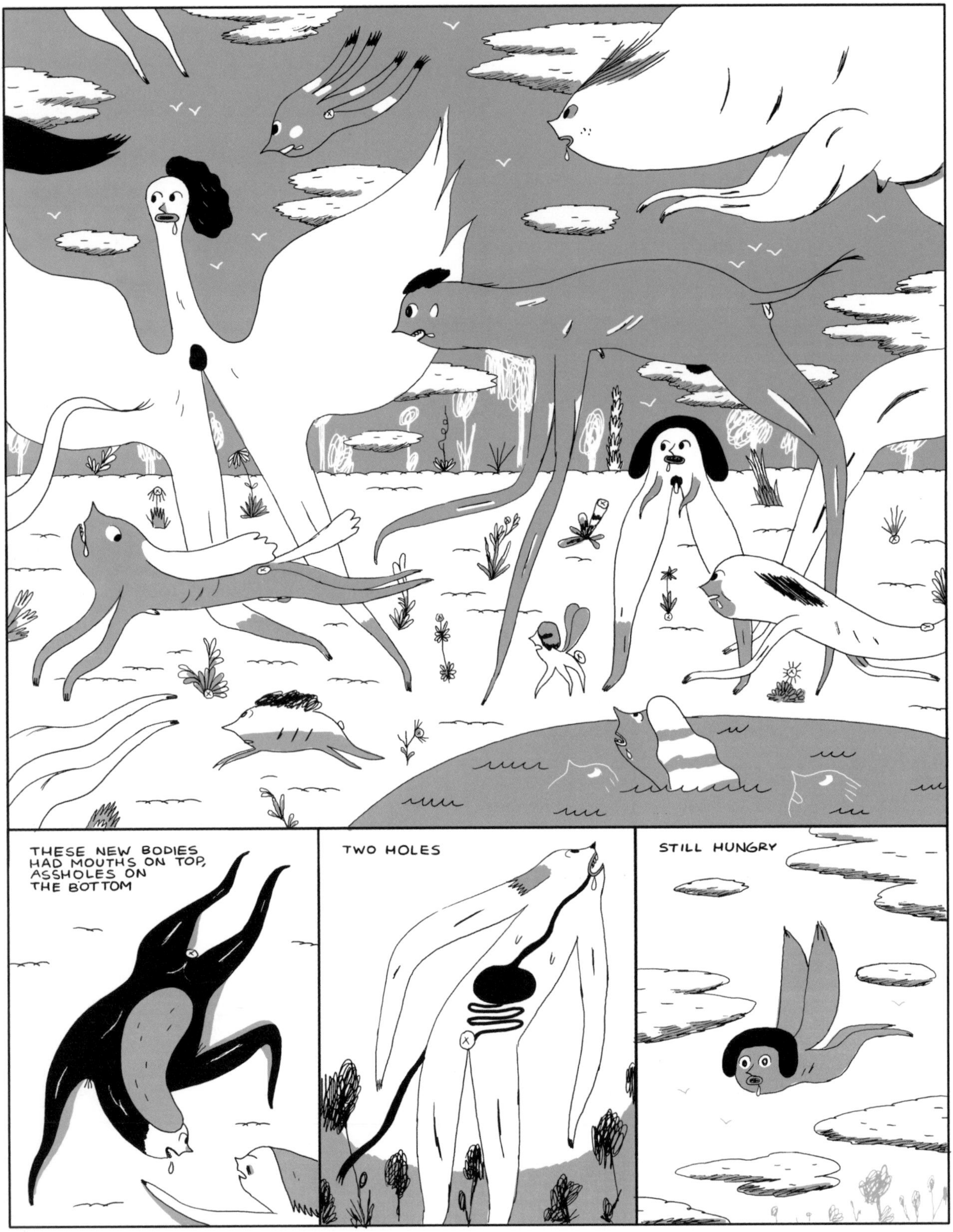
THESE NEW BODIES HAD MOUTHS ON TOP, ASSHOLES ON THE BOTTOM
TWO HOLES
STILL HUNGRY

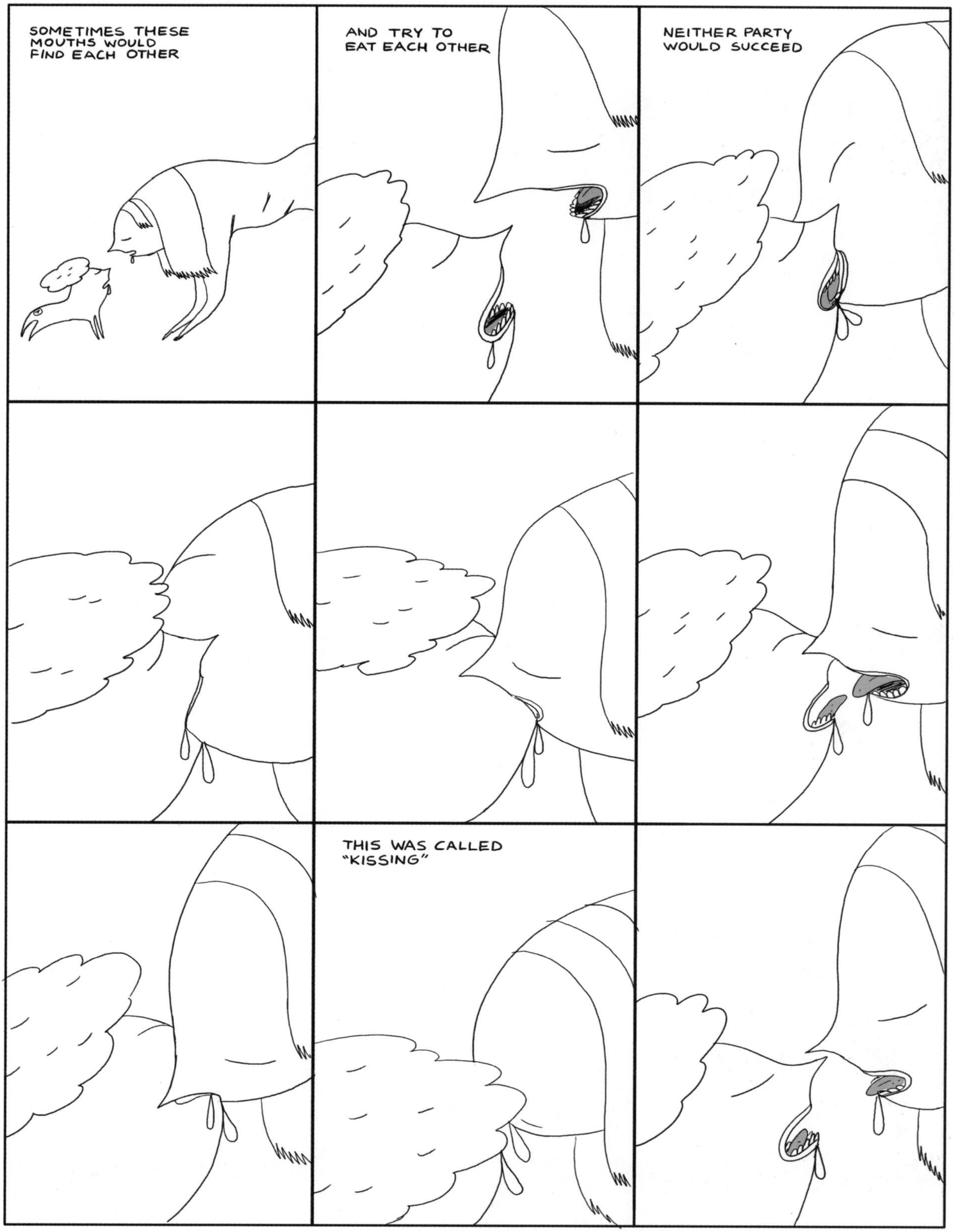
SOMETIMES THESE MOUTHS WOULD FIND EACH OTHER
AND TRY TO EAT EACH OTHER
NEITHER PARTY WOULD SUCCEED
THIS WAS CALLED "KISSING"

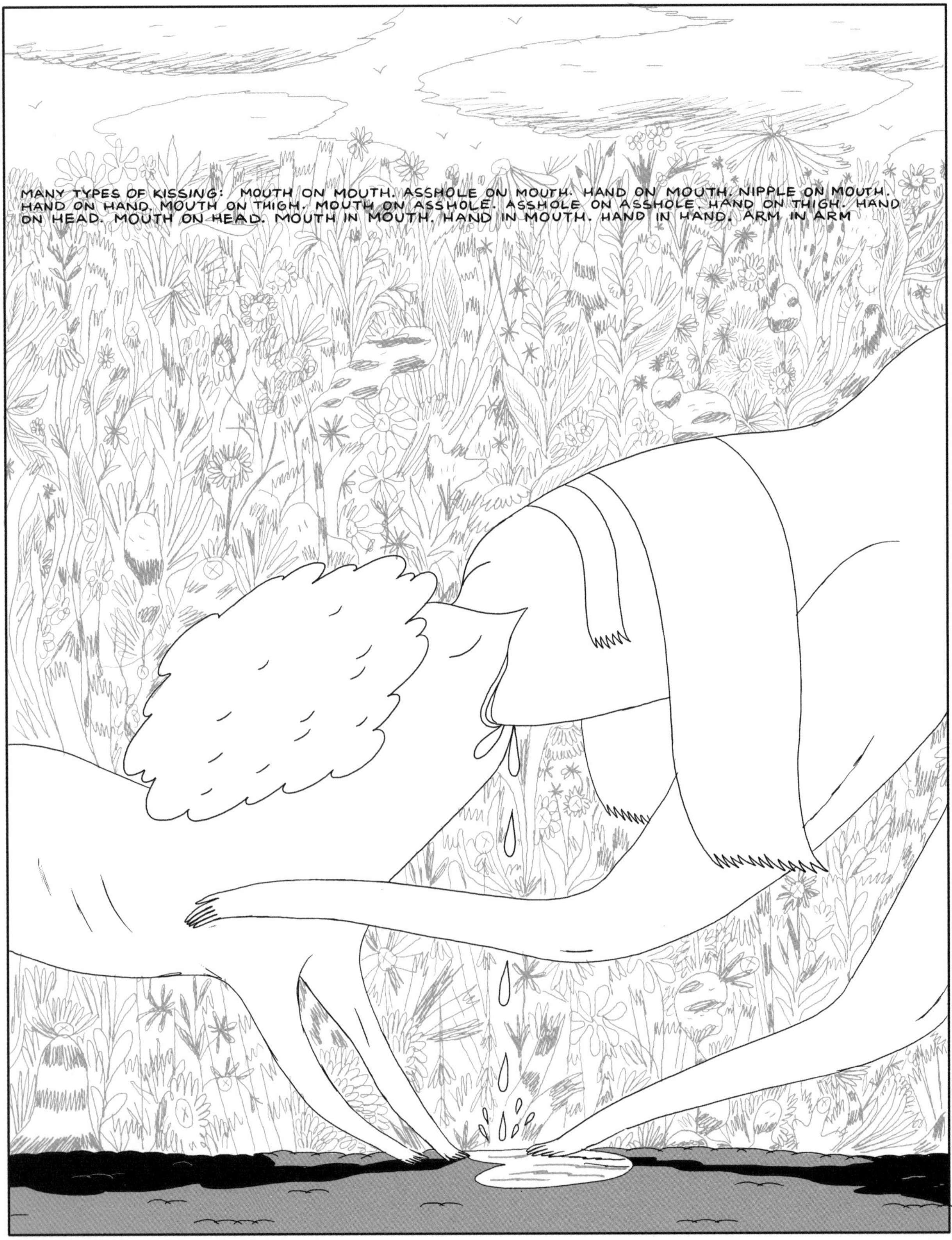
MANY TYPES OF KISSING: MOUTH ON MOUTH. ASSHOLE ON MOUTH. HAND ON MOUTH. NIPPLE ON MOUTH. HAND ON HAND. MOUTH ON THIGH. MOUTH ON ASSHOLE. ASSHOLE ON ASSHOLE. HAND ON THIGH. HAND ON HEAD. MOUTH ON HEAD. MOUTH IN MOUTH. HAND IN MOUTH. HAND IN HAND. ARM IN ARM

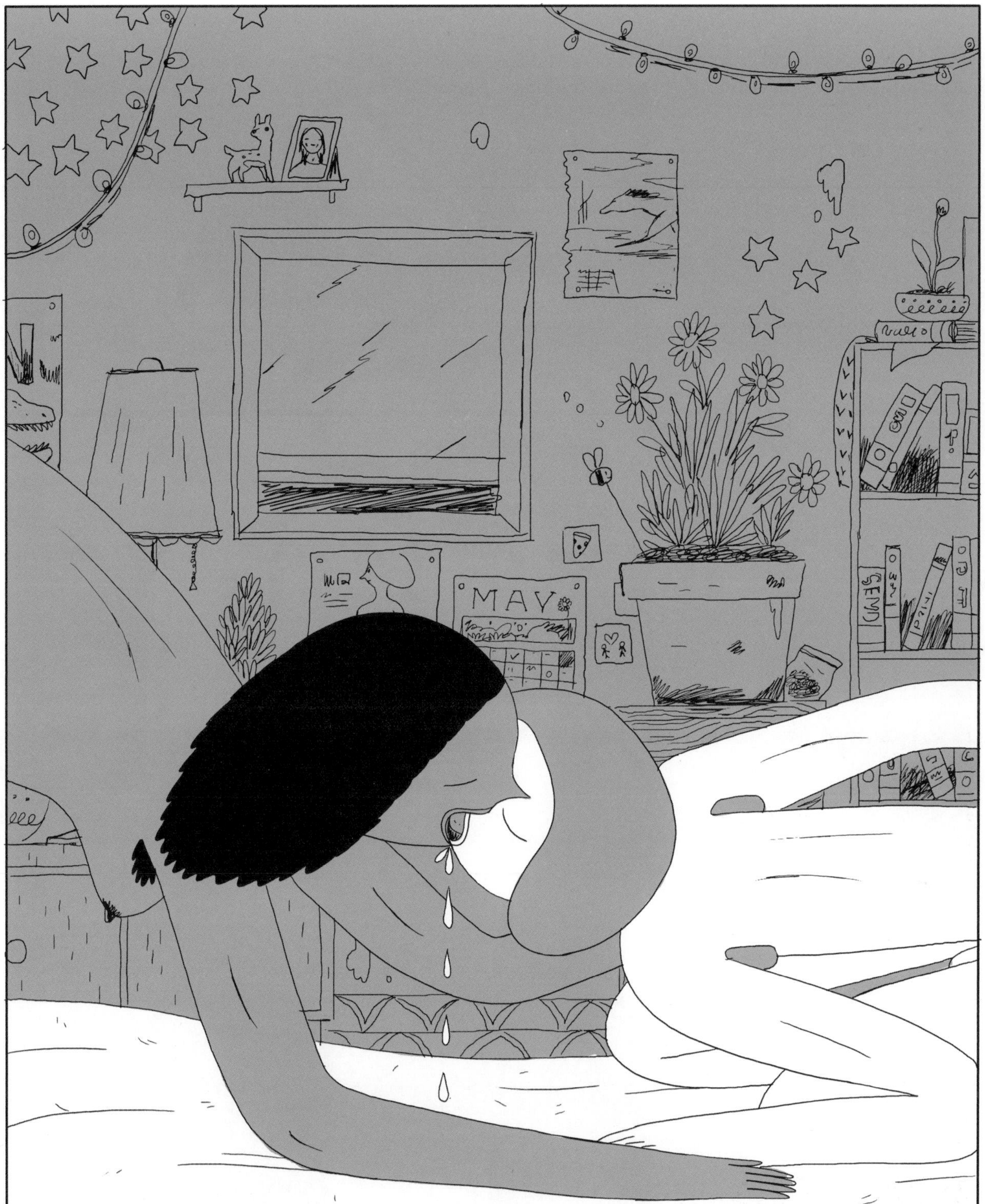
MAY

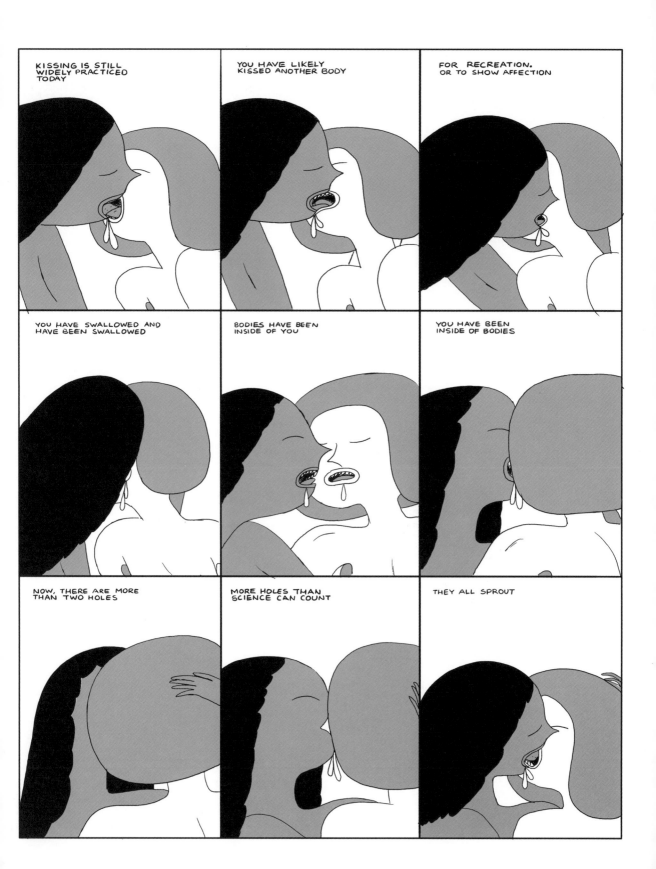

KISSING IS STILL WIDELY PRACTICED TODAY

YOU HAVE LIKELY KISSED ANOTHER BODY

FOR RECREATION, OR TO SHOW AFFECTION

YOU HAVE SWALLOWED AND HAVE BEEN SWALLOWED

BODIES HAVE BEEN INSIDE OF YOU

YOU HAVE BEEN INSIDE OF BODIES

NOW, THERE ARE MORE THAN TWO HOLES

MORE HOLES THAN SCIENCE CAN COUNT

THEY ALL SPROUT

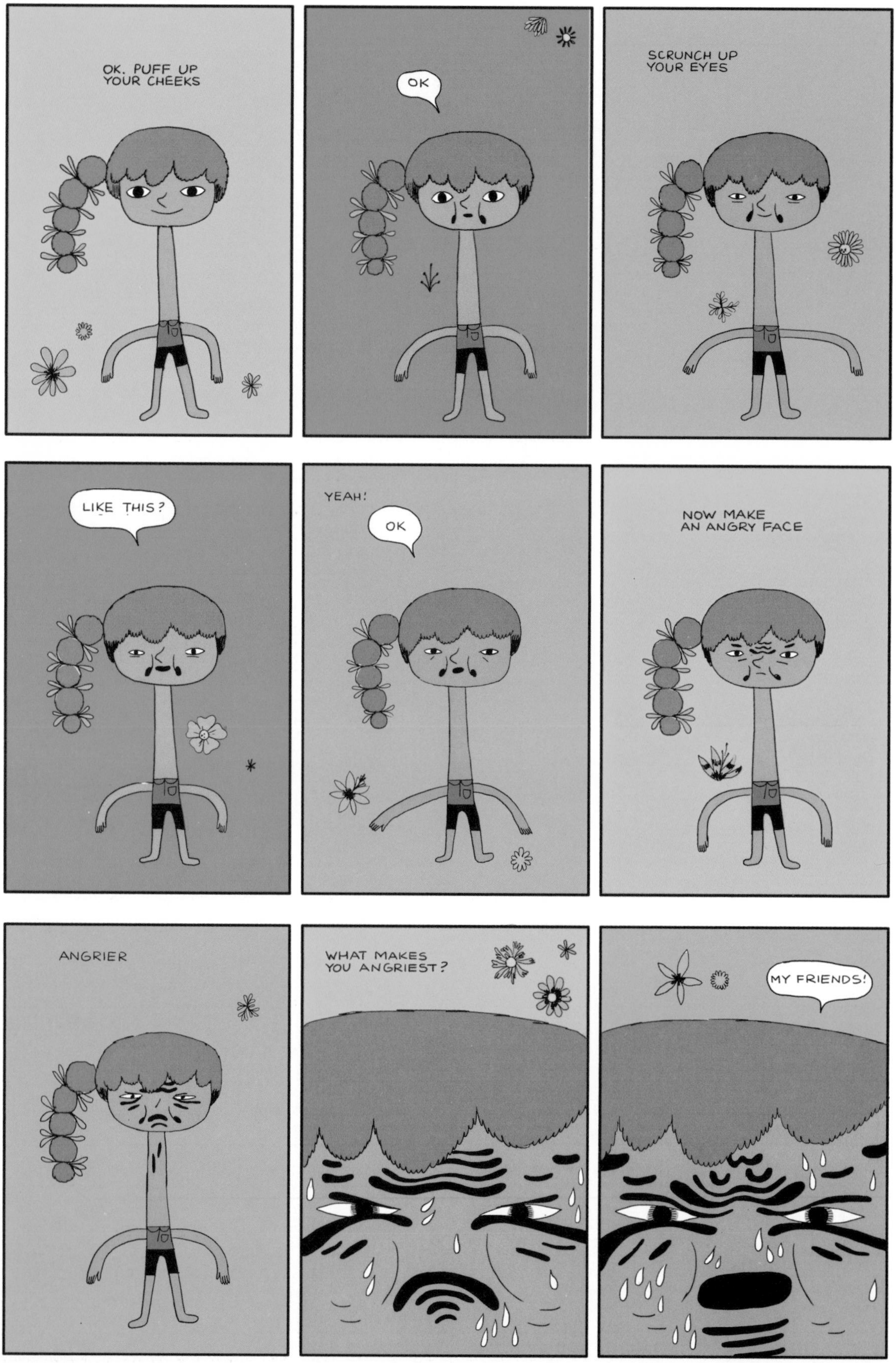
OK. PUFF UP YOUR CHEEKS
OK
SCRUNCH UP YOUR EYES
LIKE THIS?
YEAH!
OK
NOW MAKE AN ANGRY FACE
ANGRIER
WHAT MAKES YOU ANGRIEST?
MY FRIENDS!

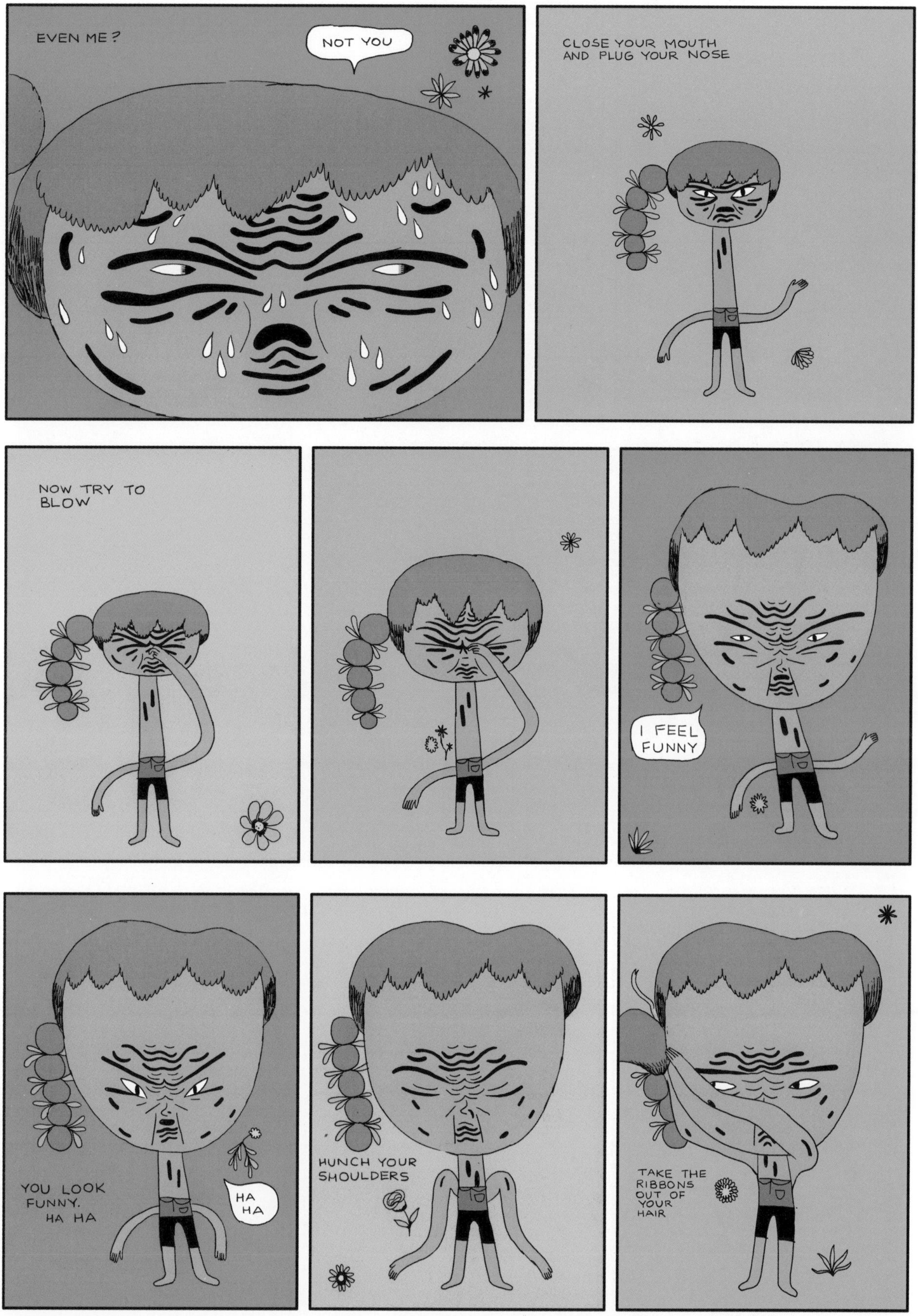
EVEN ME?
NOT YOU
CLOSE YOUR MOUTH AND PLUG YOUR NOSE
NOW TRY TO BLOW
I FEEL FUNNY
YOU LOOK FUNNY. HA HA
HA HA
HUNCH YOUR SHOULDERS
TAKE THE RIBBONS OUT OF YOUR HAIR

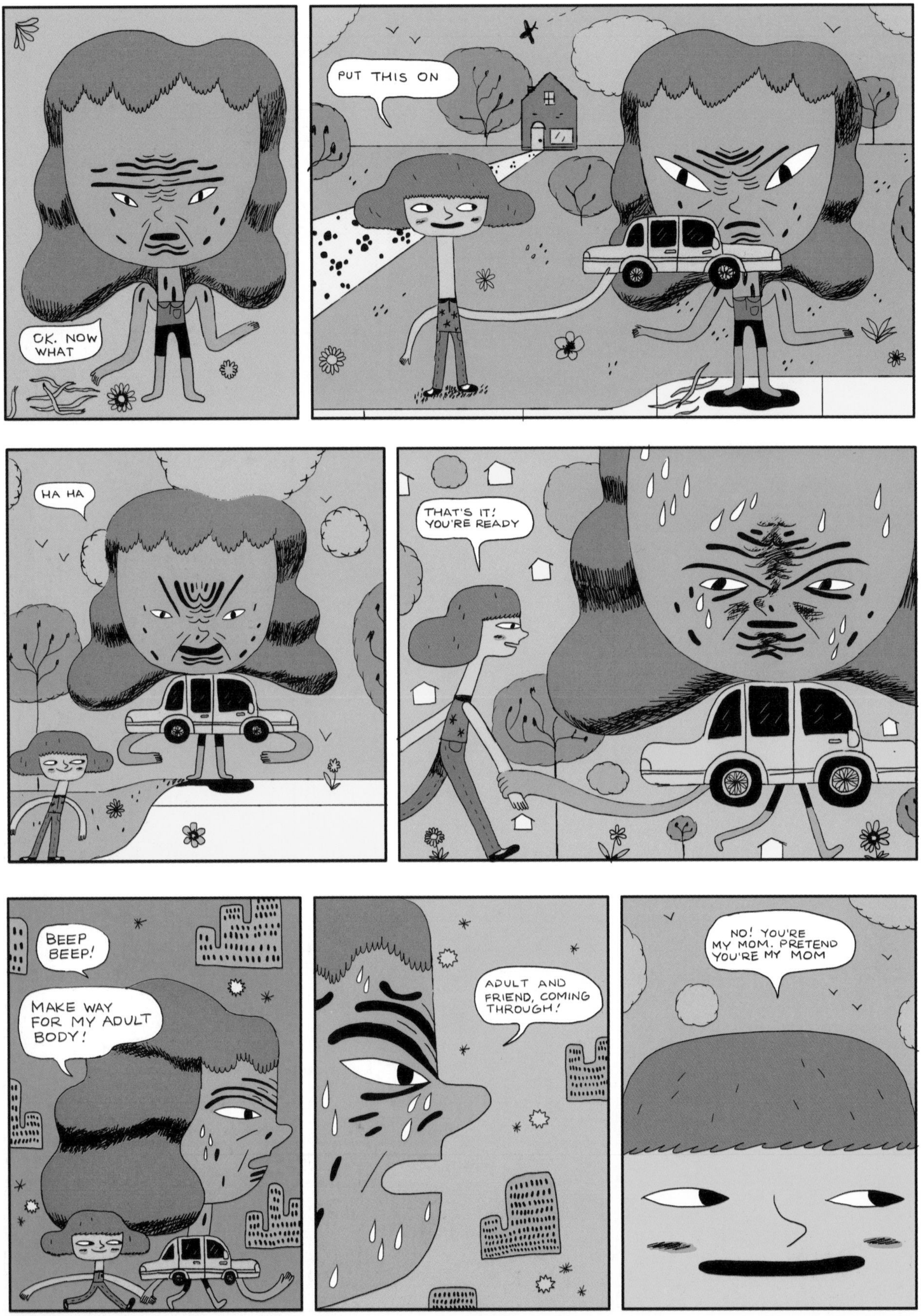
OK. NOW WHAT
PUT THIS ON
HA HA
THAT'S IT! YOU'RE READY
BEEP BEEP!
MAKE WAY FOR MY ADULT BODY!
ADULT AND FRIEND, COMING THROUGH!
NO! YOU'RE MY MOM. PRETEND YOU'RE MY MOM

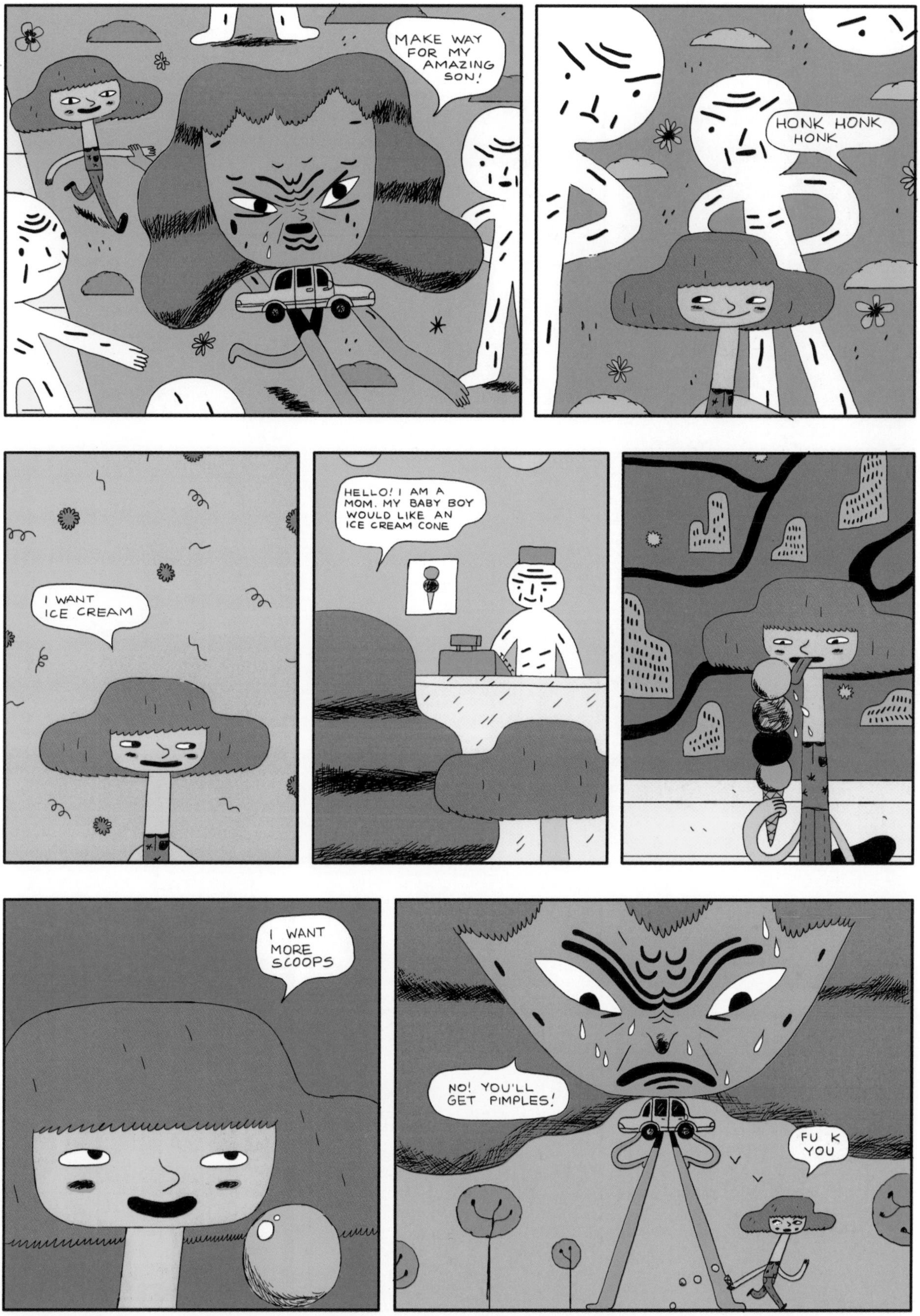
MAKE WAY FOR MY AMAZING SON!
HONK HONK HONK
I WANT ICE CREAM
HELLO! I AM A MOM. MY BABY BOY WOULD LIKE AN ICE CREAM CONE
I WANT MORE SCOOPS
NO! YOU'LL GET PIMPLES!
FU K YOU

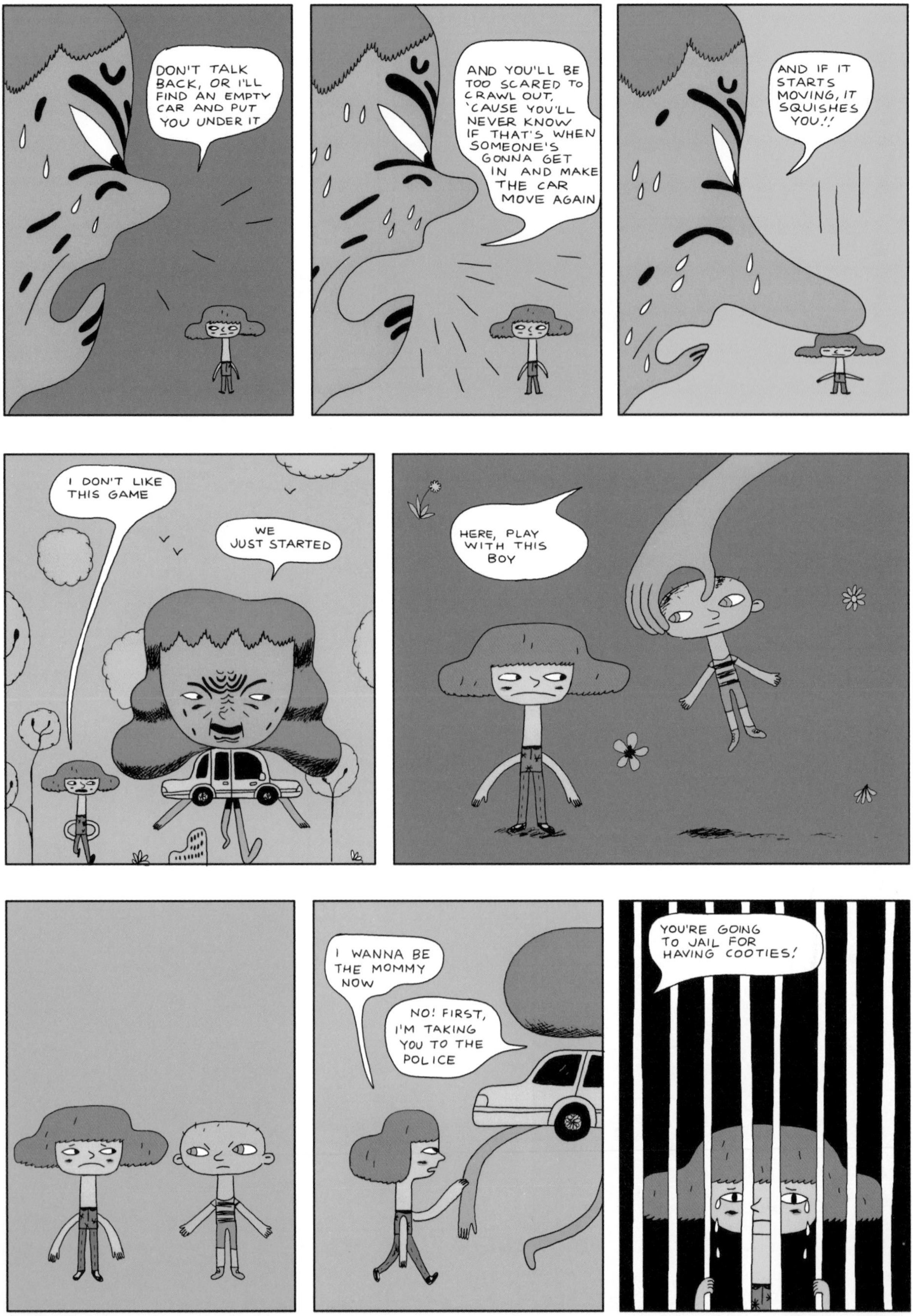
DON'T TALK BACK, OR I'LL FIND AN EMPTY CAR AND PUT YOU UNDER IT
AND YOU'LL BE TOO SCARED TO CRAWL OUT, 'CAUSE YOU'LL NEVER KNOW IF THAT'S WHEN SOMEONE'S GONNA GET IN AND MAKE THE CAR MOVE AGAIN
AND IF IT STARTS MOVING, IT SQUISHES YOU!!
I DON'T LIKE THIS GAME
WE JUST STARTED
HERE, PLAY WITH THIS BOY
I WANNA BE THE MOMMY NOW
NO! FIRST, I'M TAKING YOU TO THE POLICE
YOU'RE GOING TO JAIL FOR HAVING COOTIES!

The
Prime
Minister
of
Canada

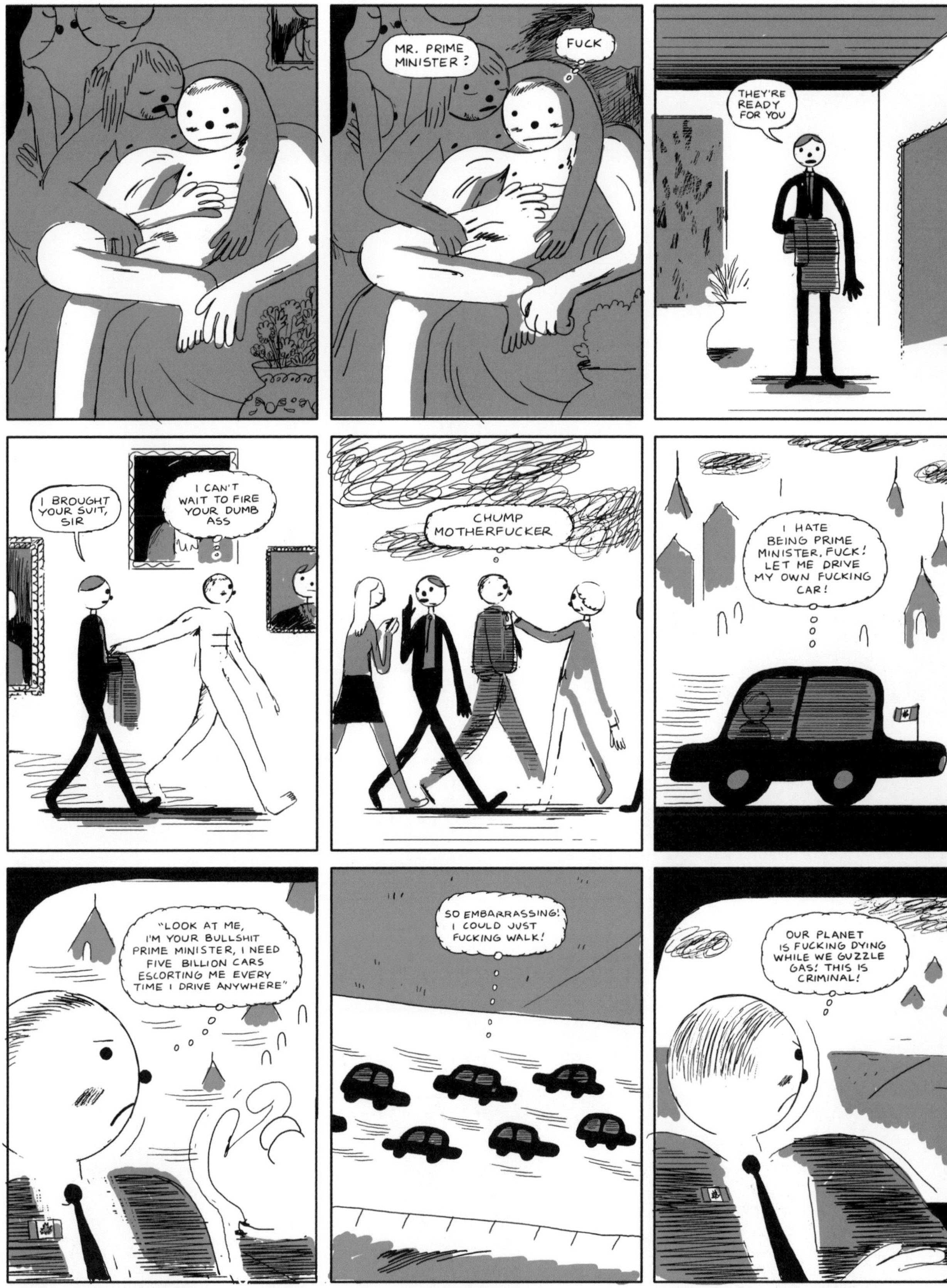
MR. PRIME MINISTER?
FUCK
THEY'RE READY FOR YOU
I BROUGHT YOUR SUIT, SIR
I CAN'T WAIT TO FIRE YOUR DUMB ASS
CHUMP MOTHERFUCKER
I HATE BEING PRIME MINISTER, FUCK! LET ME DRIVE MY OWN FUCKING CAR!
"LOOK AT ME, I'M YOUR BULLSHIT PRIME MINISTER, I NEED FIVE BILLION CARS ESCORTING ME EVERY TIME I DRIVE ANYWHERE"
SO EMBARRASSING! I COULD JUST FUCKING WALK!
OUR PLANET IS FUCKING DYING WHILE WE GUZZLE GAS! THIS IS CRIMINAL!

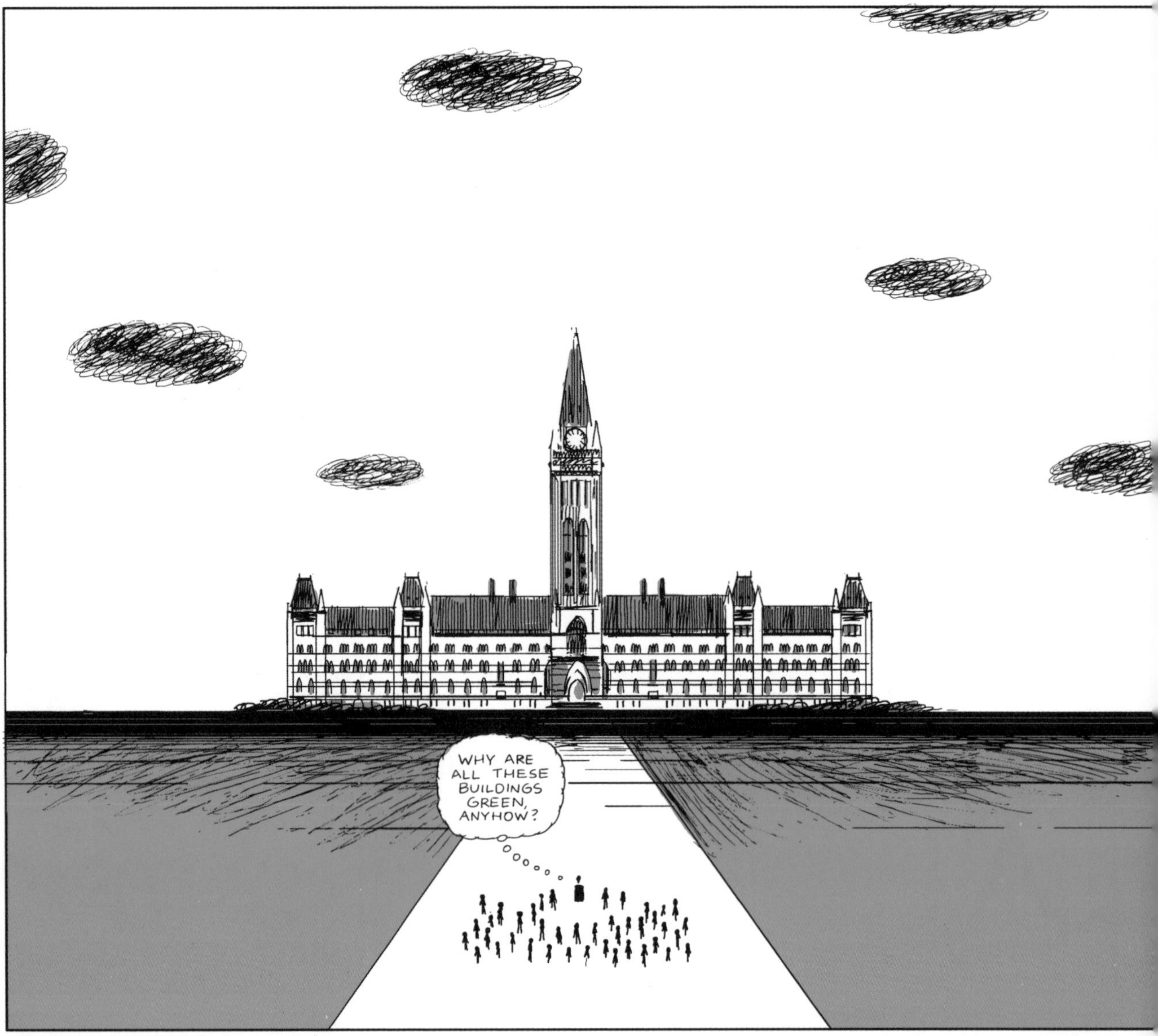
WHY ARE ALL THESE BUILDINGS GREEN, ANYHOW?

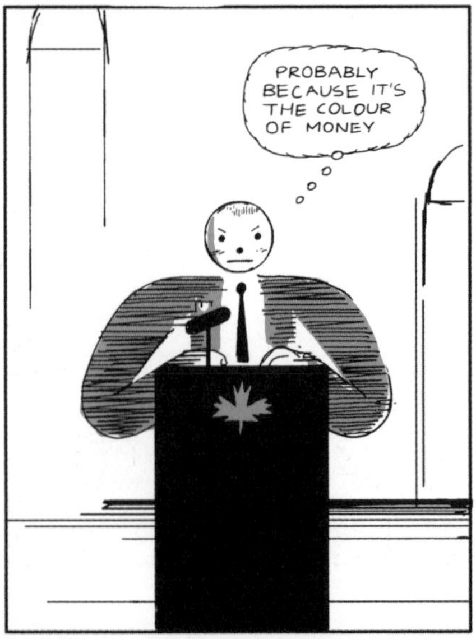
PROBABLY BECAUSE IT'S THE COLOUR OF MONEY

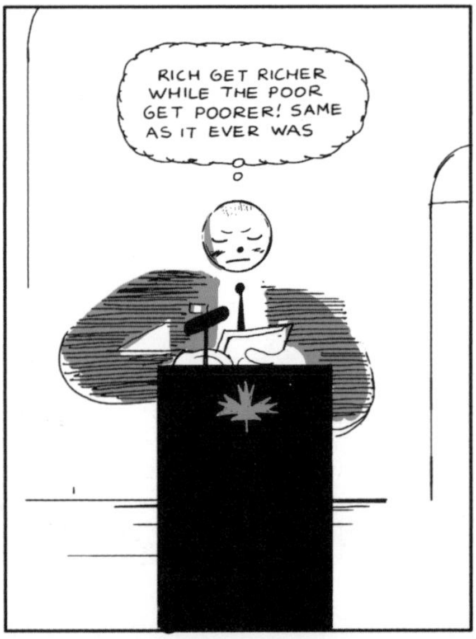
RICH GET RICHER WHILE THE POOR GET POORER! SAME AS IT EVER WAS

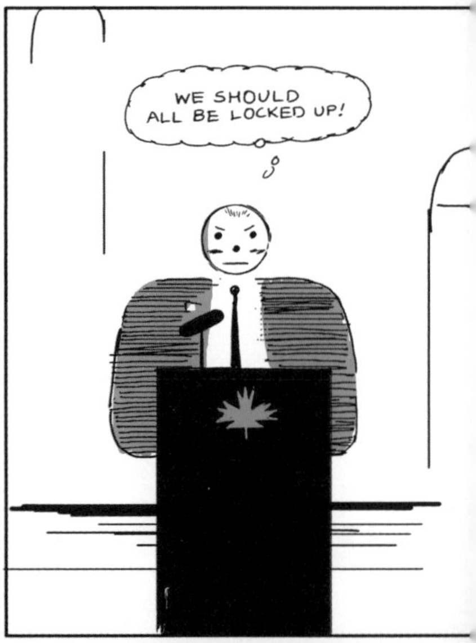
WE SHOULD ALL BE LOCKED UP!

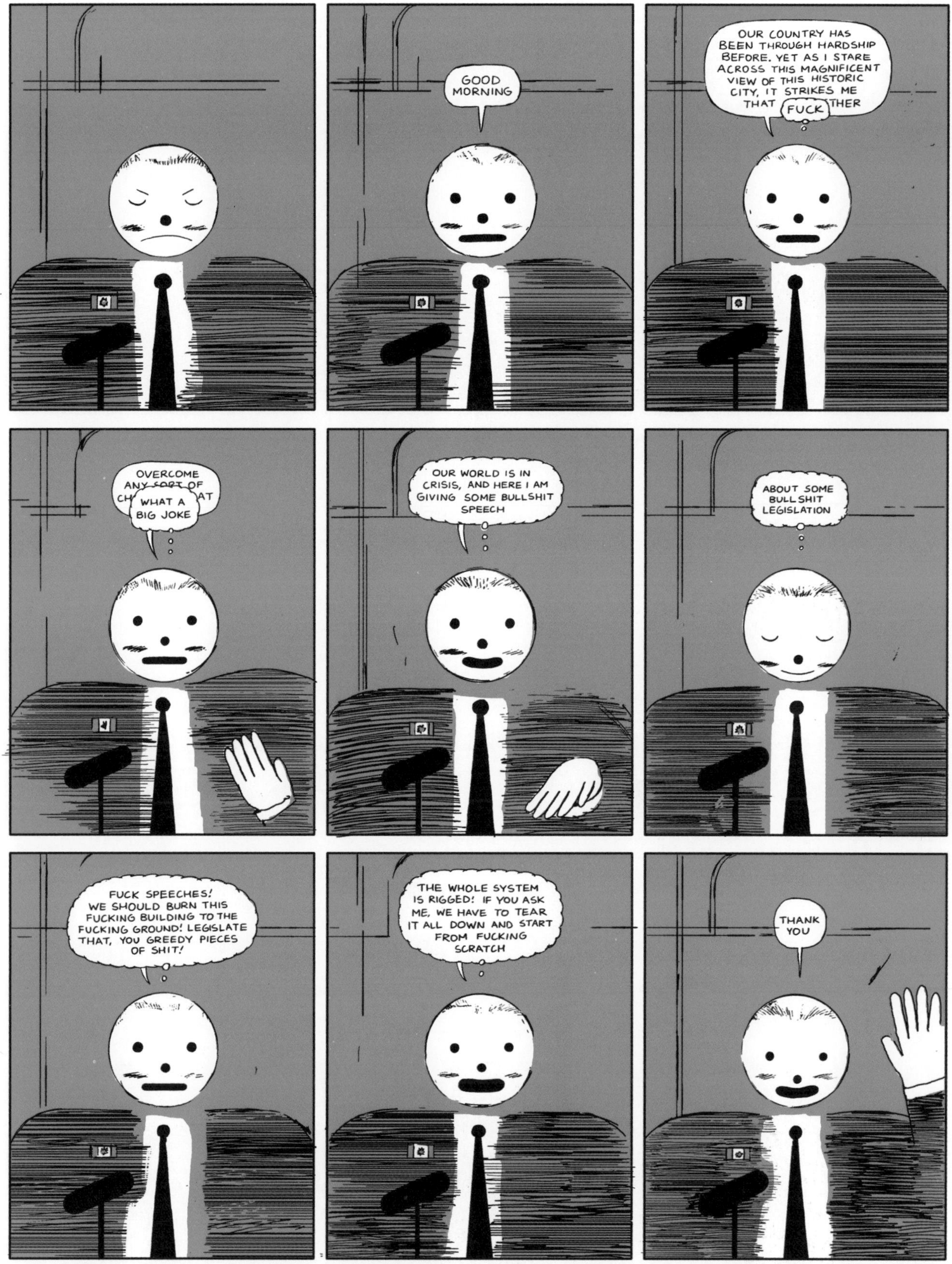
GOOD MORNING
OUR COUNTRY HAS BEEN THROUGH HARDSHIP BEFORE. YET AS I STARE ACROSS THIS MAGNIFICENT VIEW OF THIS HISTORIC CITY, IT STRIKES ME THAT THER
FUCK
OVERCOME ANY SORT OF CH AT
WHAT A BIG JOKE
OUR WORLD IS IN CRISIS, AND HERE I AM GIVING SOME BULLSHIT SPEECH
ABOUT SOME BULLSHIT LEGISLATION
FUCK SPEECHES! WE SHOULD BURN THIS FUCKING BUILDING TO THE FUCKING GROUND! LEGISLATE THAT, YOU GREEDY PIECES OF SHIT!
THE WHOLE SYSTEM IS RIGGED! IF YOU ASK ME, WE HAVE TO TEAR IT ALL DOWN AND START FROM FUCKING SCRATCH
THANK YOU

I FEEL SO MUCH BETTER NAKED
I SHOULD PASS A LAW THAT SAYS ONE DAY A MONTH, IT'S ILLEGAL TO WEAR CLOTHING
DICKS ARE SO WEIRD
WHERE'S THAT REMOTE
CLICK
--CONFLICT ABOUT WHETHER OR NOT CANADA WILL BE LENDING TROOPS TO THE PEACEKEEPING ---
BREAKING NEWS
UGH! I CAN'T STAND THIS STUFF

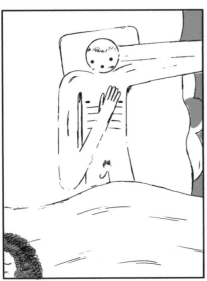

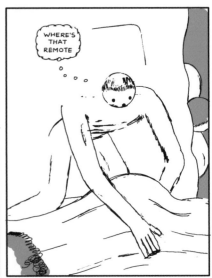

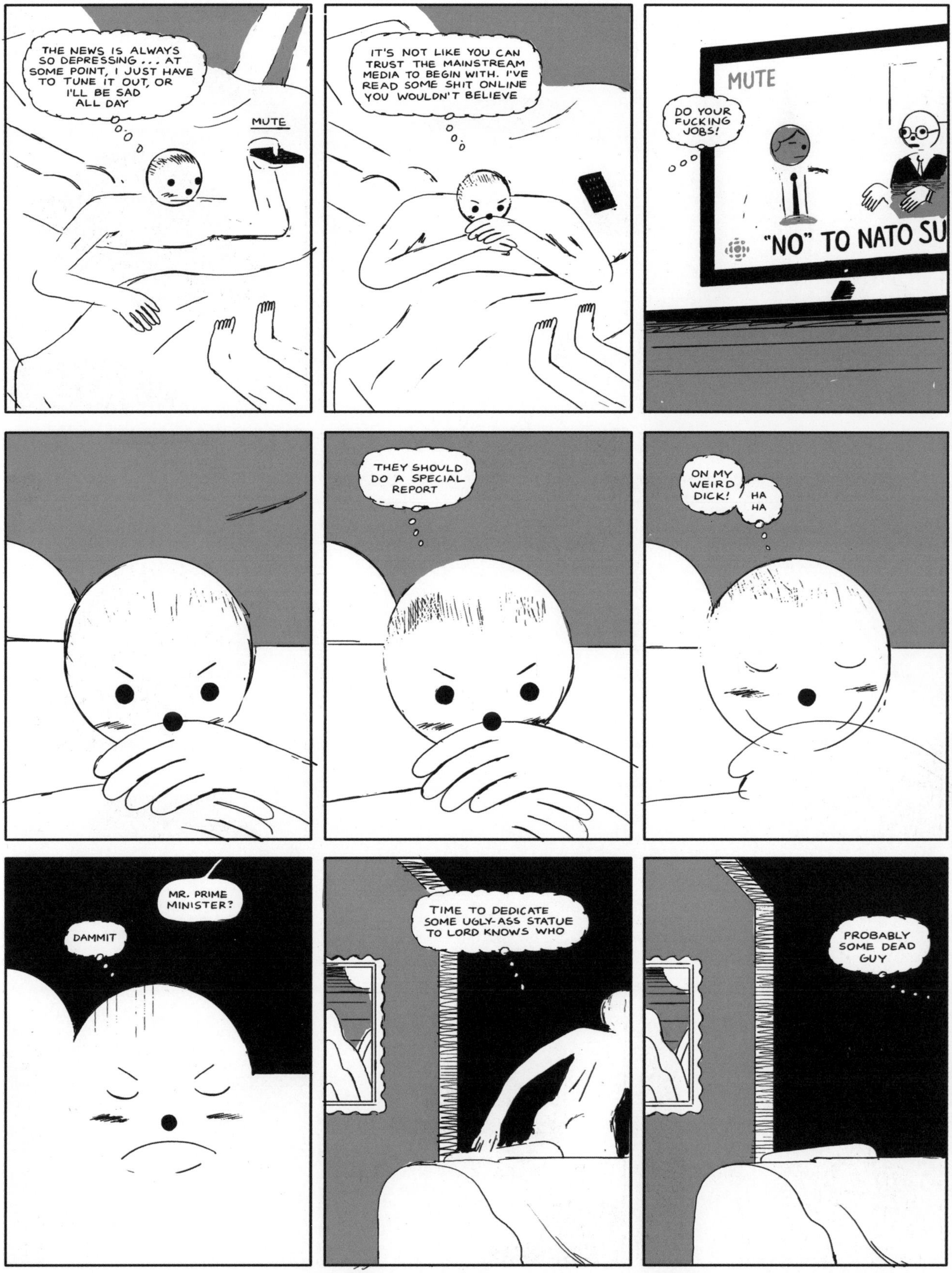
THE NEWS IS ALWAYS SO DEPRESSING... AT SOME POINT, I JUST HAVE TO TUNE IT OUT, OR I'LL BE SAD ALL DAY
MUTE
IT'S NOT LIKE YOU CAN TRUST THE MAINSTREAM MEDIA TO BEGIN WITH. I'VE READ SOME SHIT ONLINE YOU WOULDN'T BELIEVE
MUTE
DO YOUR FUCKING JOBS!
"NO" TO NATO SU
THEY SHOULD DO A SPECIAL REPORT
ON MY WEIRD DICK!
HA HA
MR. PRIME MINISTER?
DAMMIT
TIME TO DEDICATE SOME UGLY-ASS STATUE TO LORD KNOWS WHO
PROBABLY SOME DEAD GUY

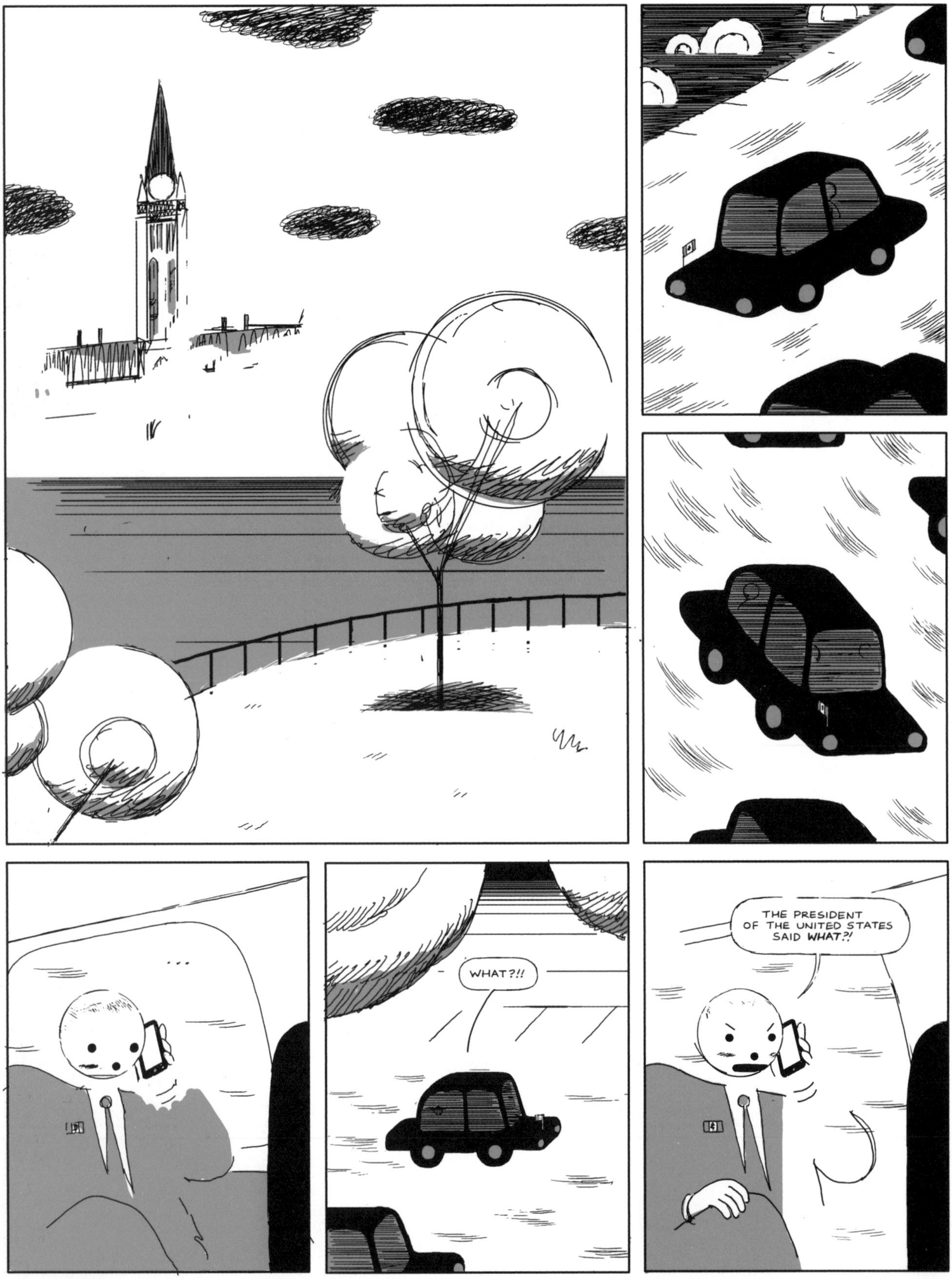
...
WHAT?!!
THE PRESIDENT OF THE UNITED STATES SAID WHAT?!

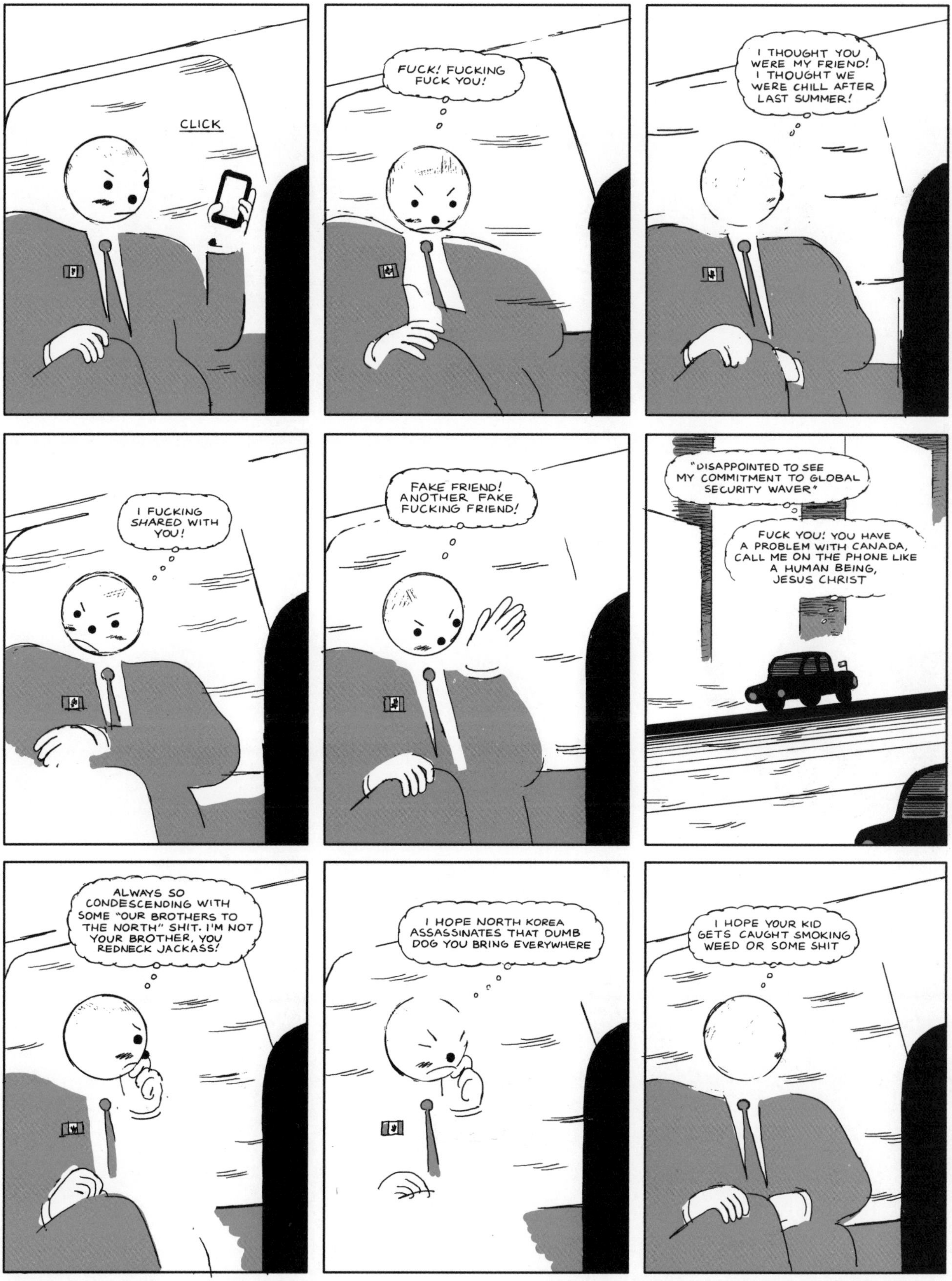
CLICK
FUCK! FUCKING FUCK YOU!
I THOUGHT YOU WERE MY FRIEND! I THOUGHT WE WERE CHILL AFTER LAST SUMMER!
I FUCKING SHARED WITH YOU!
FAKE FRIEND! ANOTHER FAKE FUCKING FRIEND!
"DISAPPOINTED TO SEE MY COMMITMENT TO GLOBAL SECURITY WAVER"
FUCK YOU! YOU HAVE A PROBLEM WITH CANADA, CALL ME ON THE PHONE LIKE A HUMAN BEING, JESUS CHRIST
ALWAYS SO CONDESCENDING WITH SOME "OUR BROTHERS TO THE NORTH" SHIT. I'M NOT YOUR BROTHER, YOU REDNECK JACKASS!
I HOPE NORTH KOREA ASSASSINATES THAT DUMB DOG YOU BRING EVERYWHERE
I HOPE YOUR KID GETS CAUGHT SMOKING WEED OR SOME SHIT

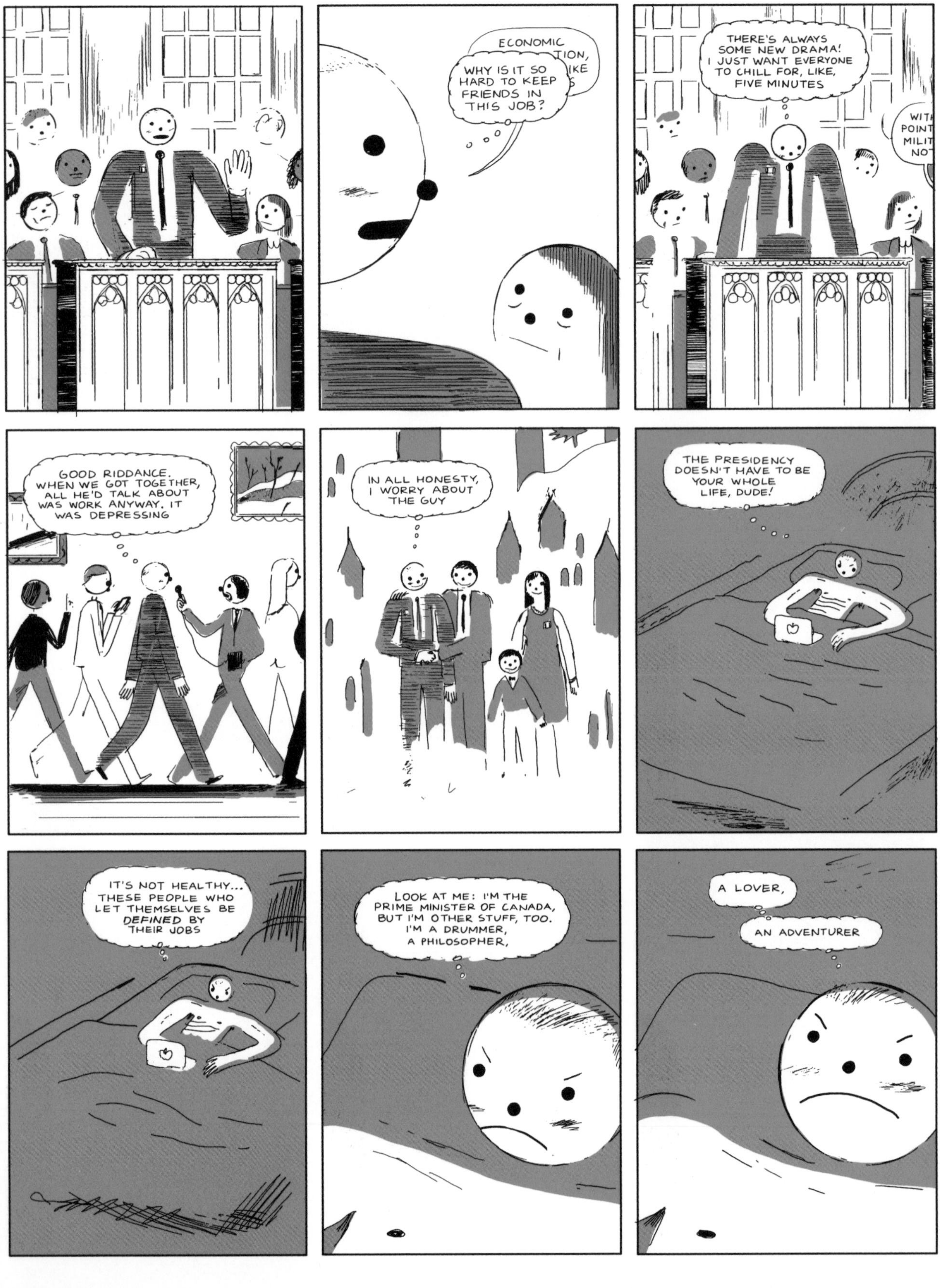
ECONOMIC
WHY IS IT SO HARD TO KEEP FRIENDS IN THIS JOB?
THERE'S ALWAYS SOME NEW DRAMA! I JUST WANT EVERYONE TO CHILL FOR, LIKE, FIVE MINUTES
GOOD RIDDANCE. WHEN WE GOT TOGETHER, ALL HE'D TALK ABOUT WAS WORK ANYWAY. IT WAS DEPRESSING
IN ALL HONESTY, I WORRY ABOUT THE GUY
THE PRESIDENCY DOESN'T HAVE TO BE YOUR WHOLE LIFE, DUDE!
IT'S NOT HEALTHY... THESE PEOPLE WHO LET THEMSELVES BE *DEFINED* BY THEIR JOBS
LOOK AT ME: I'M THE PRIME MINISTER OF CANADA, BUT I'M OTHER STUFF, TOO. I'M A DRUMMER, A PHILOSOPHER,
A LOVER,
AN ADVENTURER

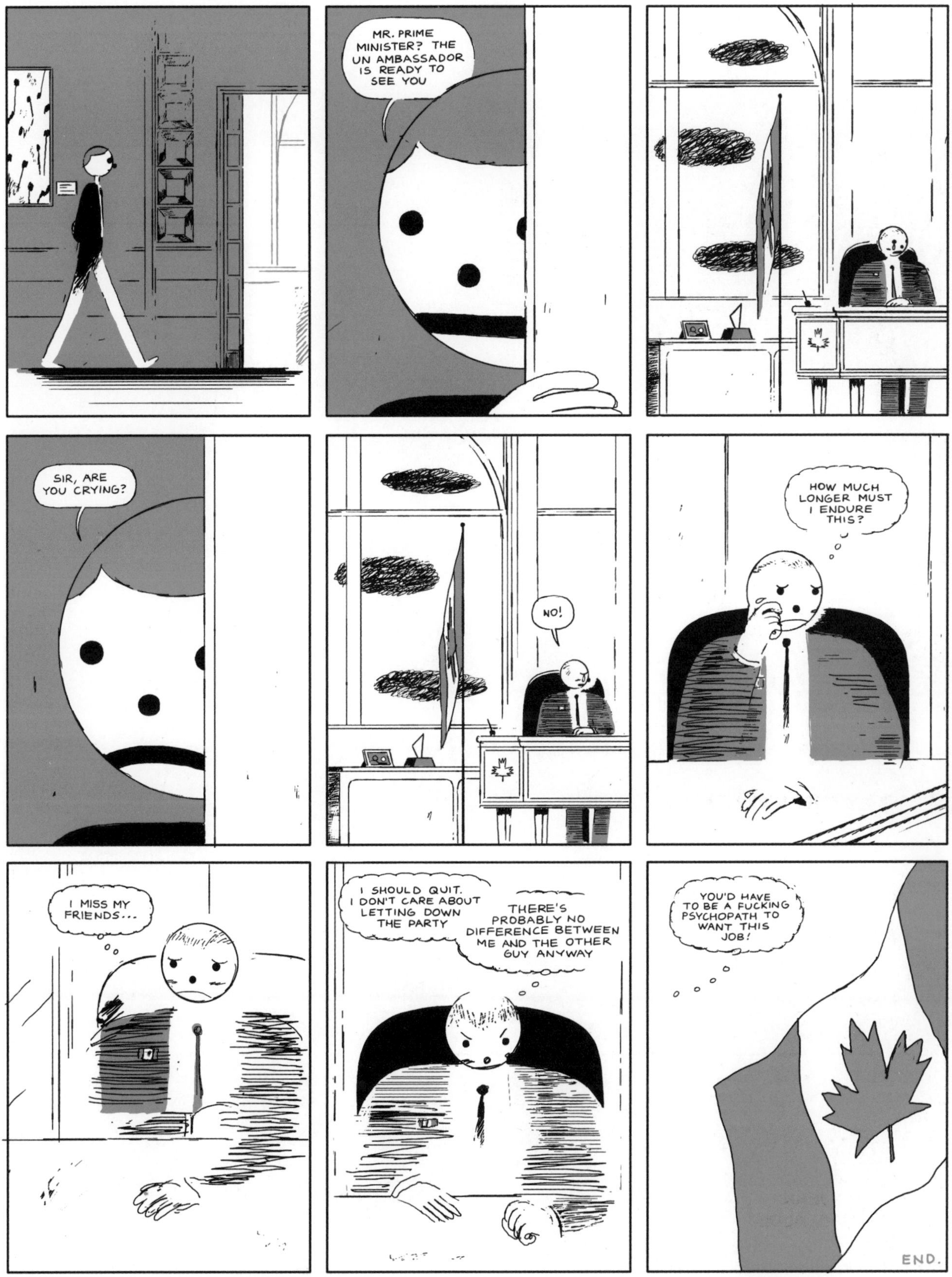
MR. PRIME MINISTER? THE UN AMBASSADOR IS READY TO SEE YOU
SIR, ARE YOU CRYING?
NO!
HOW MUCH LONGER MUST I ENDURE THIS?
I MISS MY FRIENDS...
I SHOULD QUIT. I DON'T CARE ABOUT LETTING DOWN THE PARTY
THERE'S PROBABLY NO DIFFERENCE BETWEEN ME AND THE OTHER GUY ANYWAY
YOU'D HAVE TO BE A FUCKING PSYCHOPATH TO WANT THIS JOB!
END.

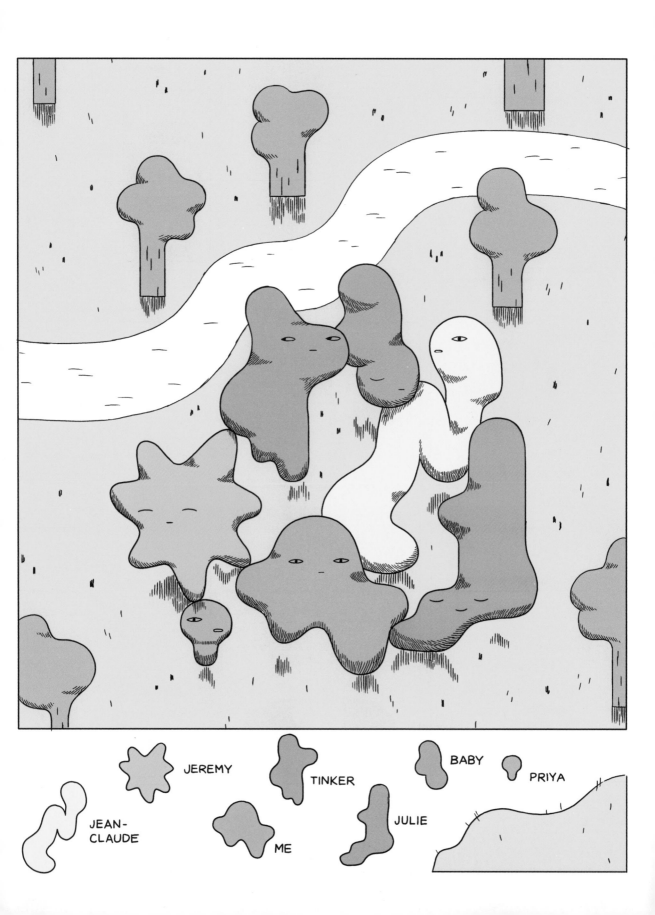

JEREMY

TINKER

BABY

PRIYA

JEAN-
CLAUDE

ME

JULIE

MY GROUP OF FRIENDS WAS UNITED BY A SHARED SET OF MUTUAL PREFERENCES – NAMELY, A PREFERENCE FOR SOFTNESS

AND, ALMOST AS IMPORTANTLY, AN AVERSION TO HARDNESS

WE ALL LIVED TOGETHER IN A SOFT VALLEY

AND WE EACH HAD A UNIQUE ROLE IN THE GROUP

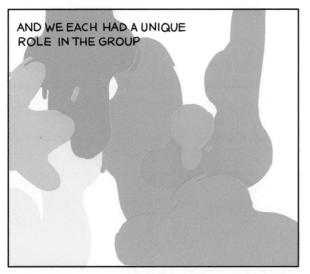

I WAS THE ARTISTIC ONE

JEAN-CLAUDE WAS THE FLIRT

PRIYA WAS THE BABY

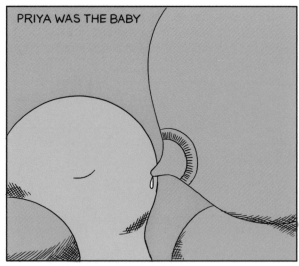

JULIE WAS THE SMART ONE

TINKER WAS THE JOCK

JEREMY WAS THE SENSITIVE ONE

BABY WAS THE FUNNY ONE, AND PRIYA'S MOM

ONE AFTERNOON, TWO HARD ANIMALS FELL FROM THE SKY

IT WAS DISCONCERTING. PRIYA AND JEREMY WERE PARTICULARLY UPSET

THE ANIMALS COULDN'T SPEAK, AS THEY HAD NO MOUTHS

BABY SWADDLED PRIYA UNTIL SHE SETTLED DOWN

WE KNEW THEY COULD HEAR US BECAUSE THEY WINCED WHEN WE SPOKE

THEY COULDN'T MOVE

THEY COULDN'T BE MOVED, BECAUSE THEIR BODIES WERE TOO HEAVY, AND THEIR EDGES WERE TOO SHARP TO HANDLE

JULIE FIGURED OUT A WAY TO MAKE THEM STAND OUT LESS

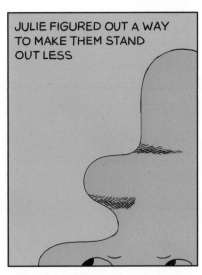

AND COVERED THEIR POINTS IN SOFT THINGS

THIS WORKED FOR A TIME. THEY BEGAN TO BLEND IN WITH THE SURROUNDING VALLEY

IT SEEMED TO CAUSE THEM SOME DISCOMFORT, BUT IT WAS THE ONLY SOLUTION WE COULD THINK OF

EVENTUALLY, THEIR SOFT EXTERIOR MADE THEM ATTRACTIVE TO JEAN-CLAUDE

HE TRIED TO LAY WITH ONE

AND WAS PUNCTURED BY ITS SPIKES

AS JEAN-CLAUDE WAS VERY TENDER

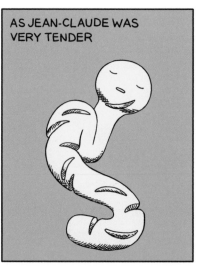

THE SOFT THINGS WERE REMOVED FROM THE HARD ANIMALS TO PREVENT FUTURE CONFUSION

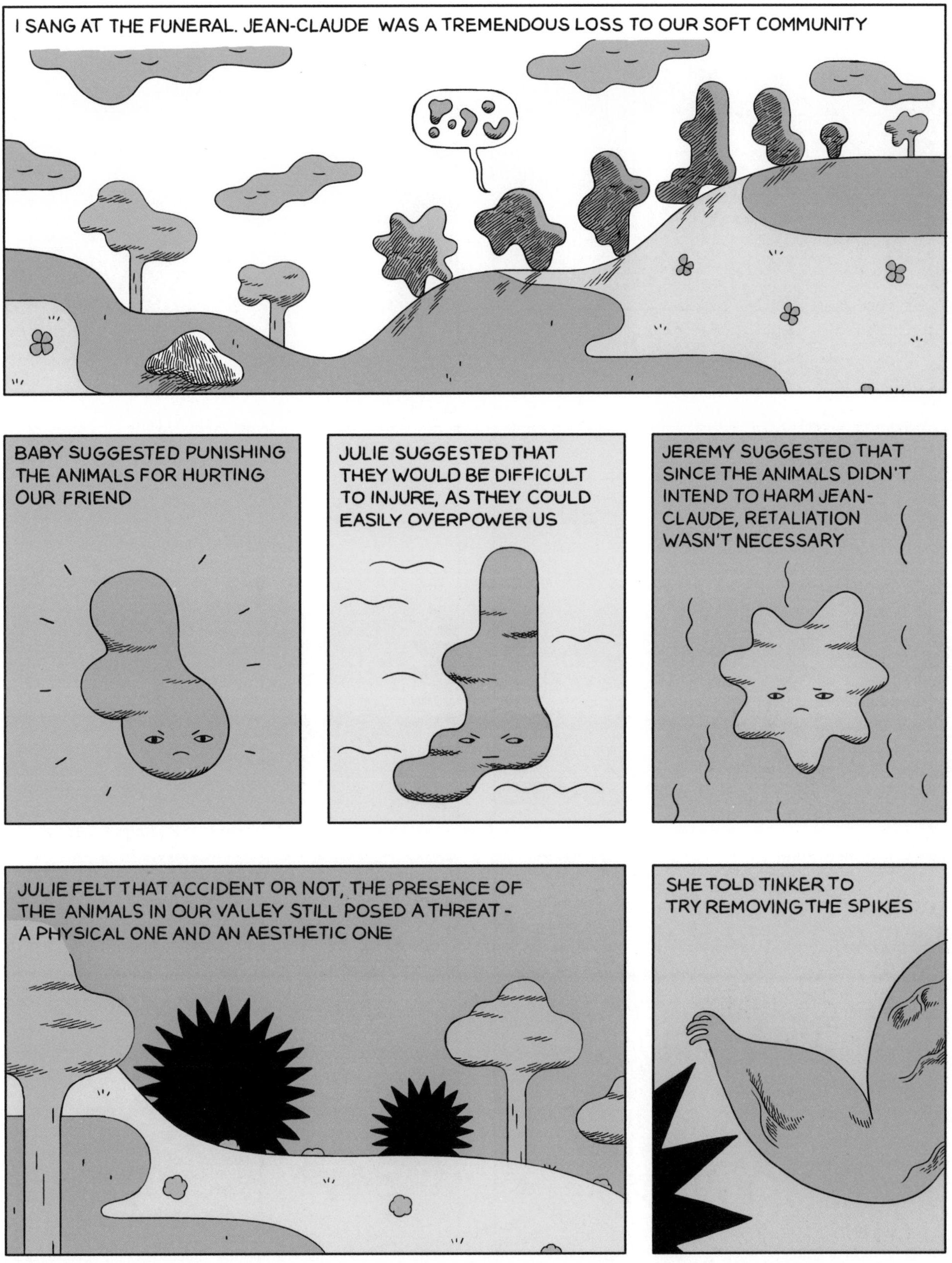
I SANG AT THE FUNERAL. JEAN-CLAUDE WAS A TREMENDOUS LOSS TO OUR SOFT COMMUNITY
BABY SUGGESTED PUNISHING THE ANIMALS FOR HURTING OUR FRIEND
JULIE SUGGESTED THAT THEY WOULD BE DIFFICULT TO INJURE, AS THEY COULD EASILY OVERPOWER US
JEREMY SUGGESTED THAT SINCE THE ANIMALS DIDN'T INTEND TO HARM JEAN-CLAUDE, RETALIATION WASN'T NECESSARY
JULIE FELT THAT ACCIDENT OR NOT, THE PRESENCE OF THE ANIMALS IN OUR VALLEY STILL POSED A THREAT - A PHYSICAL ONE AND AN AESTHETIC ONE
SHE TOLD TINKER TO TRY REMOVING THE SPIKES

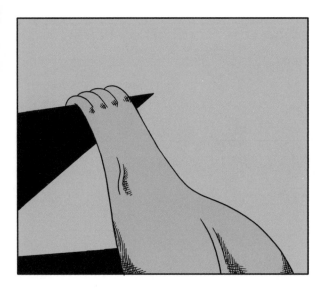

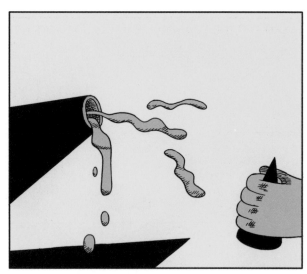

THE HARD ANIMAL'S INNARDS
SPILLED ONTO THE GROUND

IT SHOOK VIOLENTLY

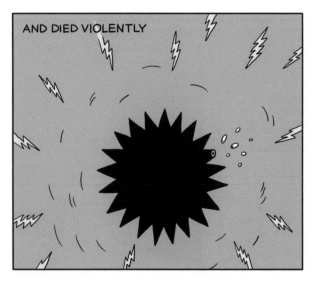

AND DIED VIOLENTLY

THE OTHER ANIMAL SOBBED AND
DID NOT STOP SOBBING FOR DAYS

THE ANIMAL'S CRYING MADE JEREMY AND PRIYA CRY. IT BECAME INCREASINGLY DIFFICULT TO SLEEP

ONE MORNING, WE WOKE UP TO FIND THAT BABY HAD LEFT THE VALLEY, NO LONGER ABLE TO BEAR THE SOUND OF HER DAUGHTER CRYING

JULIE BECAME CONCERNED WITH THE ANIMAL'S CRIES. WEEKS HAD PASSED AND IT WAS STILL UPSET

SHE THOUGHT KILLING IT WOULD BE BEST. JEREMY REASONED WITH HER

HE SUGGESTED THAT IT WAS THE SIGHT OF ITS PARTNER'S CORPSE THAT WAS UPSETTING THE ANIMAL

AND THAT IF IT COULD NO LONGER SEE THE CORPSE IT WOULD STOP CRYING

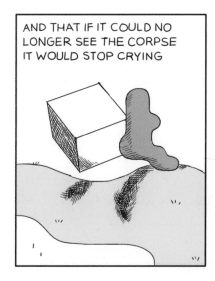

SO WE PUT A BOX OVER THE ANIMAL

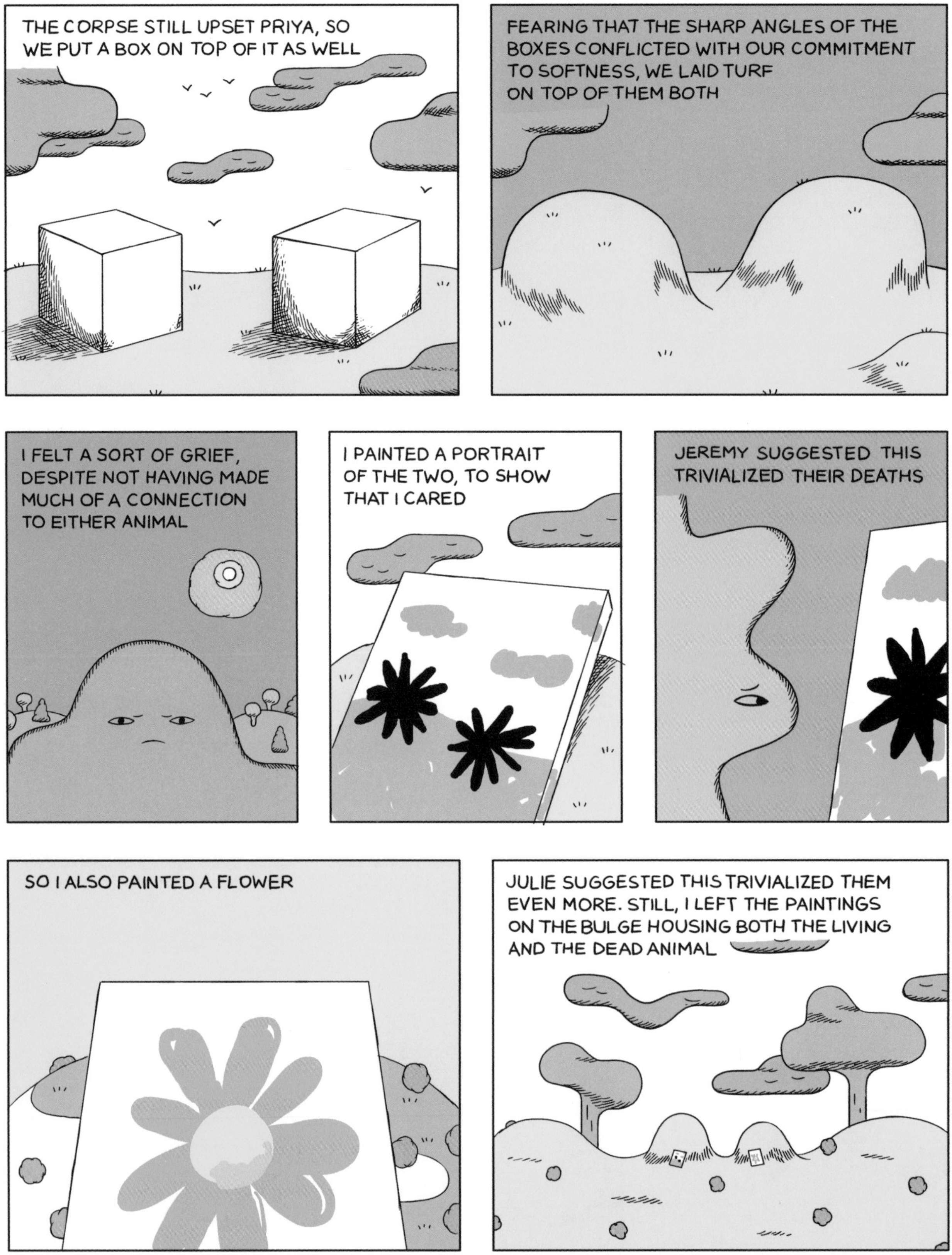
THE CORPSE STILL UPSET PRIYA, SO WE PUT A BOX ON TOP OF IT AS WELL
FEARING THAT THE SHARP ANGLES OF THE BOXES CONFLICTED WITH OUR COMMITMENT TO SOFTNESS, WE LAID TURF ON TOP OF THEM BOTH
I FELT A SORT OF GRIEF, DESPITE NOT HAVING MADE MUCH OF A CONNECTION TO EITHER ANIMAL
I PAINTED A PORTRAIT OF THE TWO, TO SHOW THAT I CARED
JEREMY SUGGESTED THIS TRIVIALIZED THEIR DEATHS
SO I ALSO PAINTED A FLOWER
JULIE SUGGESTED THIS TRIVIALIZED THEM EVEN MORE. STILL, I LEFT THE PAINTINGS ON THE BULGE HOUSING BOTH THE LIVING AND THE DEAD ANIMAL

JULIE EVENTUALLY FLED THE VALLEY, STILL FEARING RETALIATION FROM OTHER HARD ANIMALS

SHE TOOK TINKER WITH HER, FOR PROTECTION PRESUMABLY

JEREMY COULDN'T BEAR ALL THE CHANGES TO OUR GROUP. OVERWHELMED WITH EMOTION, HE LEFT AS WELL

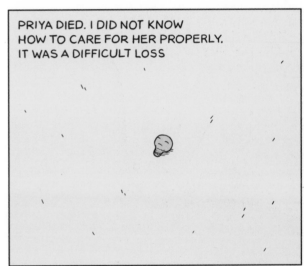

PRIYA DIED. I DID NOT KNOW HOW TO CARE FOR HER PROPERLY. IT WAS A DIFFICULT LOSS

I STILL LIVE AND WORK IN THE VALLEY

I AM SOFT. I AM SOFT, WHICH IS DIFFERENT FROM BEING TENDER, WHICH I'M NOT, AND IS DIFFERENT FROM BEING WEAK, WHICH I AM

I FEEL SOFT, WHICH IS DIFFERENT FROM BEING SOFT. THAT IS TO SAY, I AM SOFT TO THE TOUCH. I CAN'T SAY IF I LOOK SOFT. OTHERS COULD — I CAN'T

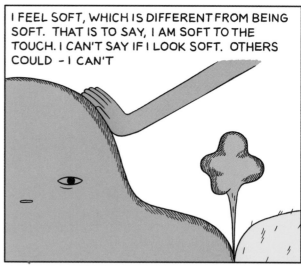

IT IS A SOFTNESS THAT IS EXPLOITED, PUSHED, PENETRATED, BREACHED, ETC. I SWALLOW EVERY FOREIGN OCCUPANT

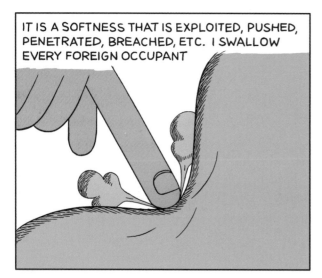

I EMBRACE EACH INTRUSION. AN EMBRACE IS DIFFERENT FROM AN INVITATION

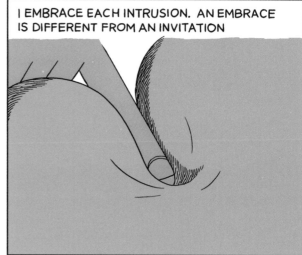

THEY ARE CONSUMED RELUCTANTLY

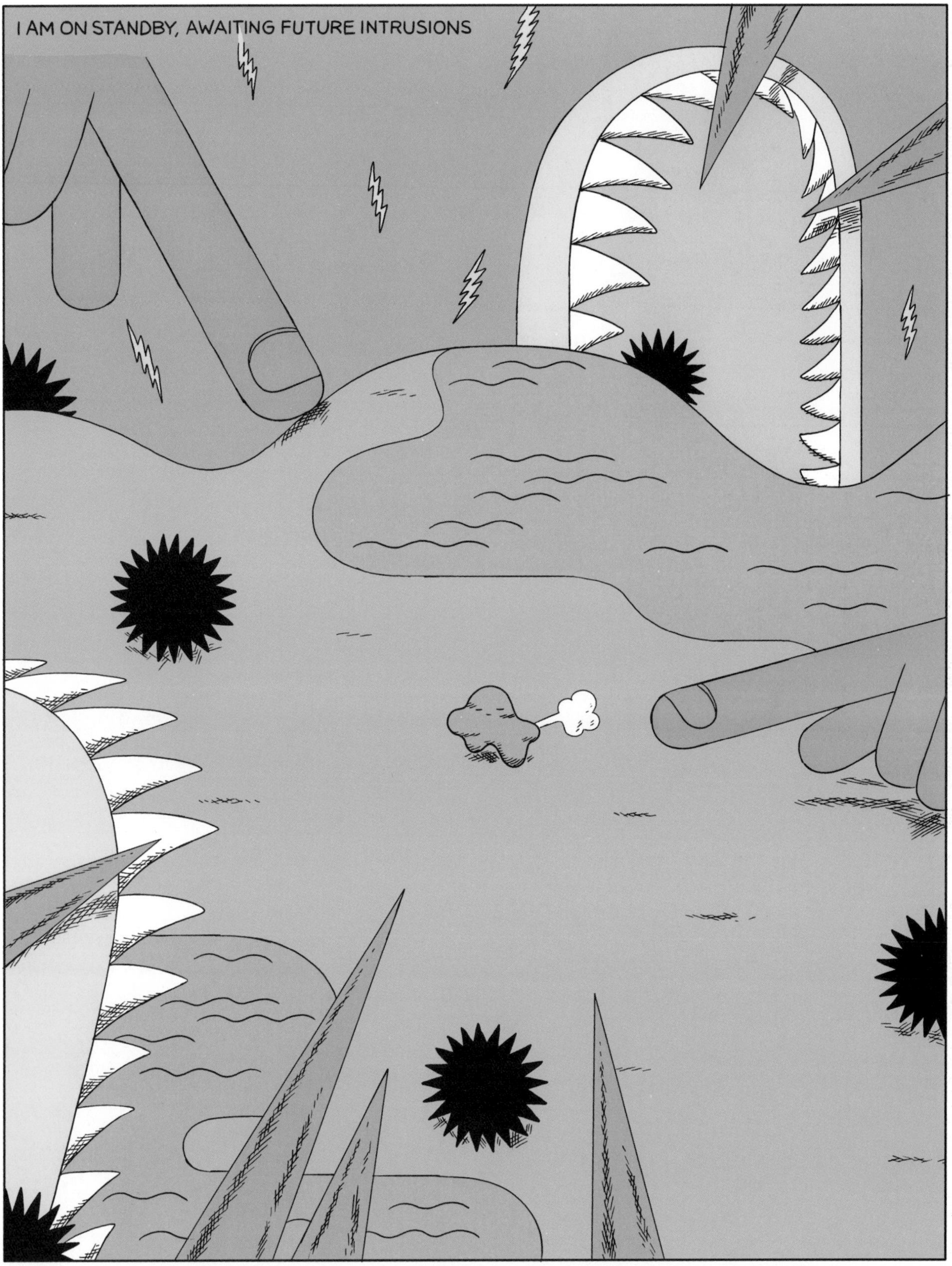
I AM ON STANDBY, AWAITING FUTURE INTRUSIONS

ALL DOGS ARE DOGS

CHAPTER 1
(A PERSON IS READING THIS PART)

"All dogs are dogs," I often repeat to myself, only sometimes believing it. I have the day off today, but I'll have to get back to it tomorrow—wading through the fur and muck and slobber, a mess of them barking as I pass, more still crawling up my legs, nipping at my wrists, gnawing at my ankles. I can't remember what it was like to have them regular. Now they are either very big or very small, these advanced dogs we couldn't wait to all have. What was so wrong with the ones we had before? What was it like to have one on your lap? To have one lick your face?

We took them for walks and we'd each carry a plastic bag in our back pocket and wrap our hand in it and pick up their shit when they shat and maybe pet them. Or we'd let them out, I guess? God, can you imagine what that would be like now? To have one just hanging around your yard, to be in constant fear of coming out to find it had been swallowed, or find it swallowing something else?

I grew up with a regular dog, but a kid down the street was the first to get one of the advanced dogs. I asked if I could walk his—this was when advanced dogs still walked, more or less. The kid said I could, and I did, and my regular one caught us. She spotted me from her dumb little lookout spot by the window. My regular dog barked and the advanced dog translated. "What the hell is this?" This was when the advanced dogs still talked, more or less.

I started going to this chat room for advanced dogs, but you had to be an advanced dog in order to join. I'd pretend. I'd stay up all night chatting and I'd hear my regular dog pawing at my door outside. My mom and dad banned me from the chats. My grades were suffering, my regular dog was suffering. It was starved, despondent—the stuff regular dogs felt. Remember when we found out they felt that way all the time? All those dogs.

So I started going to the chat rooms during computers class at school. I developed this really intense friendship with one advanced dog. It felt like the sort of correspondence that would get collected in a book someday. Some grand dialogue, or epic romance. I'd get such a charge seeing its username lit in green on my contacts list.

Eventually the dog suggested meeting in person. I kept ignoring the requests and changing the subject. When the dog persisted, I panicked and stopped responding to its messages and e-mails. The dog looked up my IP address and tracked me to my school's computer lab. One spring day, it burst through the door, barking and sputtering dial tone noises, piercing everyone's ears. It scanned the room and could tell from the expression on my face who I was and what I'd been up to. The jig was up.

I still feel awful about it, despite all the shit that's happened since, despite the journal articles, despite my mom, despite the sickness, despite everything. I broke its dumb heart. And all dogs are dogs.

CHAPTER 2
(A DOG IS READING
THIS PART)

We all had a pretty regular stretch, all of us regular dogs, for a very long time. Then everyone got tired of us, which in retrospect, we should have anticipated.

It's not like we didn't respond. We prettied ourselves up a little. Fabric, hair dye, patterns, textures. We'd try being shapes for a little while, or we'd try being people or trains or other shit that might have made us a little more likeable. Superficial changes. Nothing could hide the rottenness in our cores, our putrid middle parts pumping all that toxic nonsense to our extremities, our wet noses and sharp fingers and sticky fur and nervous tails. All these points and pricks jutting out, biting, wagging, panting. It's a wonder nobody let on before.

When I got booted from my house, I got weird in a forest for a while. I'd chew up a discarded magazine or a squirrel or a dead thing and kind of kick around, sucking dicks, foraging, whatever. I don't know. It's not like we had much direction before. Eventually, a lot of us discarded ones got together and got organized. We didn't have names anymore, so it was still a little hectic. A leaderless operation. We'd get confused—

some of our dicks or pussies or asses looked similar, or the patterns on our ears looked similar, or our voices let out similar barks. And we'd get distracted in that way regular dogs do. But we still managed to put something pretty nice together. We were proud. I'm still proud. We made a whole house together. An entire house. It was all sticks and bones and dried clay but it wasn't nothing. It was something. I'm sure it was something.

We didn't have an architect or any real plan so the house was full of these mazes that led to dead ends, corridors that led to dirt moats, doors that opened into enormous fields. Every room looked completely different from every other room. You'd turn a corner and your head would bump into some funny French curve. You'd follow a hallway off a cliff.

We started recruiting from the town nearby. There were so many town dogs walking around there with no home. Real scrappy types, fighting over a slice in a parking lot, biting each other like a bunch of dog-biters, terrorizing children—sad dog stuff. We'd roll into town and take a few back with us. They'd have a hard time fitting in. They'd get into fights about their old homes, about people, about old man politics stuff.

CHAPTER 3
(ANOTHER DOG IS READING
THIS PART)

At this point, we stopped being able to walk, so we'd just sort of scramble around, pushing our bodies forward, dragging our asses. I can't imagine what it looked like, all of these advanced dogs descending on a compound of regulars. I don't think we intended it to be any type of "showdown."

We just wanted to go over there and talk. They were the ones breaking the rules. No groups of three or more regular dogs. We thought they should either disperse or let us in and kick it with them whenever we wanted. But they wouldn't, and that's how the fight broke out. It wasn't a fair one. We advanced dogs were good at fighting—light torsos and heavy limbs, limbs so dense those dog-biters would break a tooth on them. We won. Losers walked and we took over the house. The big ones (like me) planted our fat asses wherever and breathed and shed and swelled until we filled entire rooms, pressing up against the walls, making them shake and tremble and crack until they eventually collapsed. The smaller dogs would burrow into the house's pores, rooting around and gnawing away at its columns and foundations until they were completely hollow and too weak to hold anything up. We basically trashed the place. Then we moved on.

But it was a mess to begin with. It was only a matter of time before those regular dogs killed each other or got killed or lost their nerve and let themselves get roped up again. They weren't running a house any better than we did. All dogs are dogs.

CHAPTER 4
(IT IS AMBIGUOUS WHO IS READING THIS PART)

When the dog plant first crept out of the manhole, it looked like pieces of furry macaroni glued together. They came out in these trails of five-inch-long elbow shapes. They clung to the sidewalk's lip and spread out a little into the road. Everyone ignored it. The stuff that spread to the road would initially get chopped up by tires. Larger shapes started growing out and displaced the manhole cover. Eventually, they grew large enough that it became apparent that the shapes were breathing and not just fussing about in the wind. Or maybe not breathing exactly, but certainly expanding and contracting, sometimes slowly and sometimes rapidly. You could hear the shapes rubbing against each other with each exhalation, fur purring against fur to create a sort of faint static.

The plant's fur was golden.

The big shapes came with a few more variations. One would be three feet tall and shaped like a drumstick. One would be five feet tall and shaped like an enormous kidney bean. One was like a blunt triangle, only two feet tall. Some new, smaller shapes started growing, too—smaller than the elbow macaroni ones—that looked like donut holes and would sometimes fall off the plant after a gust of wind. They'd spill into the streets and roll down hills and sometimes get swallowed by regular dogs or collected and traded by neighbourhood children.

Cars were having a difficult time driving around the plant, until eventually the whole road was blocked off and residents had to park outside the cul-de-sac and walk to their houses from there. The neighbourhood took a vote to try to chop the plant down. Small businesses wanted to keep it, and the mayor wanted to keep it, thinking it could be some big tourist attraction. The vote still passed and the plant was axed. The base of the plant was not very thick, and the shapes were all just soft meat, so it only took two swings of an axe to separate it. With each swing, the plant's shapes—not just the ones still attached to the plant, but all the smaller, shed shapes around it—did this strange little jump in the air, like a hiccup. And then they were still.

Bureaucracy is bureaucracy and months had passed between the vote being proposed and the vote being voted on and the town actually doing the thing. So by the time it was chopped, two more dog plants had sprouted in neighbouring cities. One had black fur and one had white fur with tan circles.

CHAPTER 5
(AN UGLY DOG IS READING
THIS PART)

No dog or man ever loved me. I started out round and featureless and two inches tall and will die lumpy and porous and two inches tall. My siblings all had uniform brown fur, but I am every colour, which makes me difficult to focus on. My face caved in on itself to make a little mouth and I grew eyes that didn't stay inside sockets but instead bulged out of my head like floppy tits. I sprouted pointy legs, and soon my body was more bodylike. I grew up with a litter of twelve other advanced dogs, all the small kind. Their features weren't so different from mine, really, but mine were off by just enough that there was something undeniably wrong-looking about my construction. "All dogs are dogs," a sibling would say to reassure me, but they had a cute face and a hot little mouth, so what did they know about anything.

Anyway, I was tasked with planting a dog plant where the collapsed house used to be, to commemorate our noble failure. In the time it took all of us to leave, have a meeting about it, and come back, a libertarian bought the property and built a grocery store there. I had to sneak through the cereal aisle and discreetly shake off a piece of my leg, which bounced on the ground and immediately started to multiply. One part, then two parts, growing in a spiral. It looked like a group of kissing caterpillars, or sausage links. Soon, it grew upward.

Since my fur is every colour, the tree came out in every colour, and since my fur is every texture, the tree came out in every texture—cola-coloured at the bottom, then pink, then something else, then pumpkin orange, then neon green, then something else, then taupe, and so on and so on. All the people in the store stopped and stared. They'd watch the plant inhale and they'd inhale with it. They'd watch the plant exhale and then exhale with it. The dogs had entered the store by now. They inhaled and exhaled, too. So did the items on the shelves. All of us, all of us breathing all of our breaths.

A woman put her hand on a dog's scruff and we all felt her hand on our necks. A boy squeezed a juice box and all of our ribcages caved in. A man rubbed his belly and we all felt the warmth. Every person, every dog, every juice box, every dog part, every apple, every plant, every tile, every ceiling fan, every plant, every person, every dog, every dog part, every person, every plant, every dog, every person, every dog, every person, everydog, every person, every dog, each dog, every dog, each and every dog, every person, every dog.

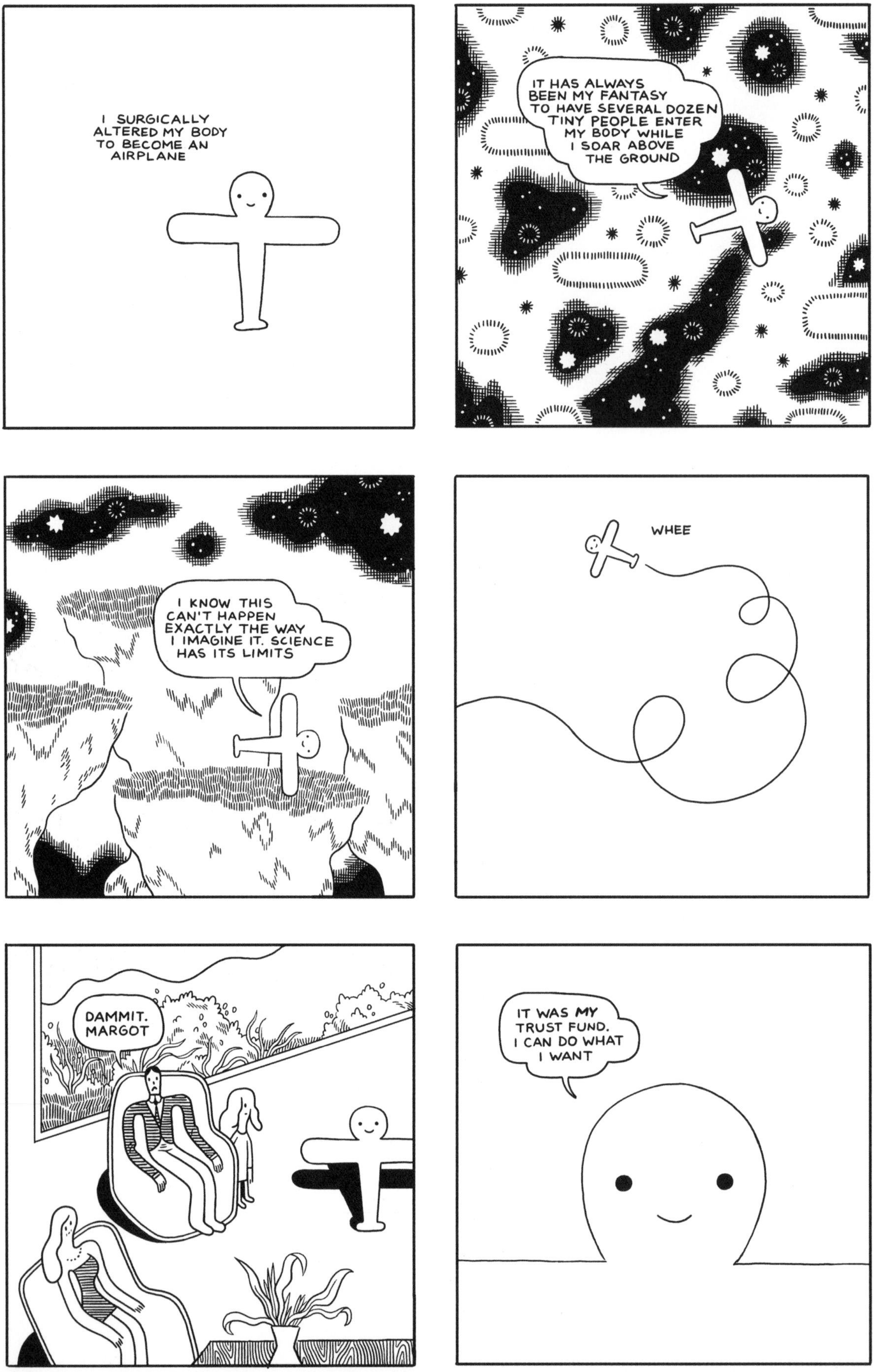
I SURGICALLY ALTERED MY BODY TO BECOME AN AIRPLANE
IT HAS ALWAYS BEEN MY FANTASY TO HAVE SEVERAL DOZEN TINY PEOPLE ENTER MY BODY WHILE I SOAR ABOVE THE GROUND
I KNOW THIS CAN'T HAPPEN EXACTLY THE WAY I IMAGINE IT. SCIENCE HAS ITS LIMITS
WHEE
DAMMIT. MARGOT
IT WAS MY TRUST FUND. I CAN DO WHAT I WANT

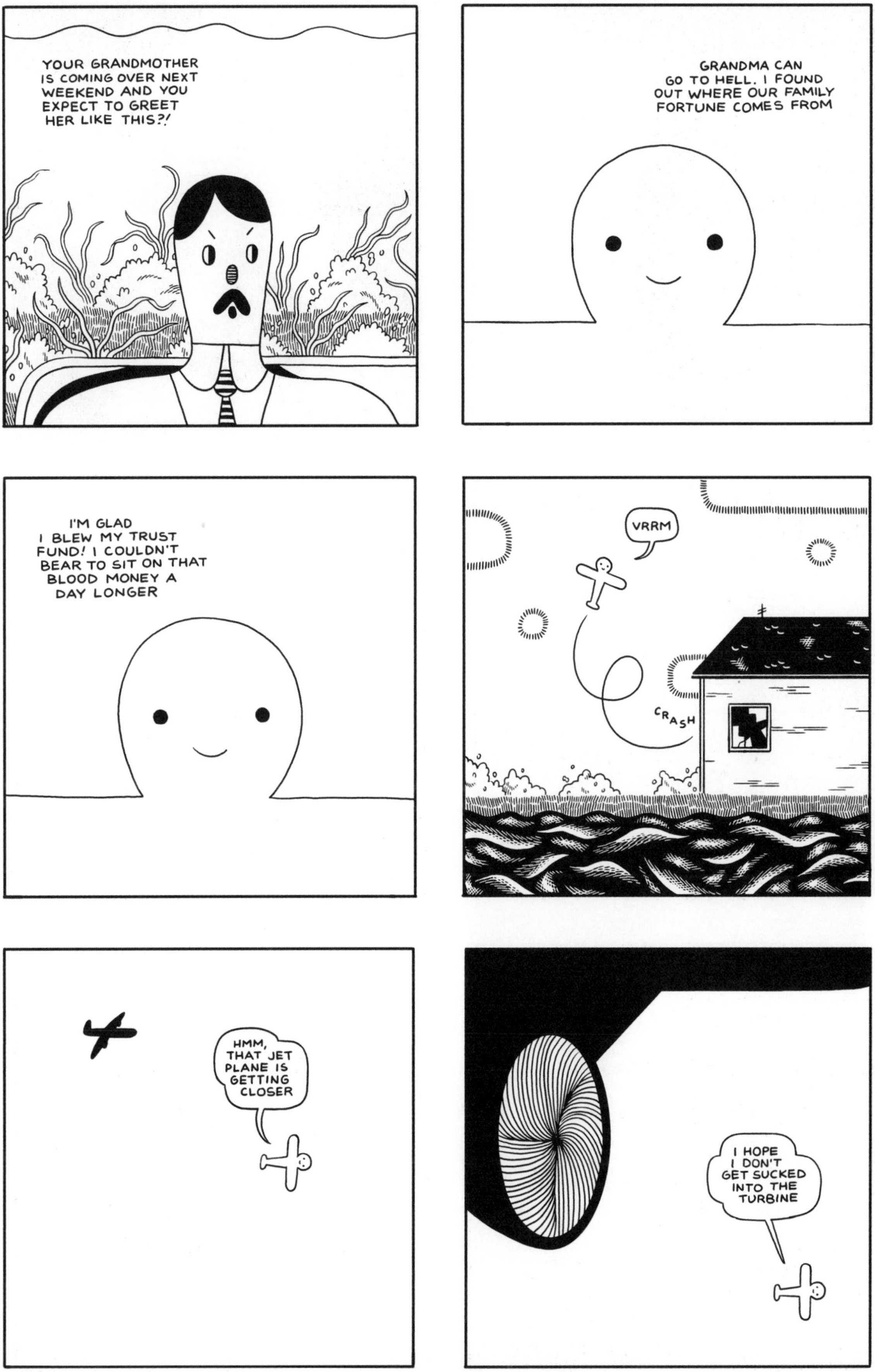
YOUR GRANDMOTHER IS COMING OVER NEXT WEEKEND AND YOU EXPECT TO GREET HER LIKE THIS?!
GRANDMA CAN GO TO HELL. I FOUND OUT WHERE OUR FAMILY FORTUNE COMES FROM
I'M GLAD I BLEW MY TRUST FUND! I COULDN'T BEAR TO SIT ON THAT BLOOD MONEY A DAY LONGER
VRRM
CRASH
HMM, THAT JET PLANE IS GETTING CLOSER
I HOPE I DON'T GET SUCKED INTO THE TURBINE

THIS IS LESS CHILL THAN I IMAGINED
OH! A BOY FROM SCHOOL I LIKE
BUT SOMETHING'S DIFFERENT ABOUT HIM
I TURNED MY BODY INTO A CAR
VROOM
BEEP BEEP

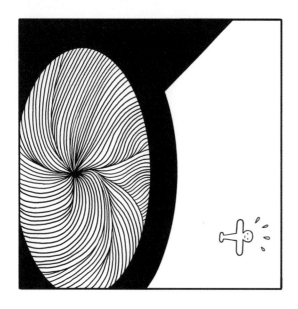

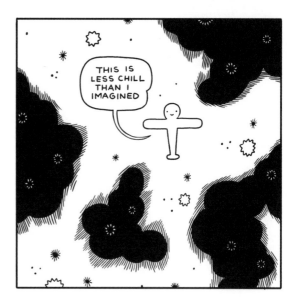

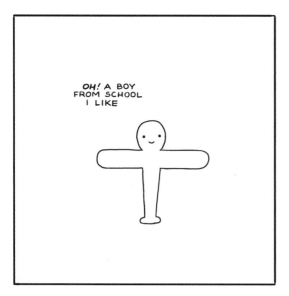

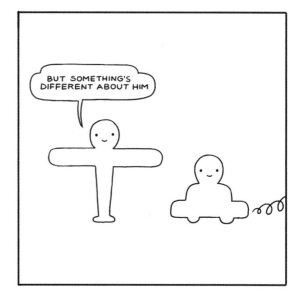

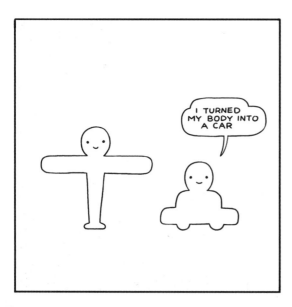

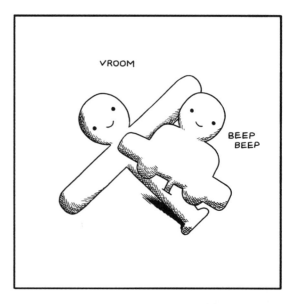

PUT
PUT PUT PUT
BRRRTT
ZOOM
WHOOSH
I BECAME AN AIRPLANE BECAUSE I NEEDED SPACE. ROY BECAME A CAR BECAUSE HE LIKED TRAFFIC JAMS-- THE FEELING OF HIS BODY SUSPENDED AMONGST HUNDREDS OF OTHERS -- PACKED TIGHT, BUT NOT QUITE TOUCHING
WE HAD DIFFERENT PRIORITIES. WE SPLIT UP.
HEY, I THINK THAT'S MY HOUSE!
OH, MAYBE NOT. IT'S HARD TO TELL

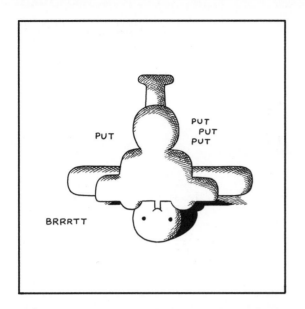

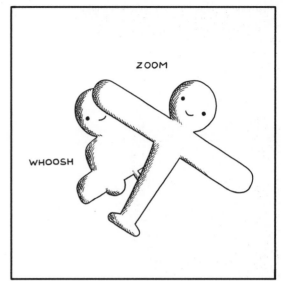

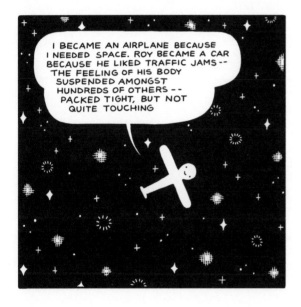

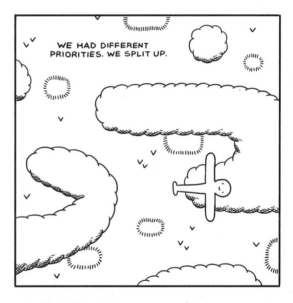

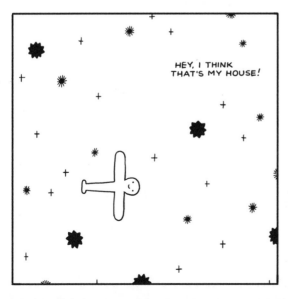

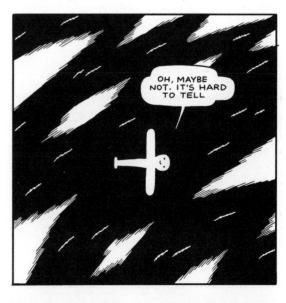

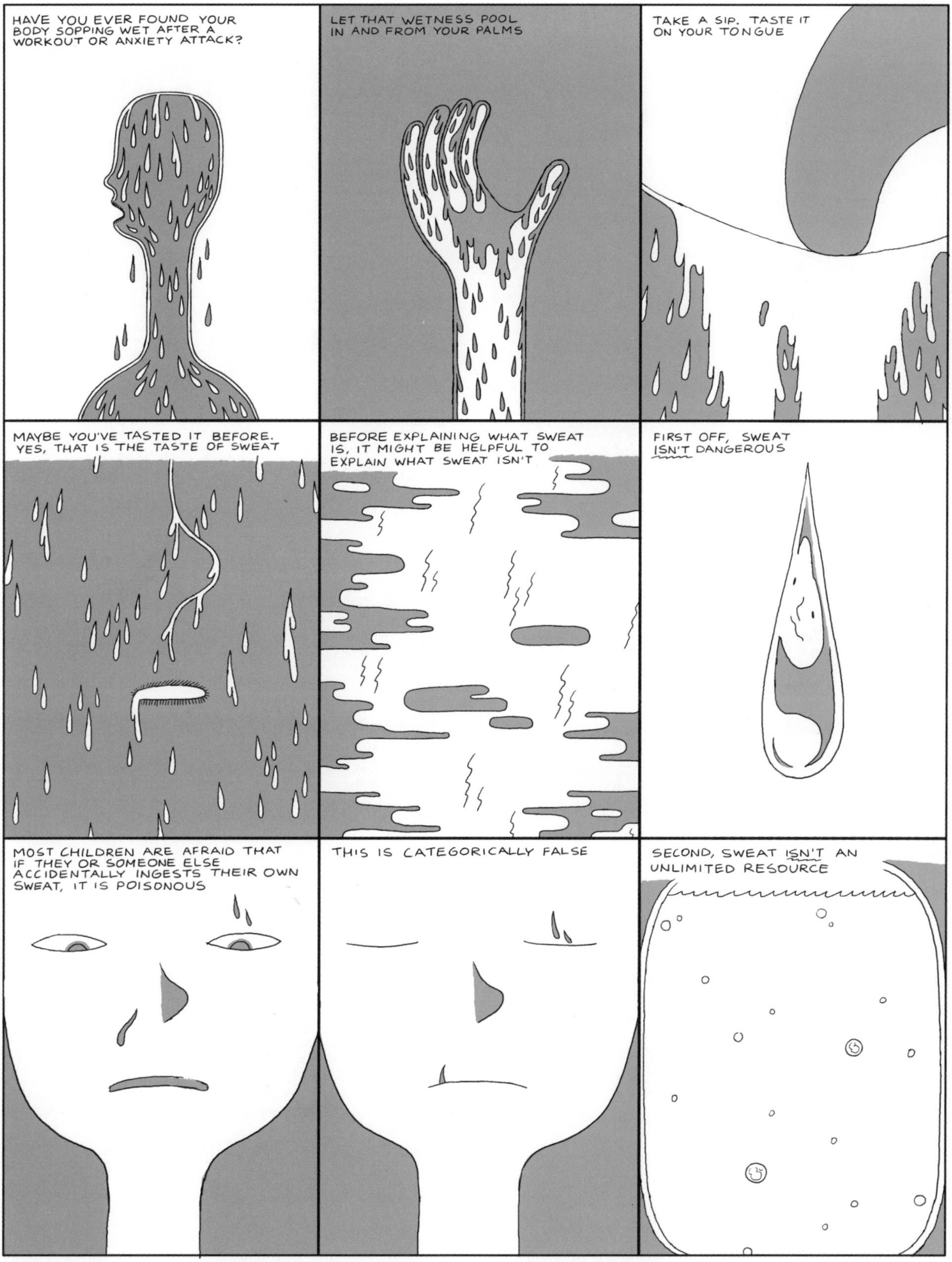
HAVE YOU EVER FOUND YOUR BODY SOPPING WET AFTER A WORKOUT OR ANXIETY ATTACK?
LET THAT WETNESS POOL IN AND FROM YOUR PALMS
TAKE A SIP. TASTE IT ON YOUR TONGUE
MAYBE YOU'VE TASTED IT BEFORE. YES, THAT IS THE TASTE OF SWEAT
BEFORE EXPLAINING WHAT SWEAT IS, IT MIGHT BE HELPFUL TO EXPLAIN WHAT SWEAT ISN'T
FIRST OFF, SWEAT ISN'T DANGEROUS
MOST CHILDREN ARE AFRAID THAT IF THEY OR SOMEONE ELSE ACCIDENTALLY INGESTS THEIR OWN SWEAT, IT IS POISONOUS
THIS IS CATEGORICALLY FALSE
SECOND, SWEAT ISN'T AN UNLIMITED RESOURCE

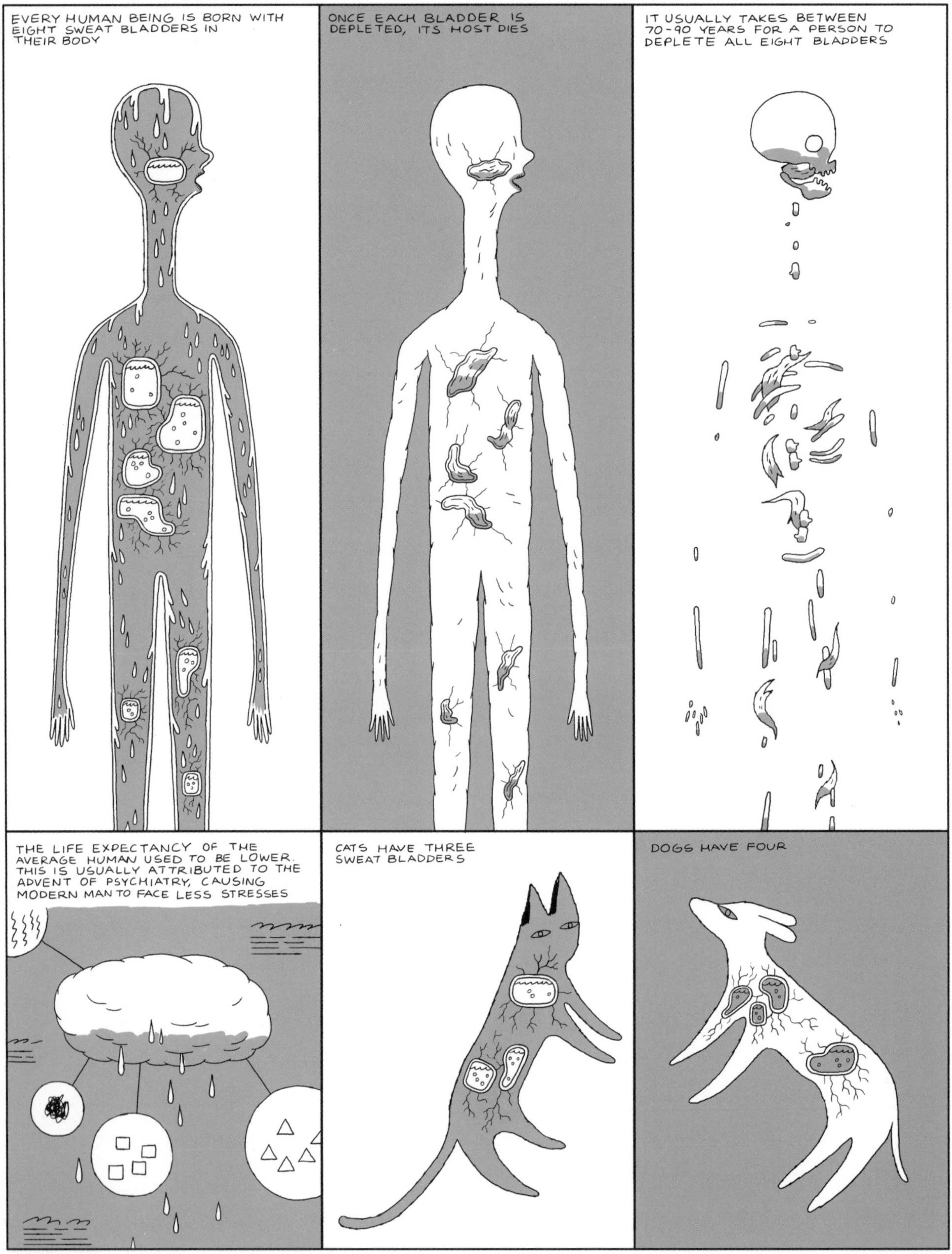
EVERY HUMAN BEING IS BORN WITH EIGHT SWEAT BLADDERS IN THEIR BODY
ONCE EACH BLADDER IS DEPLETED, ITS HOST DIES
IT USUALLY TAKES BETWEEN 70-90 YEARS FOR A PERSON TO DEPLETE ALL EIGHT BLADDERS
THE LIFE EXPECTANCY OF THE AVERAGE HUMAN USED TO BE LOWER. THIS IS USUALLY ATTRIBUTED TO THE ADVENT OF PSYCHIATRY, CAUSING MODERN MAN TO FACE LESS STRESSES
CATS HAVE THREE SWEAT BLADDERS
DOGS HAVE FOUR

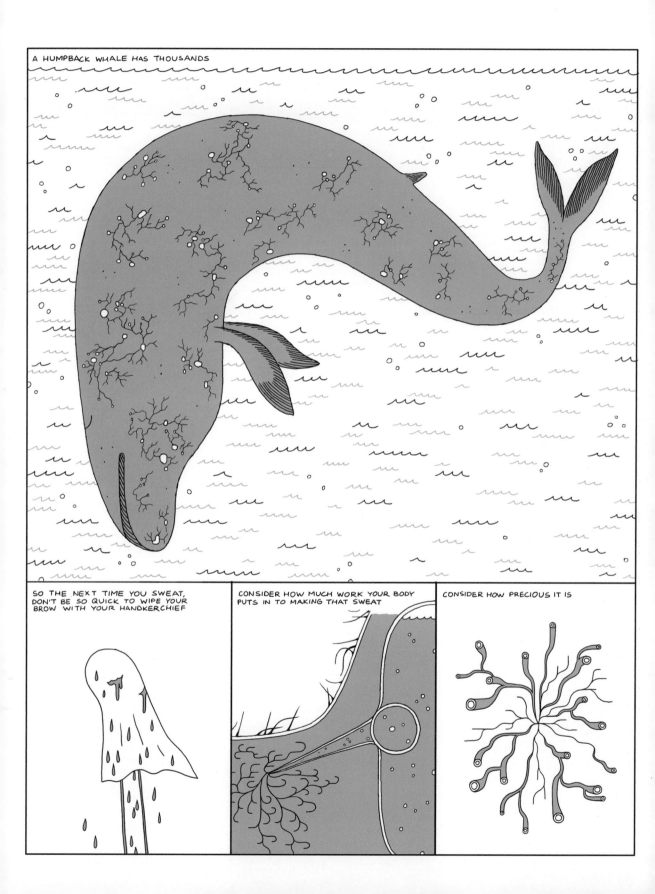

A HUMPBACK WHALE HAS THOUSANDS

SO THE NEXT TIME YOU SWEAT, DON'T BE SO QUICK TO WIPE YOUR BROW WITH YOUR HANDKERCHIEF

CONSIDER HOW MUCH WORK YOUR BODY PUTS IN TO MAKING THAT SWEAT

CONSIDER HOW PRECIOUS IT IS

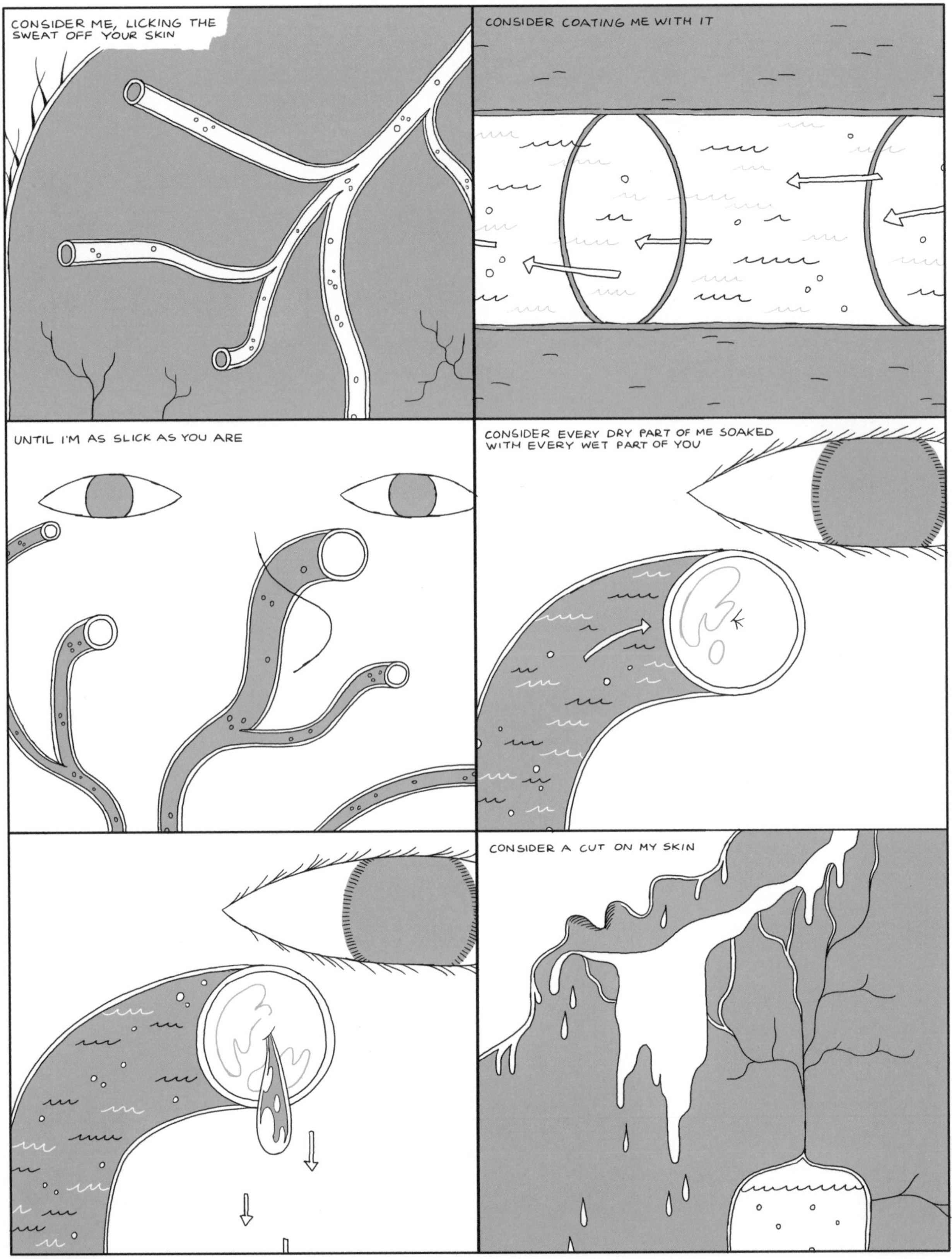
CONSIDER ME, LICKING THE SWEAT OFF YOUR SKIN
CONSIDER COATING ME WITH IT
UNTIL I'M AS SLICK AS YOU ARE
CONSIDER EVERY DRY PART OF ME SOAKED WITH EVERY WET PART OF YOU
CONSIDER A CUT ON MY SKIN

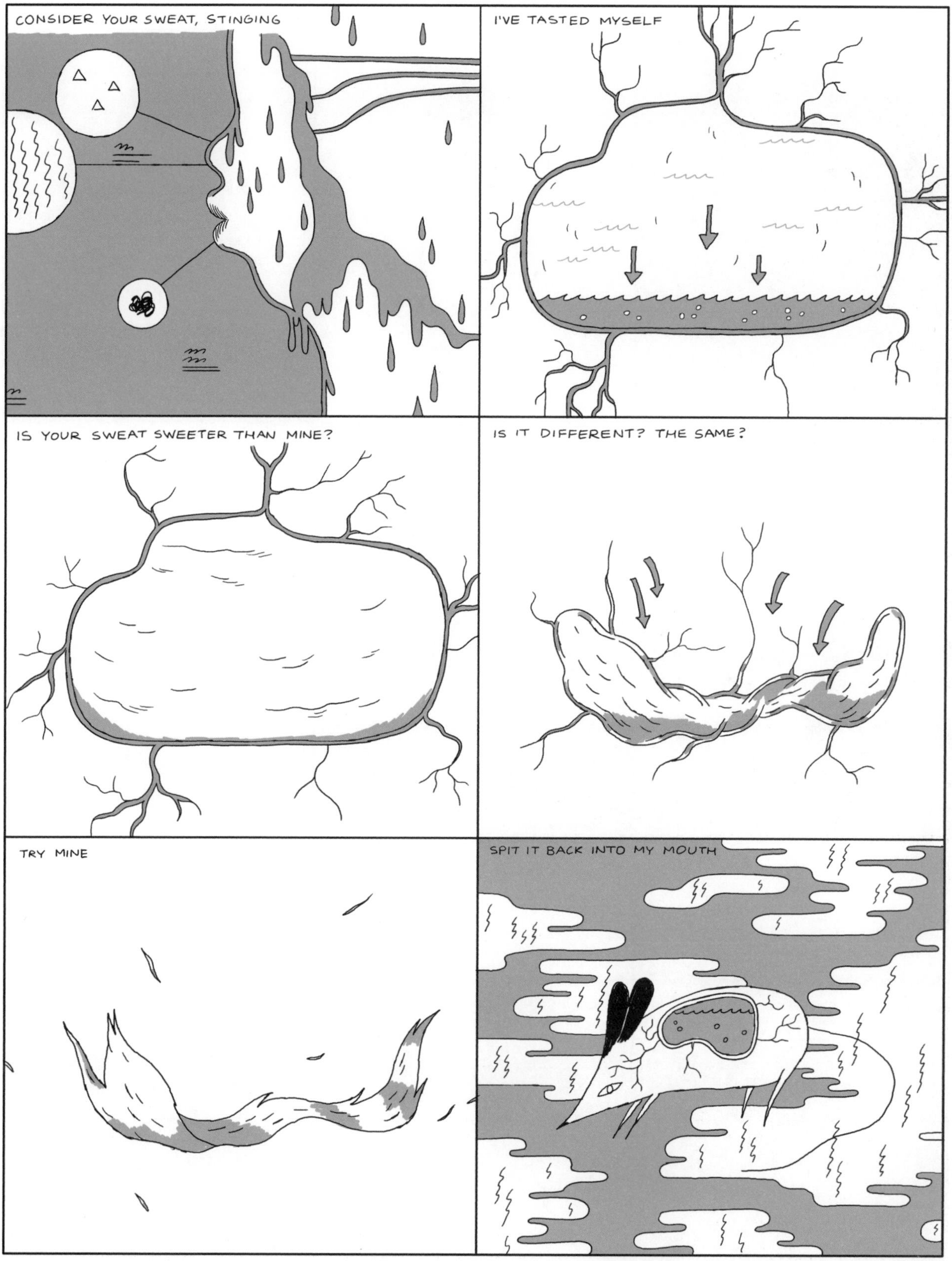
CONSIDER YOUR SWEAT, STINGING
I'VE TASTED MYSELF
IS YOUR SWEAT SWEETER THAN MINE?
IS IT DIFFERENT? THE SAME?
TRY MINE
SPIT IT BACK INTO MY MOUTH

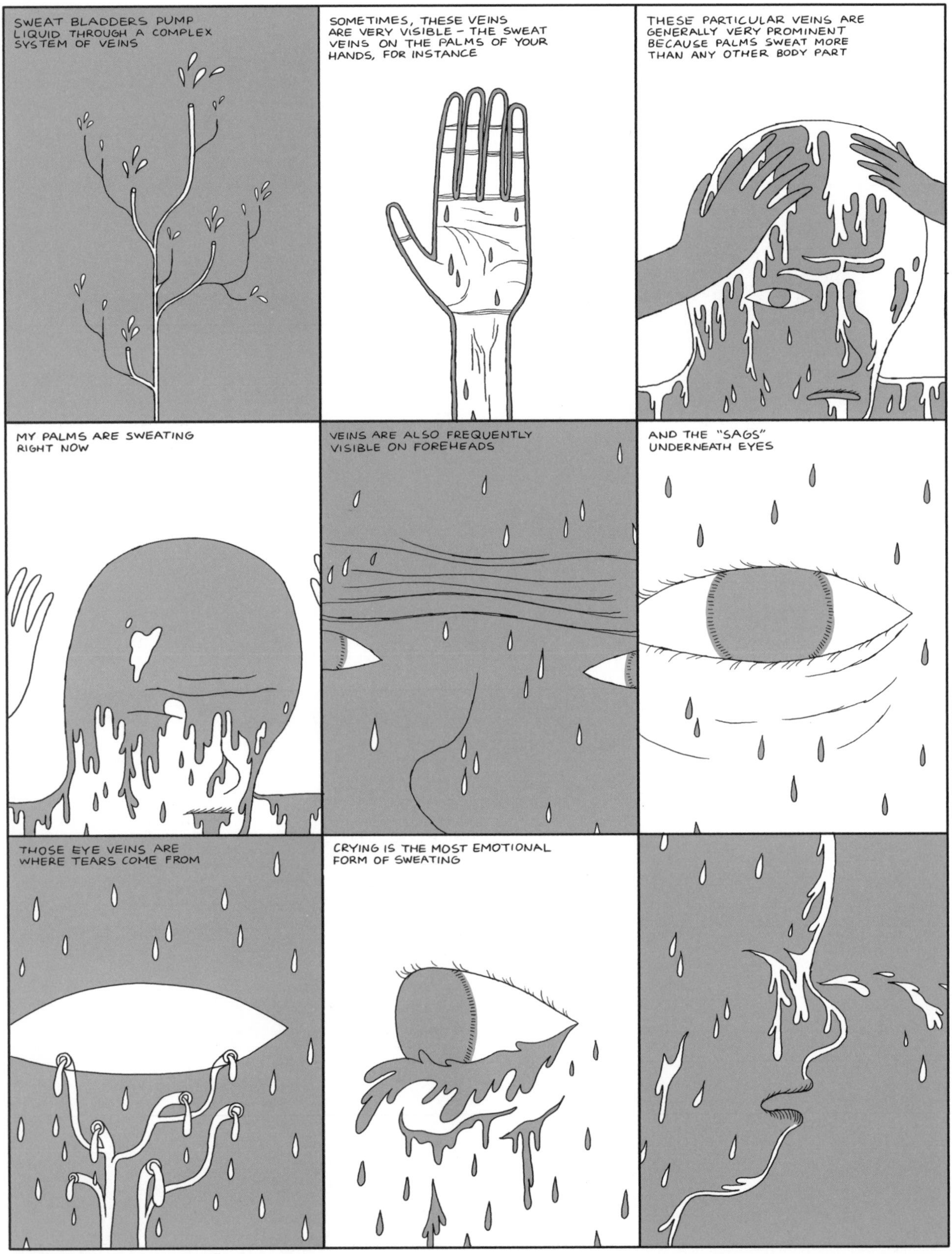
SWEAT BLADDERS PUMP LIQUID THROUGH A COMPLEX SYSTEM OF VEINS
SOMETIMES, THESE VEINS ARE VERY VISIBLE – THE SWEAT VEINS ON THE PALMS OF YOUR HANDS, FOR INSTANCE
THESE PARTICULAR VEINS ARE GENERALLY VERY PROMINENT BECAUSE PALMS SWEAT MORE THAN ANY OTHER BODY PART
MY PALMS ARE SWEATING RIGHT NOW
VEINS ARE ALSO FREQUENTLY VISIBLE ON FOREHEADS
AND THE "SAGS" UNDERNEATH EYES
THOSE EYE VEINS ARE WHERE TEARS COME FROM
CRYING IS THE MOST EMOTIONAL FORM OF SWEATING

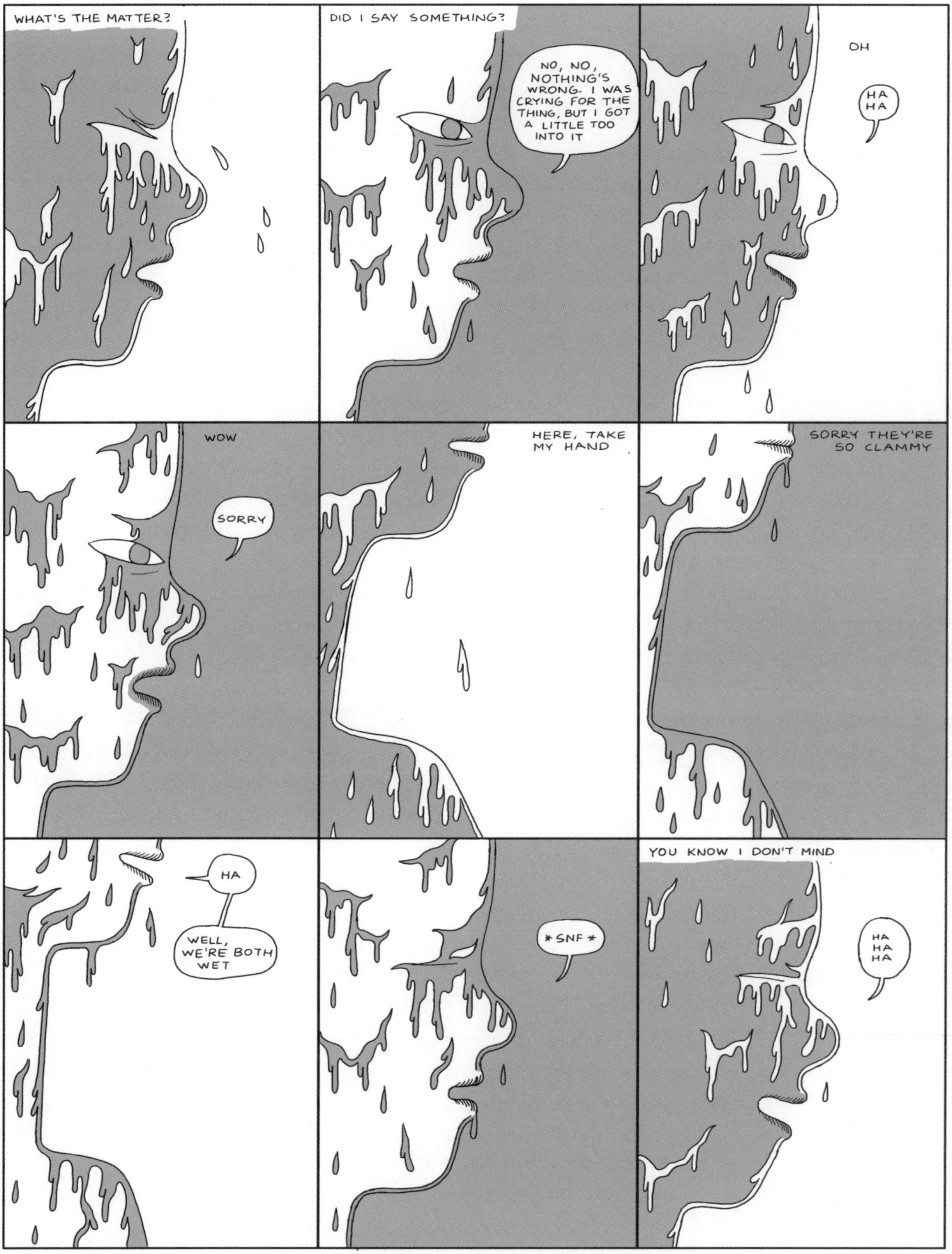
WHAT'S THE MATTER?
DID I SAY SOMETHING?
NO, NO, NOTHING'S WRONG. I WAS CRYING FOR THE THING, BUT I GOT A LITTLE TOO INTO IT
OH
HA HA
WOW
SORRY
HERE, TAKE MY HAND
SORRY THEY'RE SO CLAMMY
HA
WELL, WE'RE BOTH WET
SNF
YOU KNOW I DON'T MIND
HA HA HA

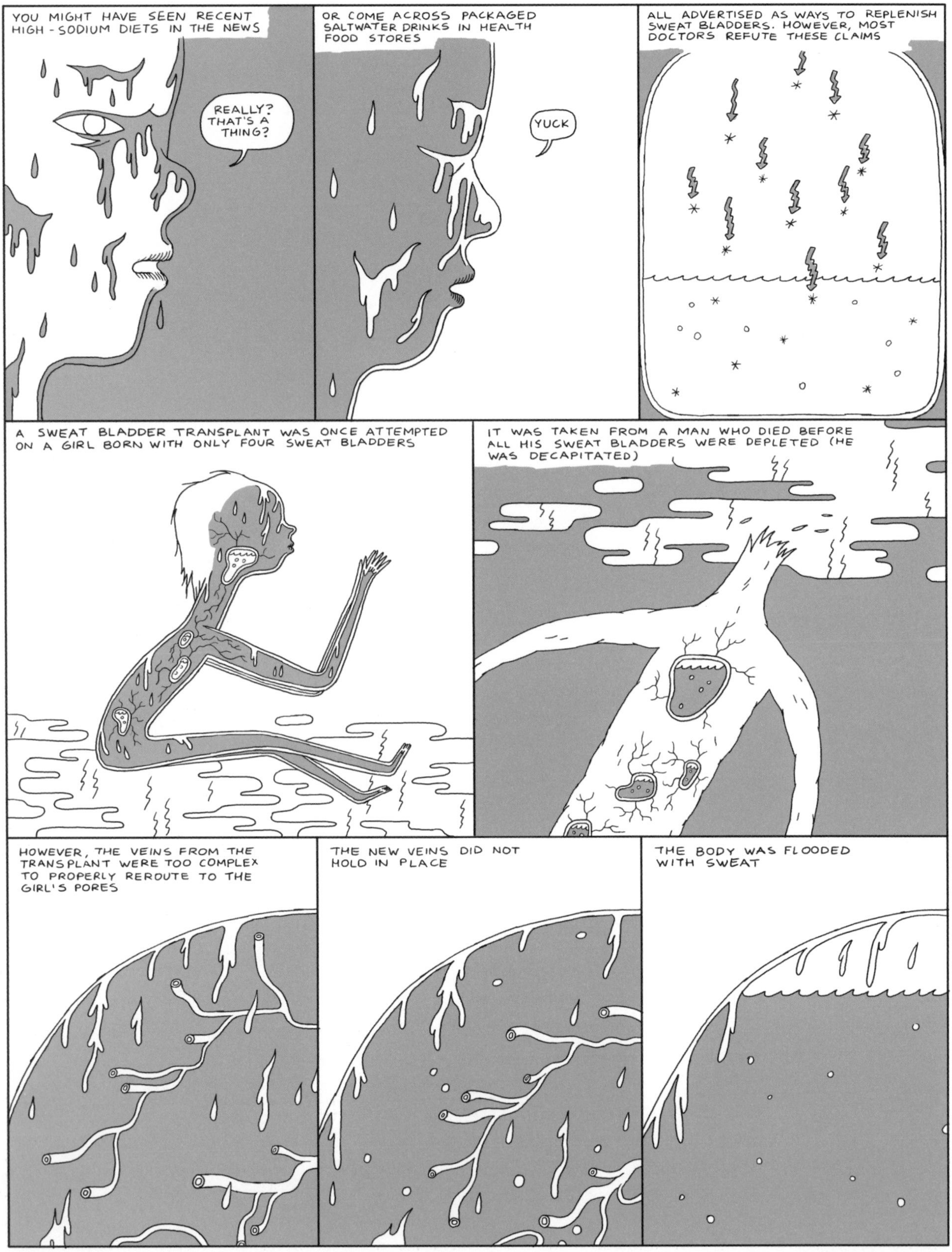
YOU MIGHT HAVE SEEN RECENT HIGH-SODIUM DIETS IN THE NEWS
REALLY? THAT'S A THING?
OR COME ACROSS PACKAGED SALTWATER DRINKS IN HEALTH FOOD STORES
YUCK
ALL ADVERTISED AS WAYS TO REPLENISH SWEAT BLADDERS. HOWEVER, MOST DOCTORS REFUTE THESE CLAIMS
A SWEAT BLADDER TRANSPLANT WAS ONCE ATTEMPTED ON A GIRL BORN WITH ONLY FOUR SWEAT BLADDERS
IT WAS TAKEN FROM A MAN WHO DIED BEFORE ALL HIS SWEAT BLADDERS WERE DEPLETED (HE WAS DECAPITATED)
HOWEVER, THE VEINS FROM THE TRANSPLANT WERE TOO COMPLEX TO PROPERLY REROUTE TO THE GIRL'S PORES
THE NEW VEINS DID NOT HOLD IN PLACE
THE BODY WAS FLOODED WITH SWEAT

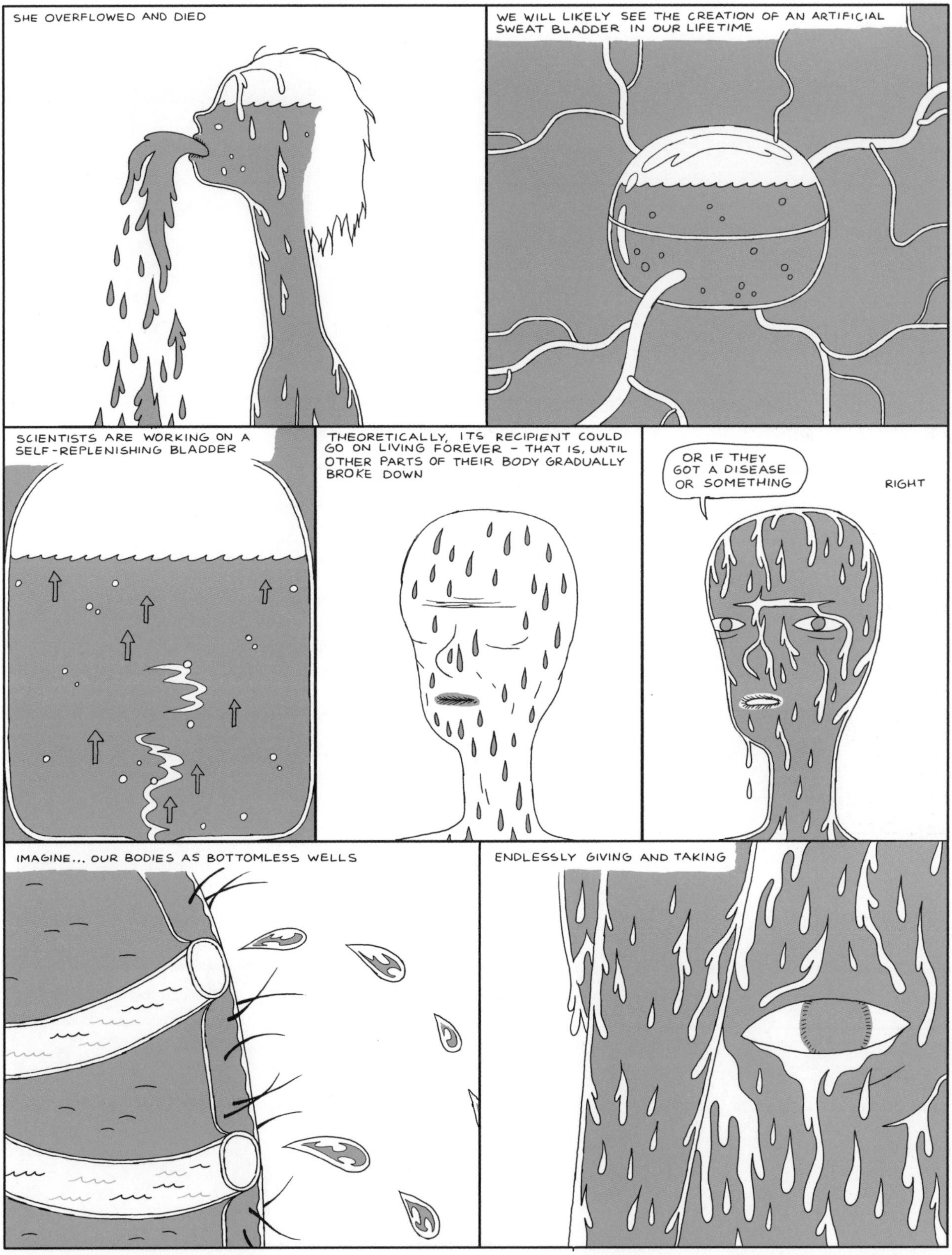
SHE OVERFLOWED AND DIED
WE WILL LIKELY SEE THE CREATION OF AN ARTIFICIAL SWEAT BLADDER IN OUR LIFETIME
SCIENTISTS ARE WORKING ON A SELF-REPLENISHING BLADDER
THEORETICALLY, ITS RECIPIENT COULD GO ON LIVING FOREVER - THAT IS, UNTIL OTHER PARTS OF THEIR BODY GRADUALLY BROKE DOWN
OR IF THEY GOT A DISEASE OR SOMETHING
RIGHT
IMAGINE... OUR BODIES AS BOTTOMLESS WELLS
ENDLESSLY GIVING AND TAKING

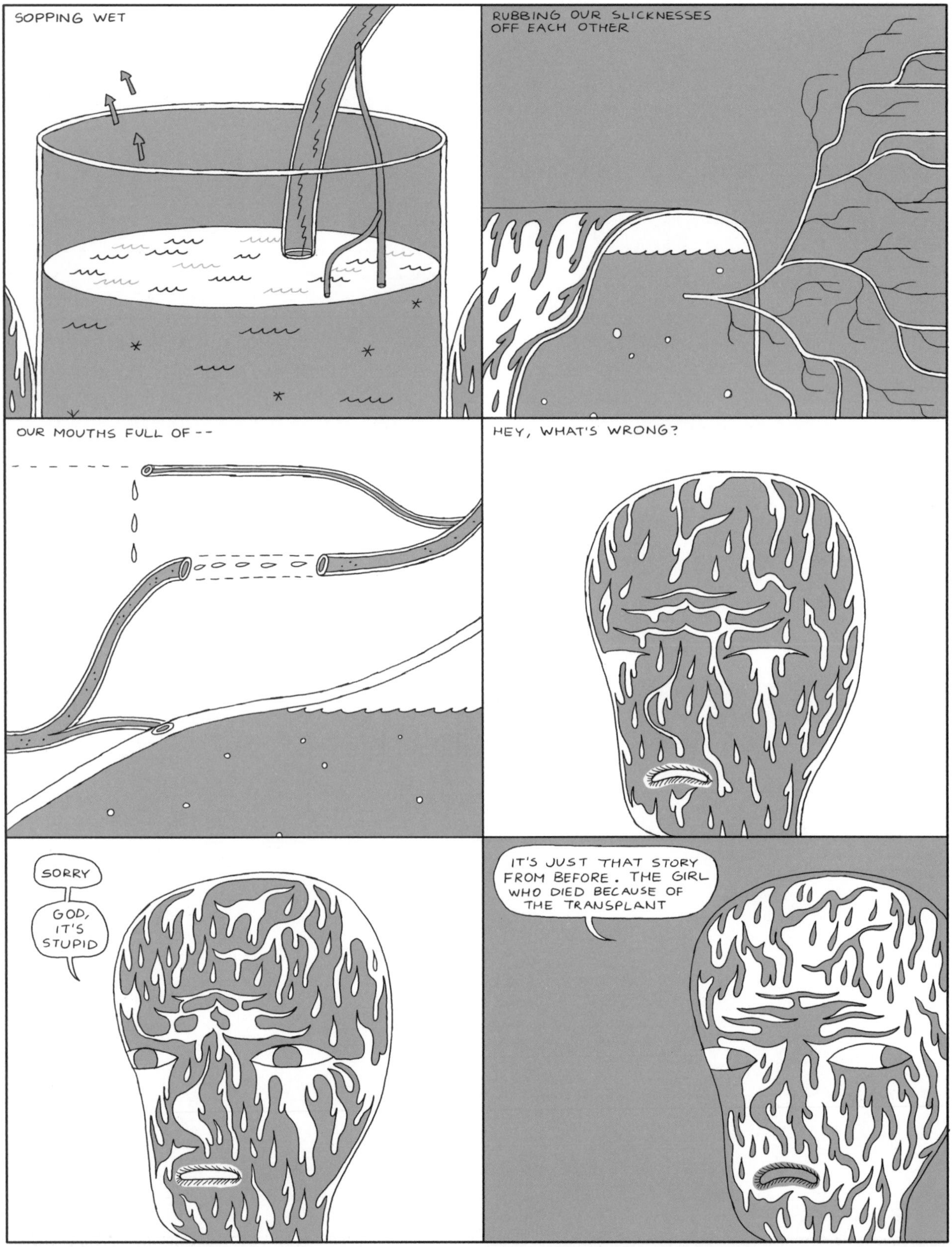
SOPPING WET
RUBBING OUR SLICKNESSES OFF EACH OTHER
OUR MOUTHS FULL OF --
HEY, WHAT'S WRONG?
SORRY
GOD, IT'S STUPID
IT'S JUST THAT STORY FROM BEFORE. THE GIRL WHO DIED BECAUSE OF THE TRANSPLANT

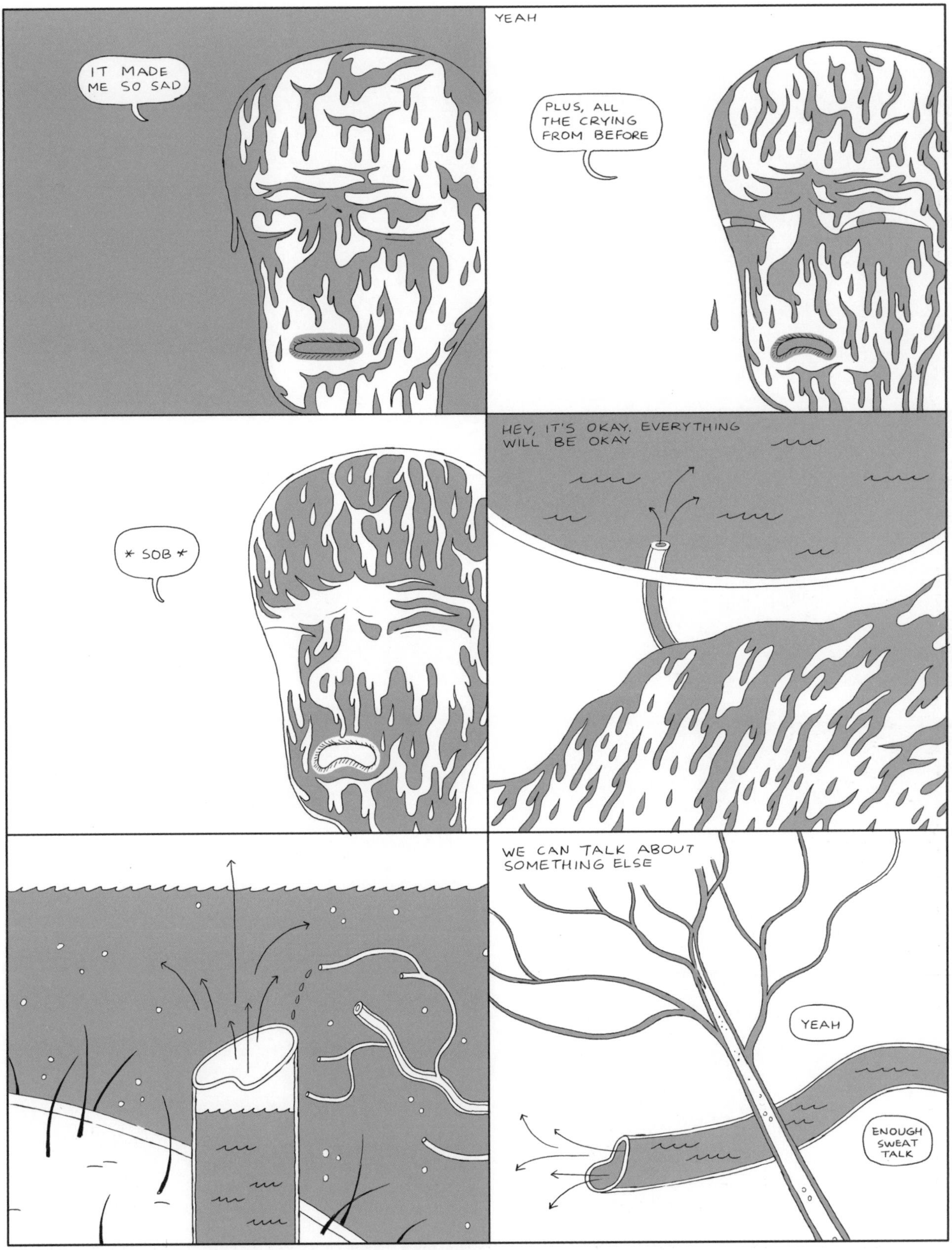
IT MADE ME SO SAD
YEAH
PLUS, ALL THE CRYING FROM BEFORE
* SOB *
HEY, IT'S OKAY. EVERYTHING WILL BE OKAY
WE CAN TALK ABOUT SOMETHING ELSE
YEAH
ENOUGH SWEAT TALK

SOME PEOPLE ARE BOYS AND ALSO CHINESE

SOME PEOPLE ARE BOYS AND ALSO NEED GLASSES

I AM A BOY WHO IS ALSO A BIRD

MY BODY IS NOT BUILT FOR FLYING, HOWEVER

I AM UNABLE TO PARTICIPATE IN MANY OF THE ACTIVITIES OTHER BOYS MY AGE TAKE PART IN. I DO NOT HAVE HANDS TO SQUEEZE BREASTS OR SMOKE JOINTS WITH, FOR INSTANCE

MY BRAIN IS BIRD-SIZED BUT MY HEAD IS BOY-SIZED

OVERALL, I WOULD SAY MY LIFE IS VERY BAD

MOST BIRDS LOOK LIKE SMALL FUCKERS TO ME

WITH SMALL DICKS (SMALLER THAN MINE)

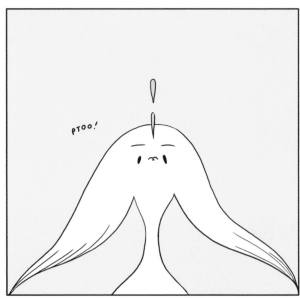

PTOO!

HEY-- DON'T DO THAT

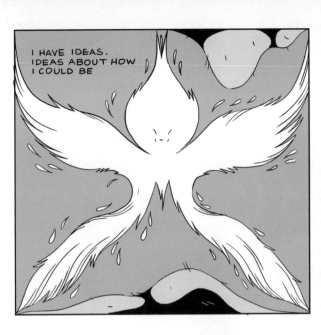

I HAVE IDEAS.
IDEAS ABOUT HOW
I COULD BE

I COULD GROW UP TO BE
VERY STRONG

I COULD GROW UP TO BE
VERY BEAUTIFUL, LIKE MY
VERY BEAUTIFUL TEACHER

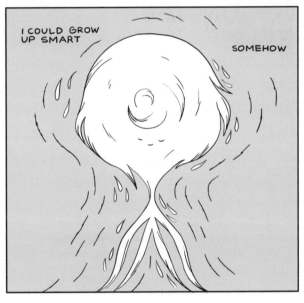

I COULD GROW
UP SMART

SOMEHOW

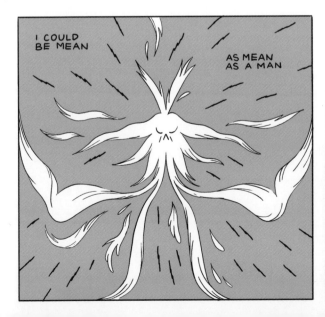

I COULD
BE MEAN

AS MEAN
AS A MAN

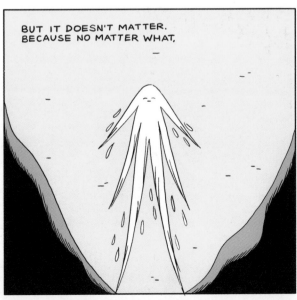

BUT IT DOESN'T MATTER.
BECAUSE NO MATTER WHAT,

I WILL BE DEFICIENT
YOU SHOULDN'T HAVE HIT THAT BIRD
NOT ALL BIRDS FLY, YOU KNOW
NOW THIS ONE DOESN'T EITHER
PENGUINS DON'T FLY. NEITHER DO OSTRICHES
AND NOW THEY'RE EXTINCT
ORNITHOLOGIST
ALWAYS BUGGING ME
I PLAN TO ASK HER OUT. HER INTEREST IN ME WOULD BE PURELY SCIENTIFIC

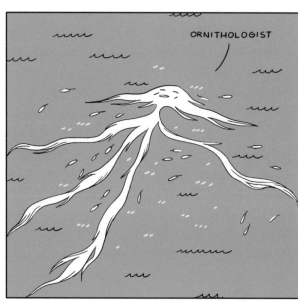

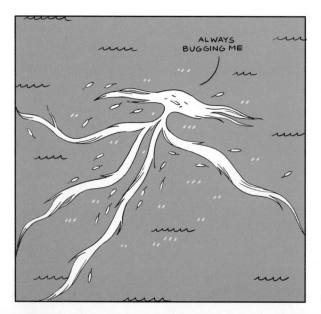

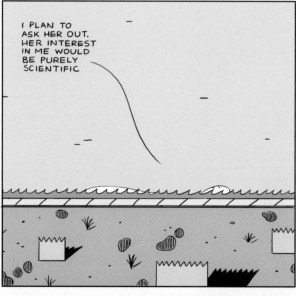

BUT I'D
SETTLE
FOR IT

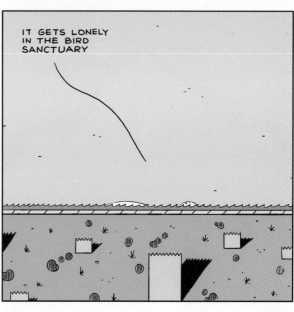

IT GETS LONELY
IN THE BIRD
SANCTUARY

AND BOYS
HAVE WANTS

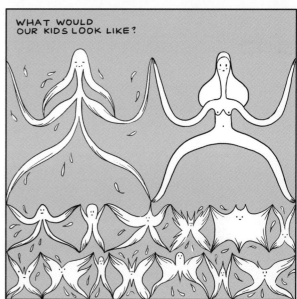

WHAT WOULD
OUR KIDS LOOK LIKE?

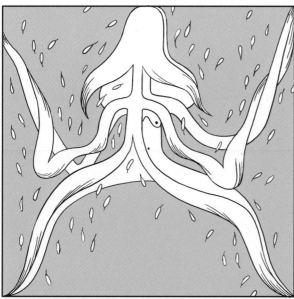

WOULD THEIR BRAINS BE
BIRD-SIZED, LIKE MINE?

OR WOULD THEIR BRAINS BE HUMAN-
SIZED AND THEIR BODIES BIRD-SIZED

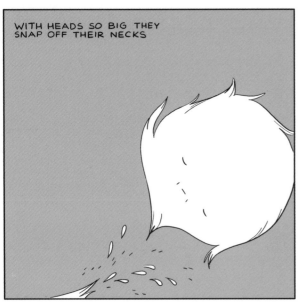

WITH HEADS SO BIG THEY
SNAP OFF THEIR NECKS

THEY'D, LIKE, ROLL DOWN HILLS.
AND KNOCK OVER OLD LADIES

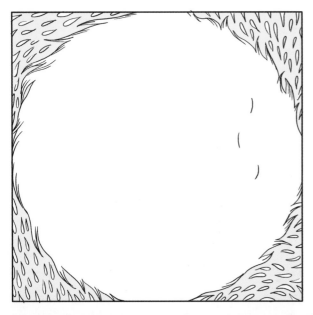

SO WILL YOU DO IT? WILL YOU
GO ON DATES WITH ME

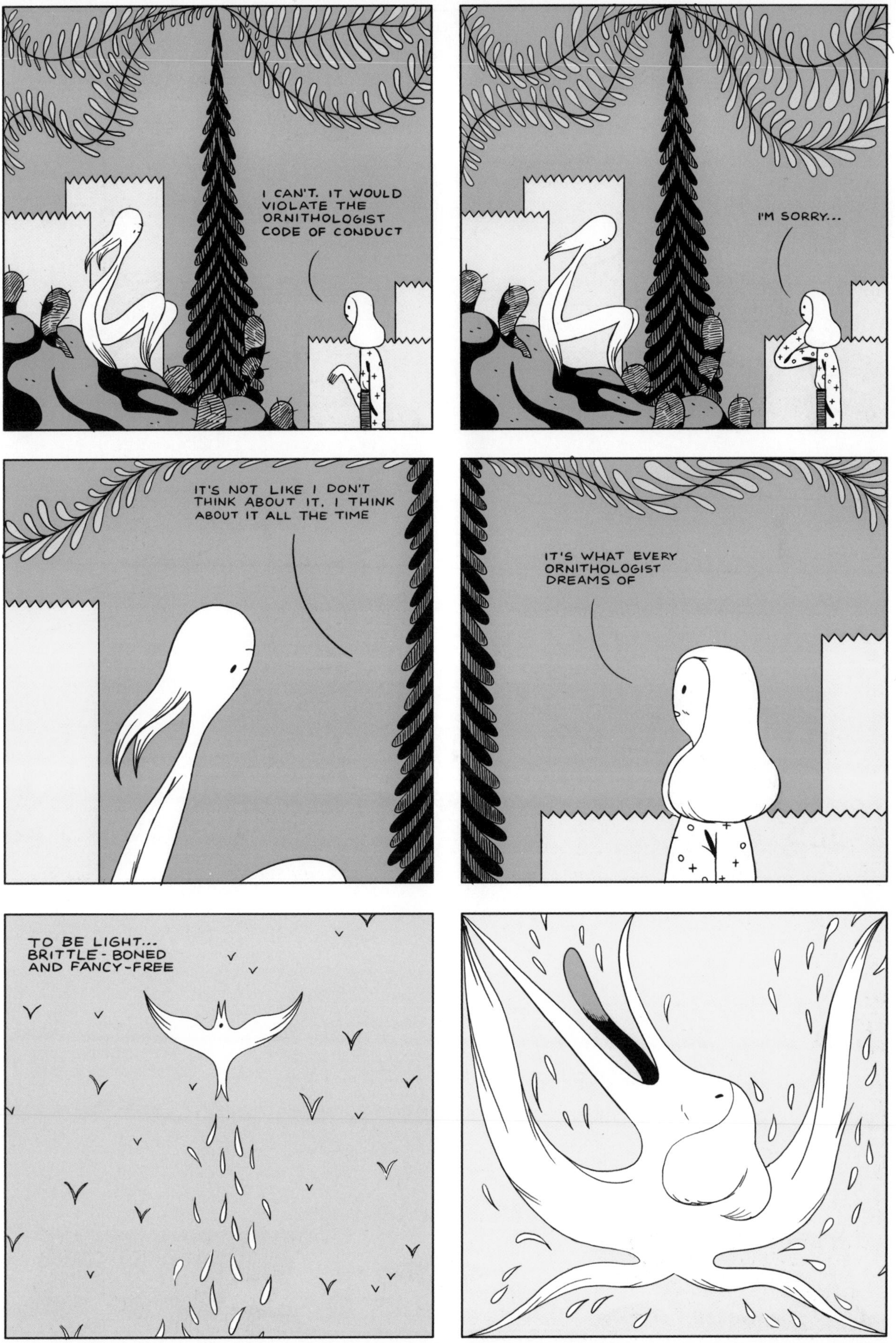
I CAN'T. IT WOULD VIOLATE THE ORNITHOLOGIST CODE OF CONDUCT
I'M SORRY...
IT'S NOT LIKE I DON'T THINK ABOUT IT. I THINK ABOUT IT ALL THE TIME
IT'S WHAT EVERY ORNITHOLOGIST DREAMS OF
TO BE LIGHT... BRITTLE-BONED AND FANCY-FREE

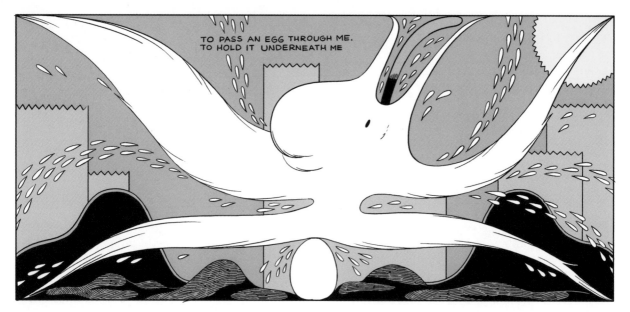

TO PASS AN EGG THROUGH ME.
TO HOLD IT UNDERNEATH ME

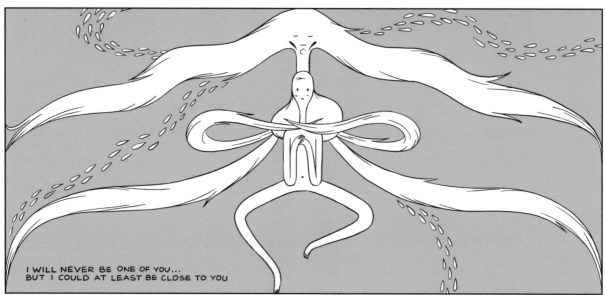

I WILL NEVER BE ONE OF YOU...
BUT I COULD AT LEAST BE CLOSE TO YOU

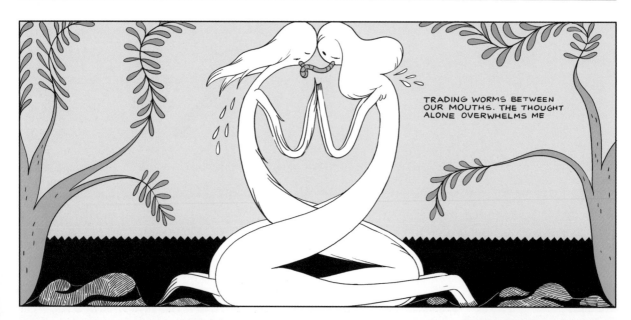

TRADING WORMS BETWEEN
OUR MOUTHS. THE THOUGHT
ALONE OVERWHELMS ME

I DON'T KNOW WHAT YOU MEAN

OF ALL THE THINGS TO BE, WHAT A DUMB THING I AM

I GET FEATHERS EVERYWHERE

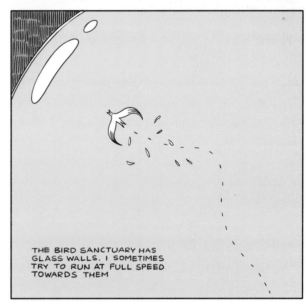

THE BIRD SANCTUARY HAS GLASS WALLS. I SOMETIMES TRY TO RUN AT FULL SPEED TOWARDS THEM

OTHER BIRDS SMACK INTO THEM AND DIE

I KNOW THE WALL IS THERE, SO I CAN NEVER QUITE HIT IT AT FULL VELOCITY. MY BODY BETRAYS ME -- IT HESITATES, INVOLUNTARILY

MY SIDES ARE COVERED IN BRUISES

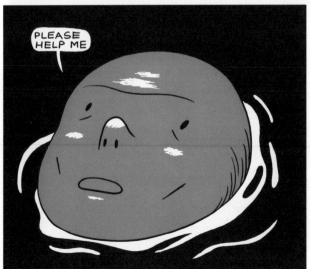

PLEASE HELP ME

I'M NOT THE ONLY ONE IN THIS QUICK SAND

THERE'S SOMETHING SQUEEZING MY ARM
A VINE, MAYBE
IT'S GETTING TIGHTER AND TIGHTER

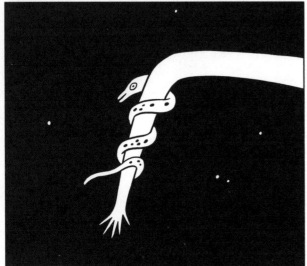

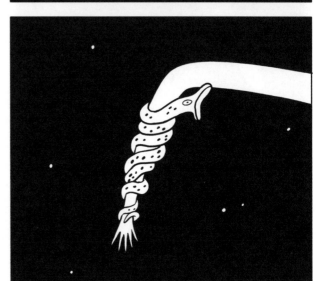

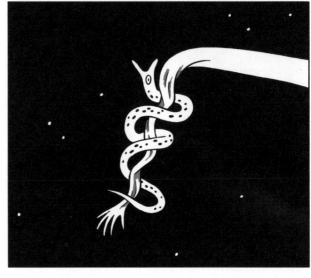

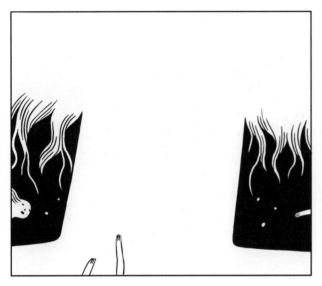

I CAN FEEL SOMETHING ON MY NECK

SOME *THINGS* MAYBE

LEAVING TINY BITES

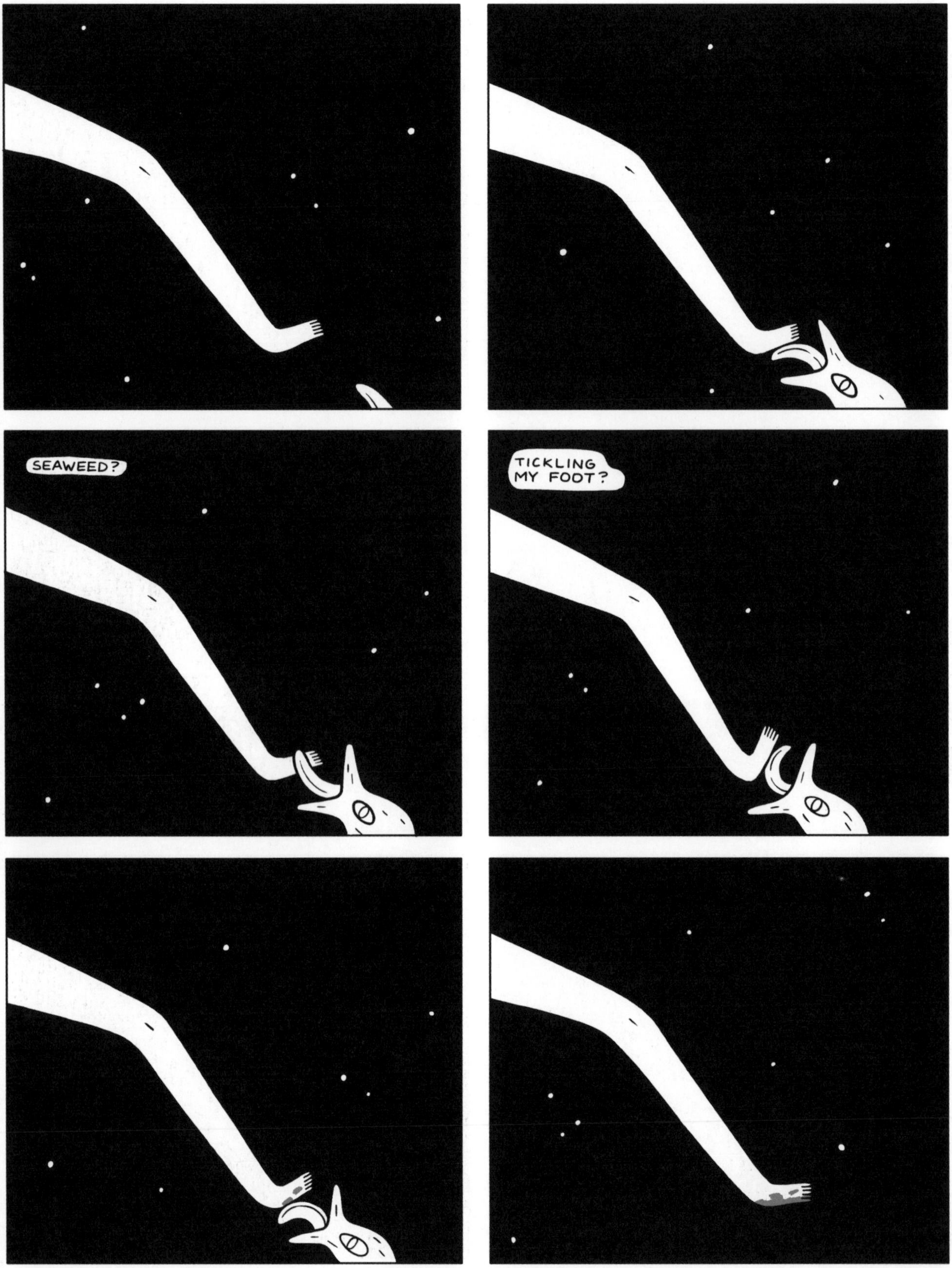
SEAWEED?
TICKLING MY FOOT?

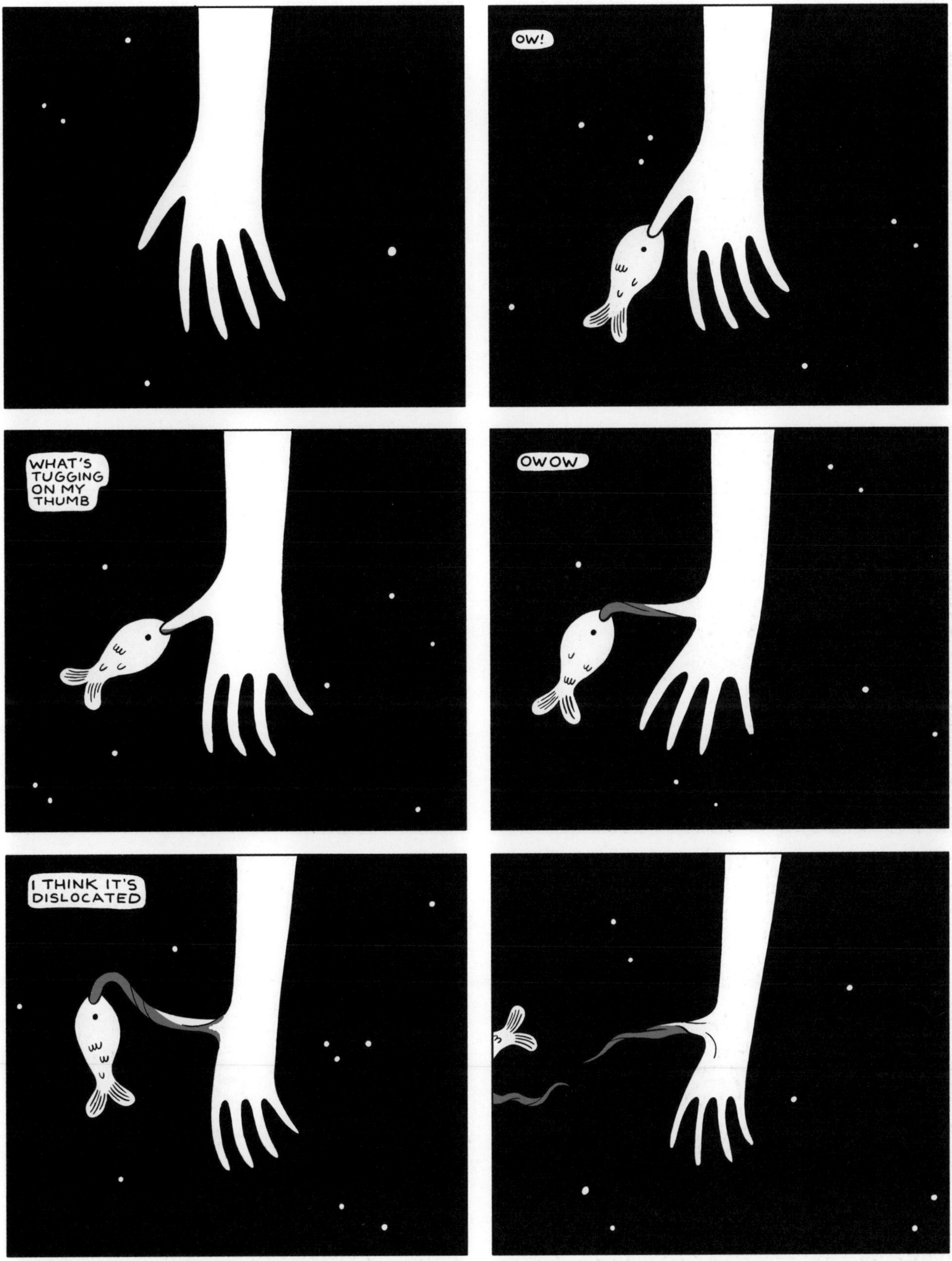
OW!
WHAT'S TUGGING ON MY THUMB
OWOW
I THINK IT'S DISLOCATED

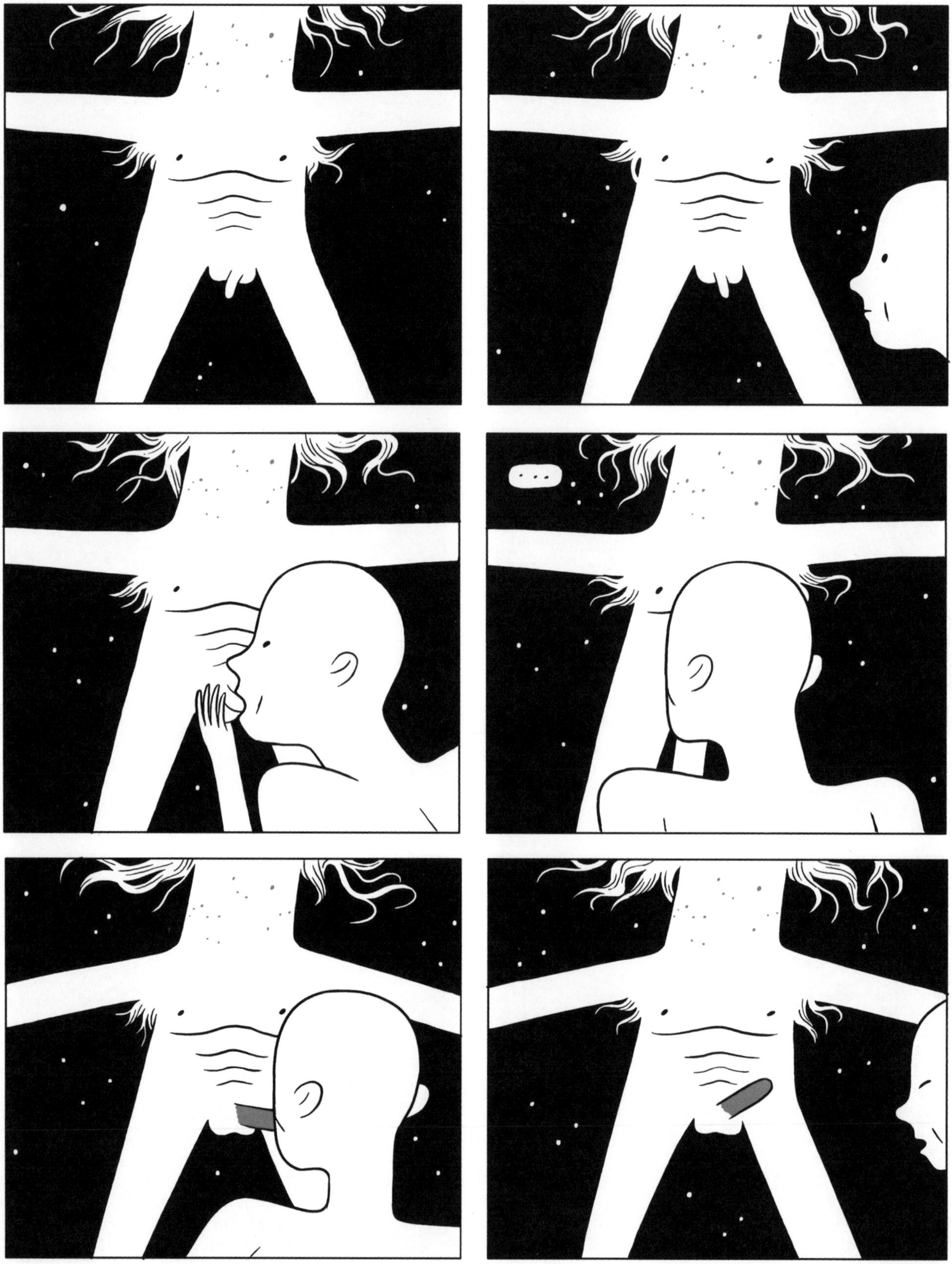
...

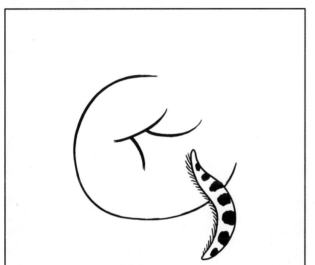

I THINK
I'M GETTING
MUD IN MY EARS

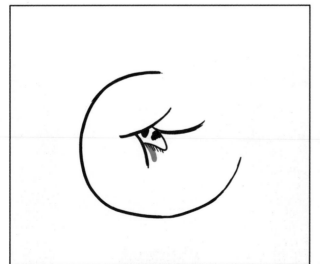

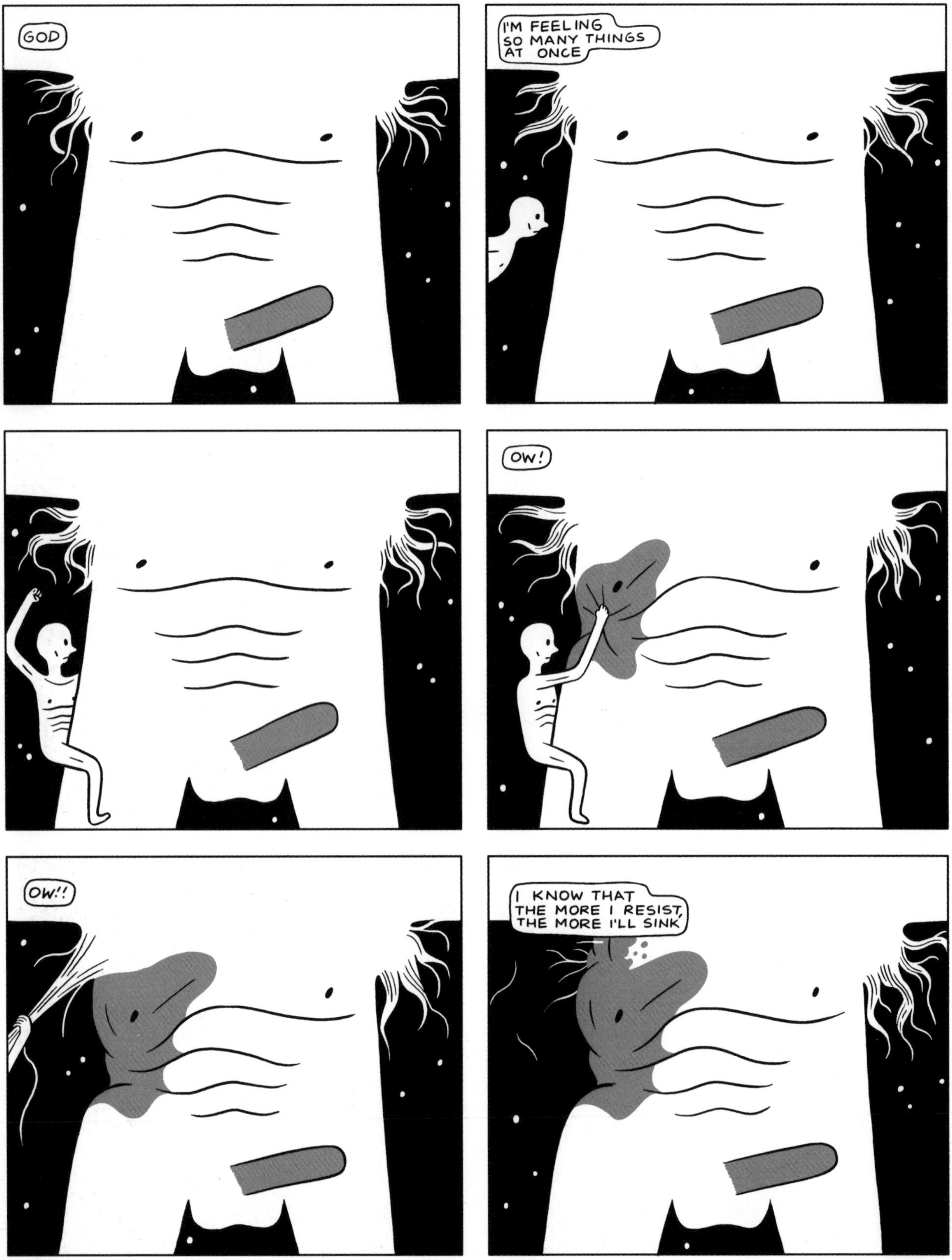
GOD
I'M FEELING SO MANY THINGS AT ONCE
OW!
OW!!
I KNOW THAT THE MORE I RESIST, THE MORE I'LL SINK

AND THE MUD IS TOO THICK TO STRUGGLE, ANYHOW

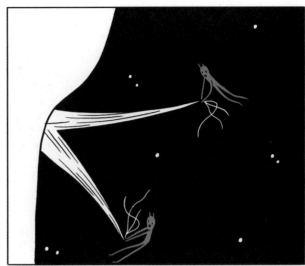

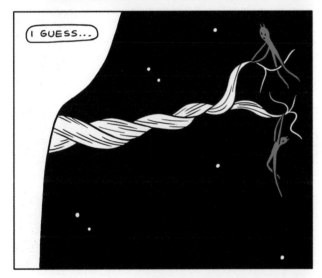

I GUESS...

IT'S NOT ALL BAD. NOT EVERY FEELING IS BAD

AND EVERY NOW AND THEN, A TREE NUT WILL FALL IN MY MOUTH

GIVING ME SUSTENANCE

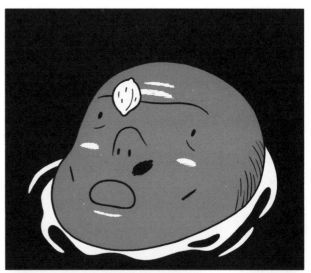

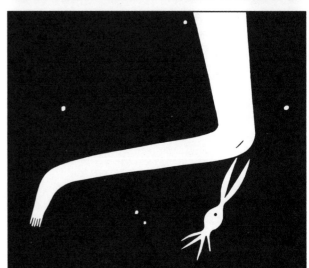

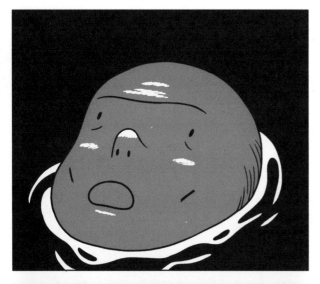

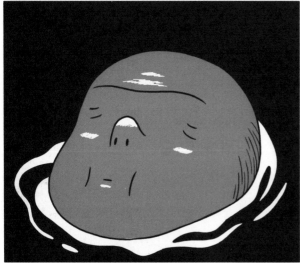

I CAN'T SEE MY BODY

OR TOUCH MY BODY WITH ANOTHER PART OF MY BODY

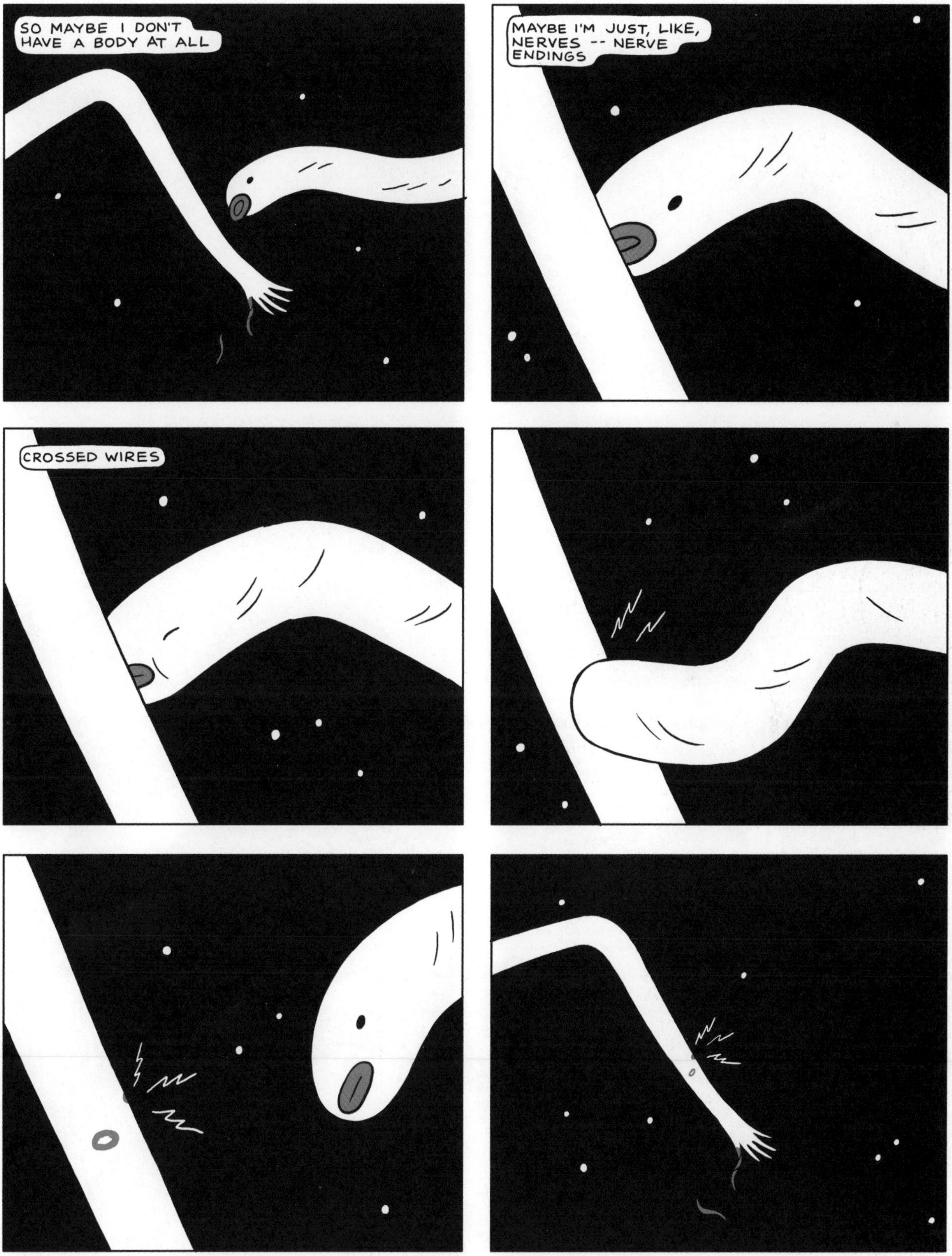
SO MAYBE I DON'T HAVE A BODY AT ALL
MAYBE I'M JUST, LIKE, NERVES -- NERVE ENDINGS
CROSSED WIRES

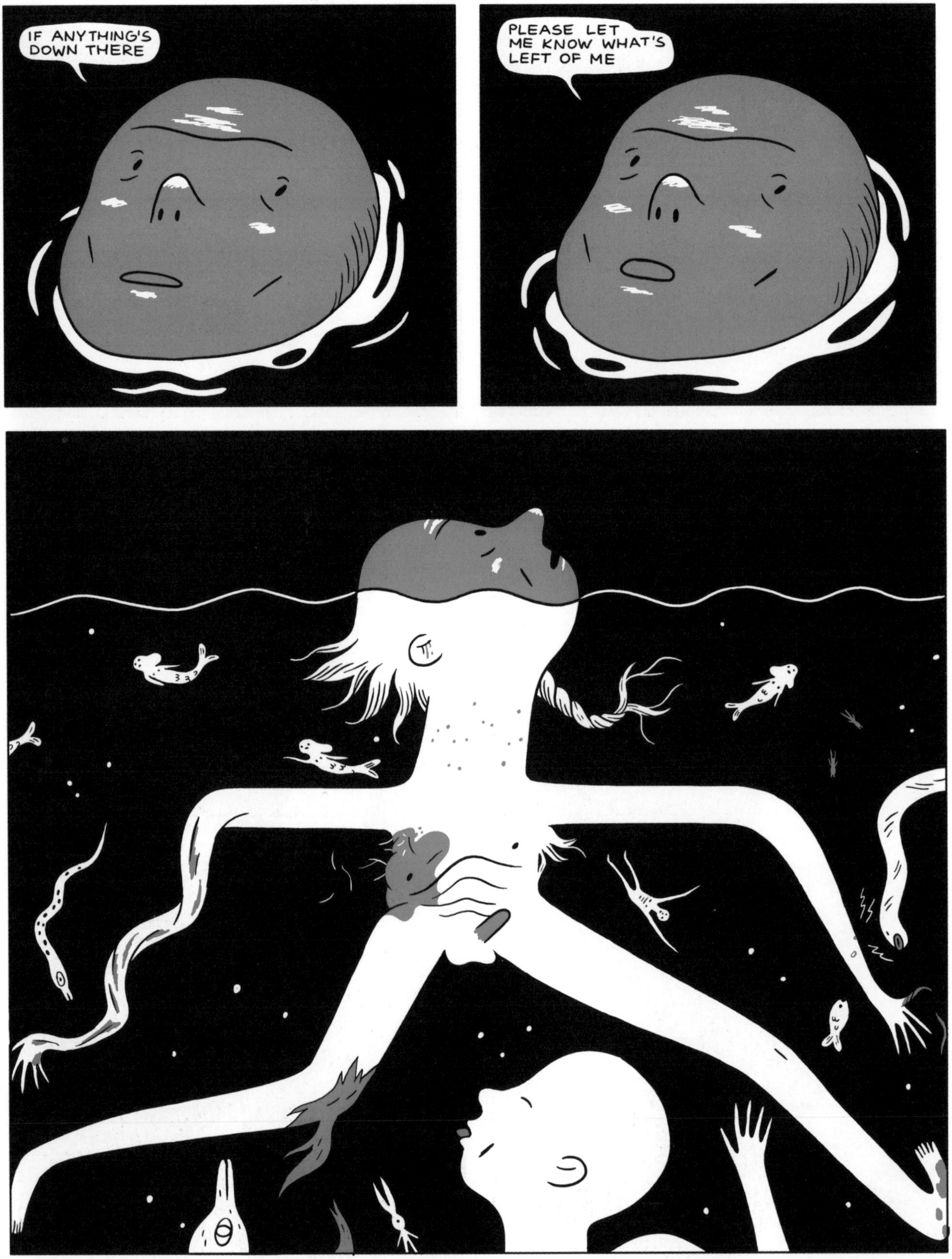
IF ANYTHING'S DOWN THERE
PLEASE LET ME KNOW WHAT'S LEFT OF ME

PLACEHOLDERS

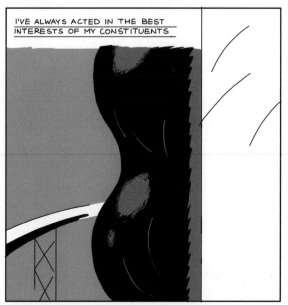

I'VE ALWAYS ACTED IN THE BEST INTERESTS OF MY CONSTITUENTS

I THINK MY RECORD REFLECTS THAT

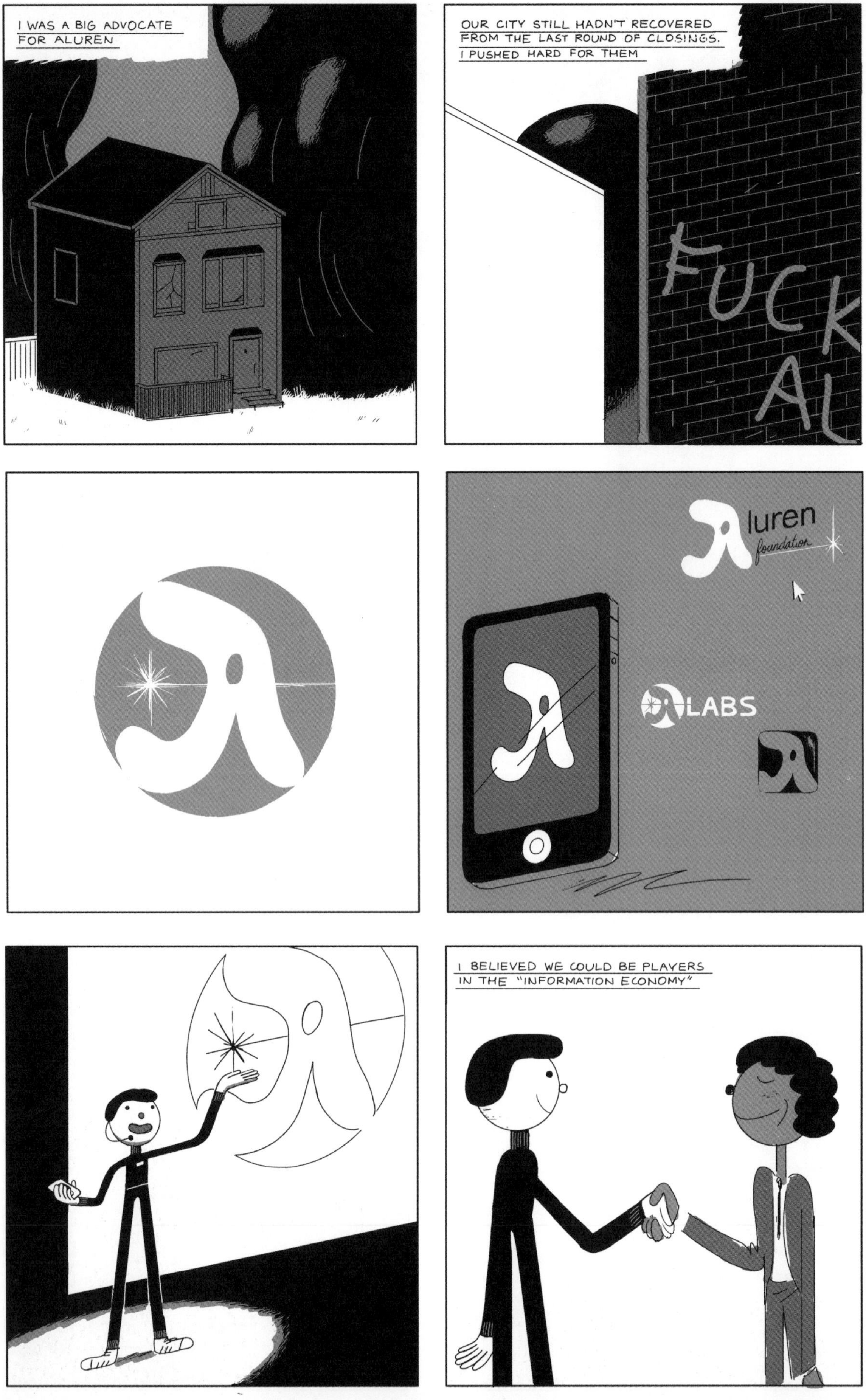
I WAS A BIG ADVOCATE FOR ALUREN
OUR CITY STILL HADN'T RECOVERED FROM THE LAST ROUND OF CLOSINGS. I PUSHED HARD FOR THEM
FUCK AL
luren
foundation
LABS
I BELIEVED WE COULD BE PLAYERS IN THE "INFORMATION ECONOMY"

ALL WE NEEDED WAS ONE MAJOR COMPANY TO GET THE BALL ROLLING

TO SEE THE POTENTIAL OUR SMALL CITY HAD

I AGGRESSIVELY PURSUED ALUREN. I KNEW THEY WERE LOOKING TO BUILD A CAMPUS ON THE EAST COAST

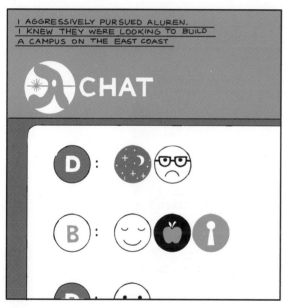

WE WEREN'T THE ONLY ONES BEING CONSIDERED

WE HAD A LOT GOING FOR US. WE WERE SAFE. WE HAD SCHOOLS. AN EDUCATED WORKFORCE. PLENTY OF SPACE

(WHAT WITH THE LAST ROUND OF CLOSINGS AND ALL)

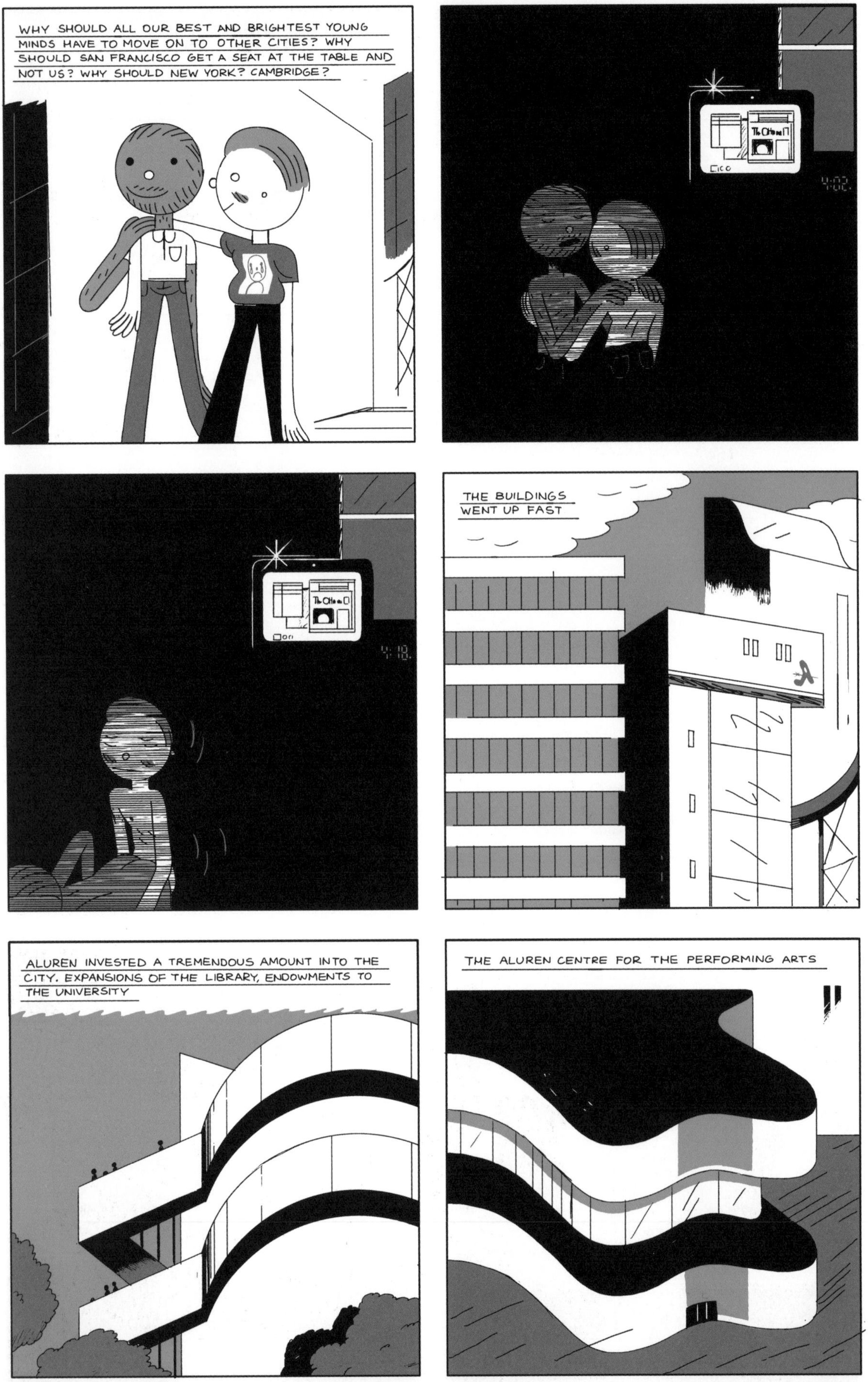
WHY SHOULD ALL OUR BEST AND BRIGHTEST YOUNG MINDS HAVE TO MOVE ON TO OTHER CITIES? WHY SHOULD SAN FRANCISCO GET A SEAT AT THE TABLE AND NOT US? WHY SHOULD NEW YORK? CAMBRIDGE?
THE BUILDINGS WENT UP FAST
ALUREN INVESTED A TREMENDOUS AMOUNT INTO THE CITY. EXPANSIONS OF THE LIBRARY, ENDOWMENTS TO THE UNIVERSITY
THE ALUREN CENTRE FOR THE PERFORMING ARTS

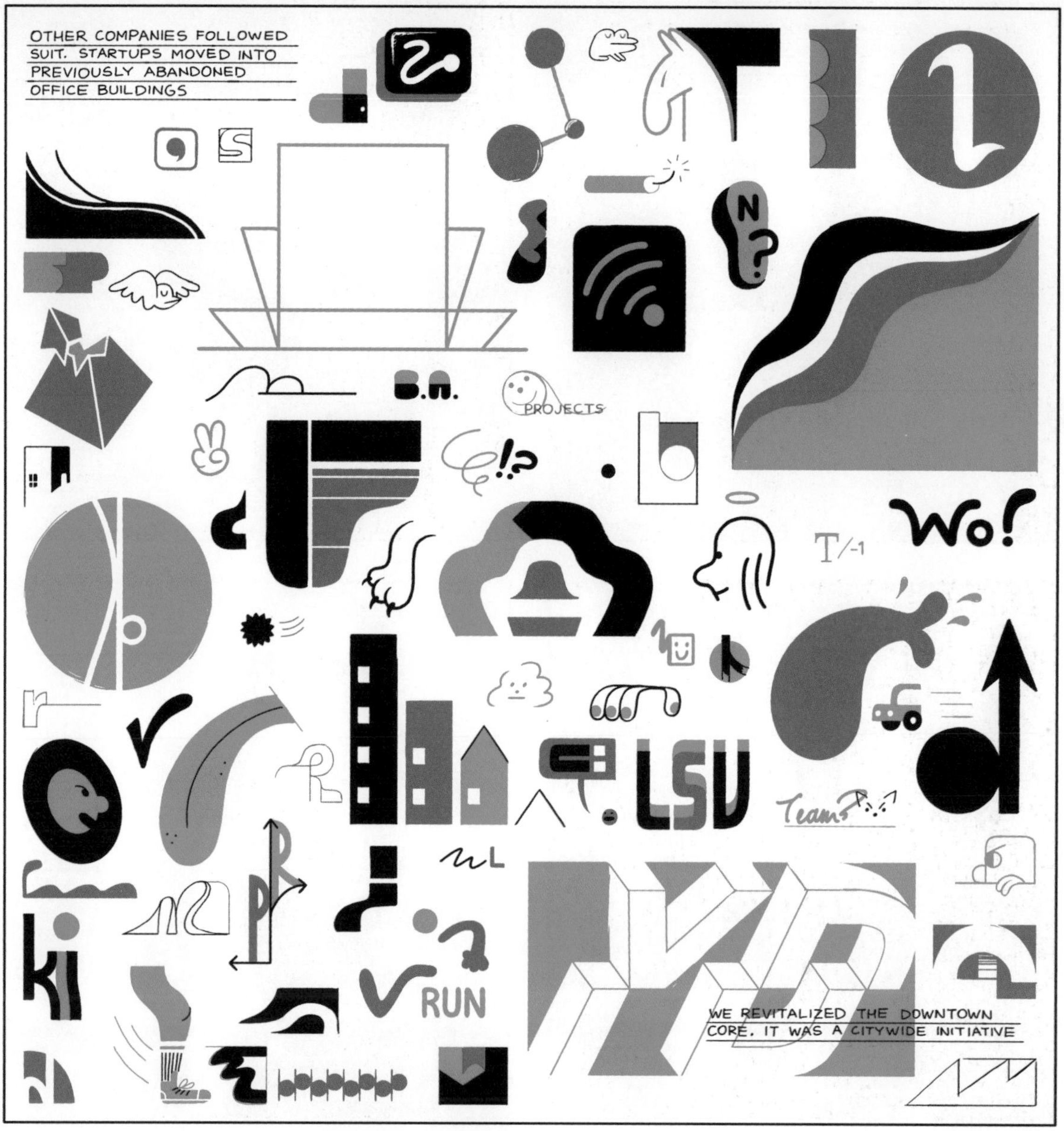
OTHER COMPANIES FOLLOWED SUIT. STARTUPS MOVED INTO PREVIOUSLY ABANDONED OFFICE BUILDINGS
PROJECTS
RUN
WE REVITALIZED THE DOWNTOWN CORE. IT WAS A CITYWIDE INITIATIVE

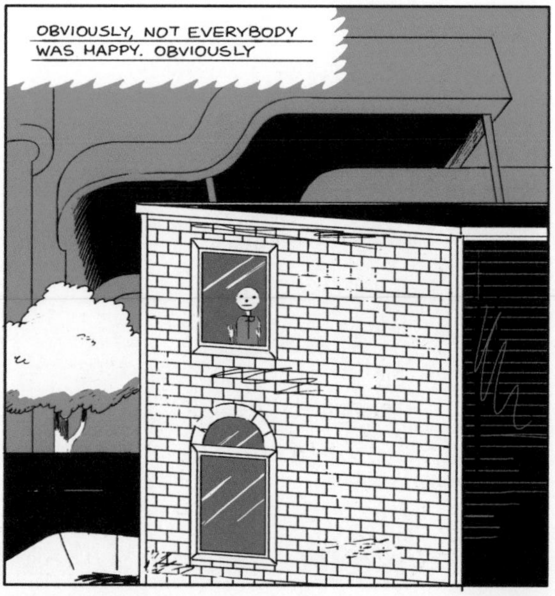
OBVIOUSLY, NOT EVERYBODY WAS HAPPY. OBVIOUSLY

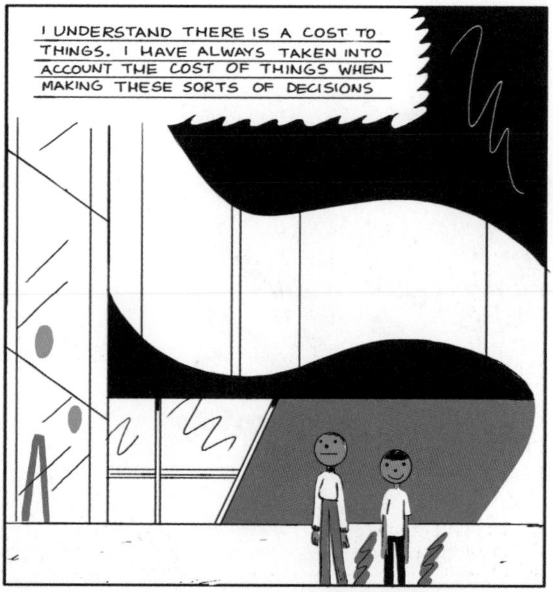
I UNDERSTAND THERE IS A COST TO THINGS. I HAVE ALWAYS TAKEN INTO ACCOUNT THE COST OF THINGS WHEN MAKING THESE SORTS OF DECISIONS

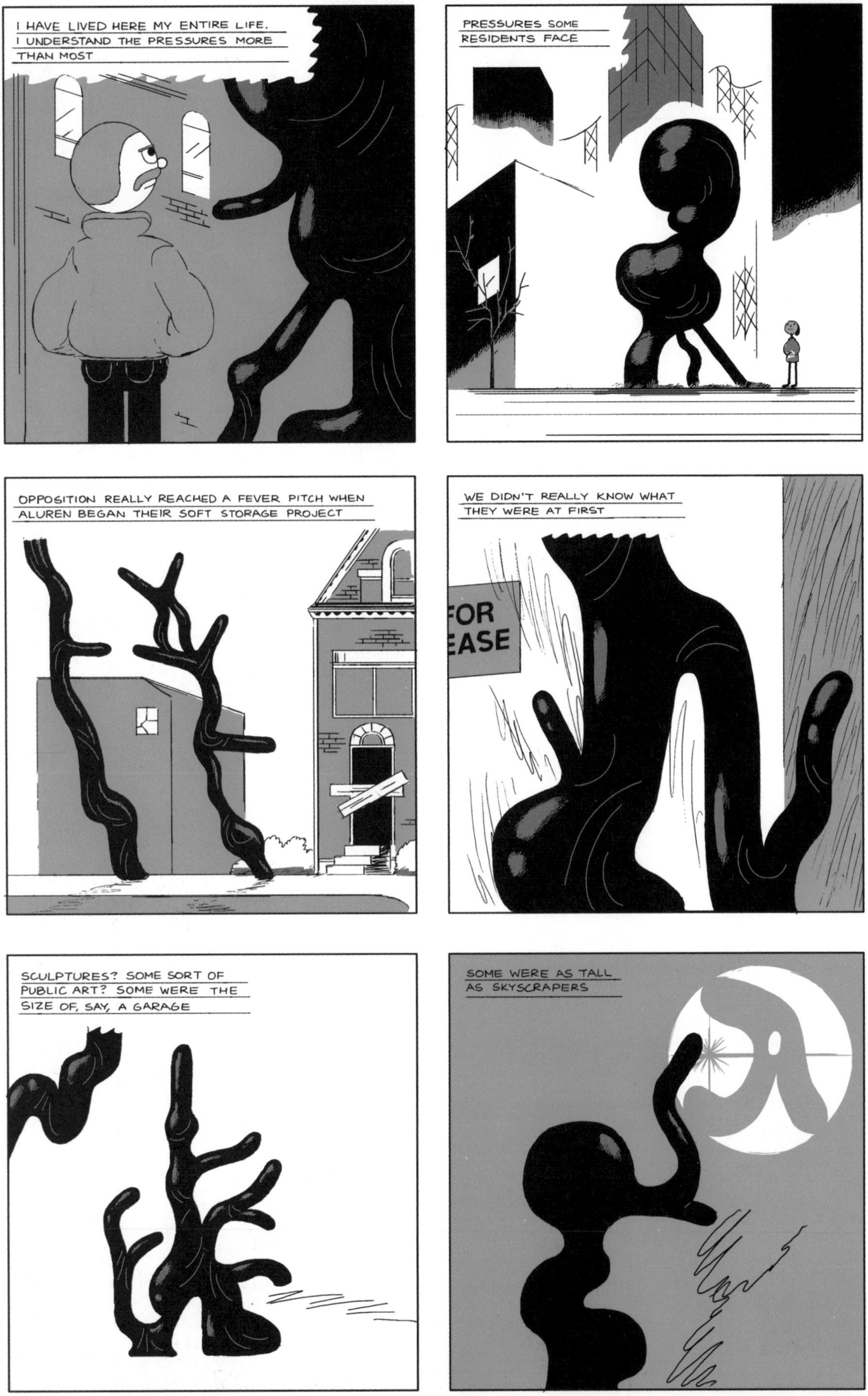
I HAVE LIVED HERE MY ENTIRE LIFE. I UNDERSTAND THE PRESSURES MORE THAN MOST
PRESSURES SOME RESIDENTS FACE
OPPOSITION REALLY REACHED A FEVER PITCH WHEN ALUREN BEGAN THEIR SOFT STORAGE PROJECT
WE DIDN'T REALLY KNOW WHAT THEY WERE AT FIRST
FOR
EASE
SCULPTURES? SOME SORT OF PUBLIC ART? SOME WERE THE SIZE OF, SAY, A GARAGE
SOME WERE AS TALL AS SKYSCRAPERS

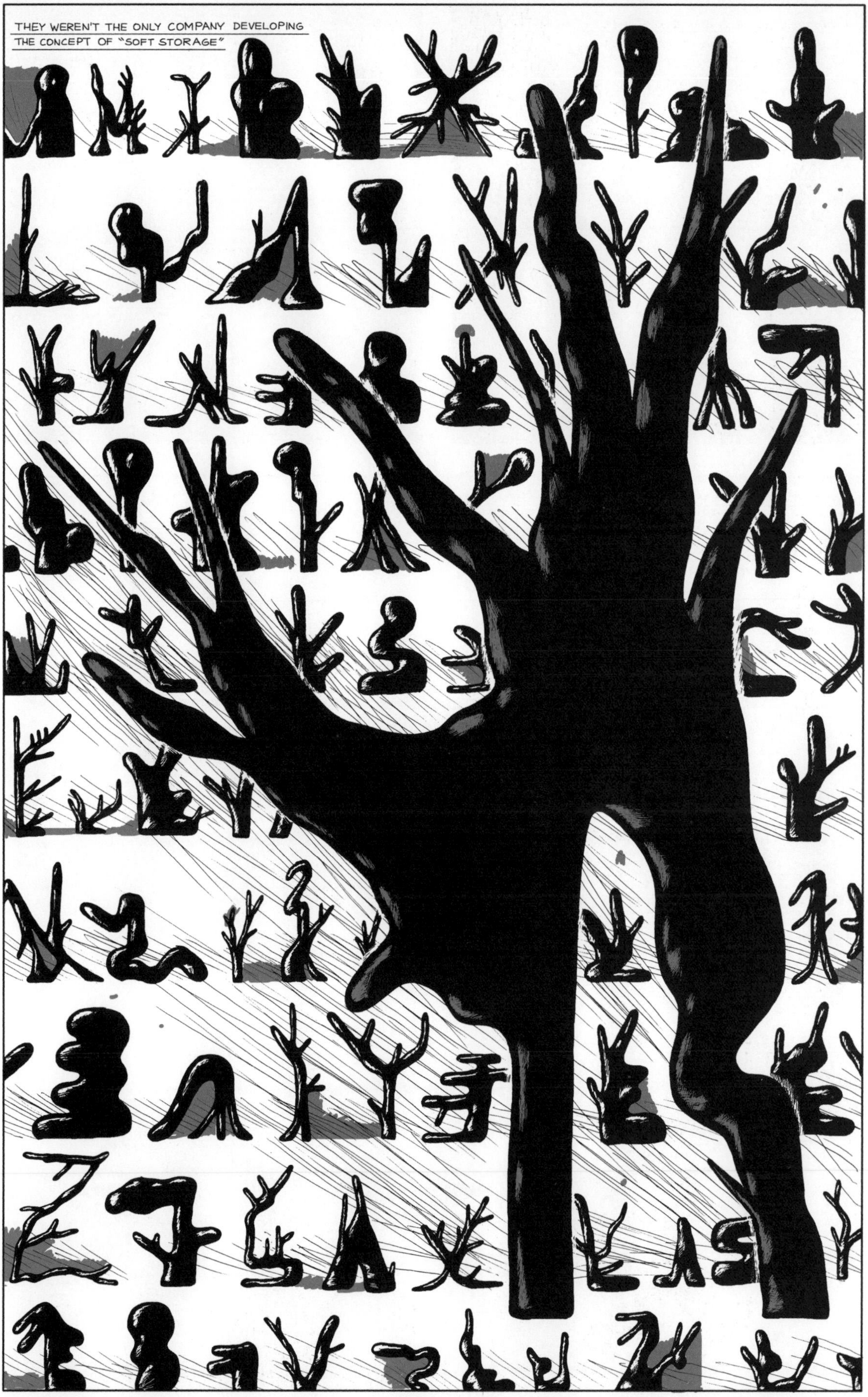
THEY WEREN'T THE ONLY COMPANY DEVELOPING
THE CONCEPT OF "SOFT STORAGE"

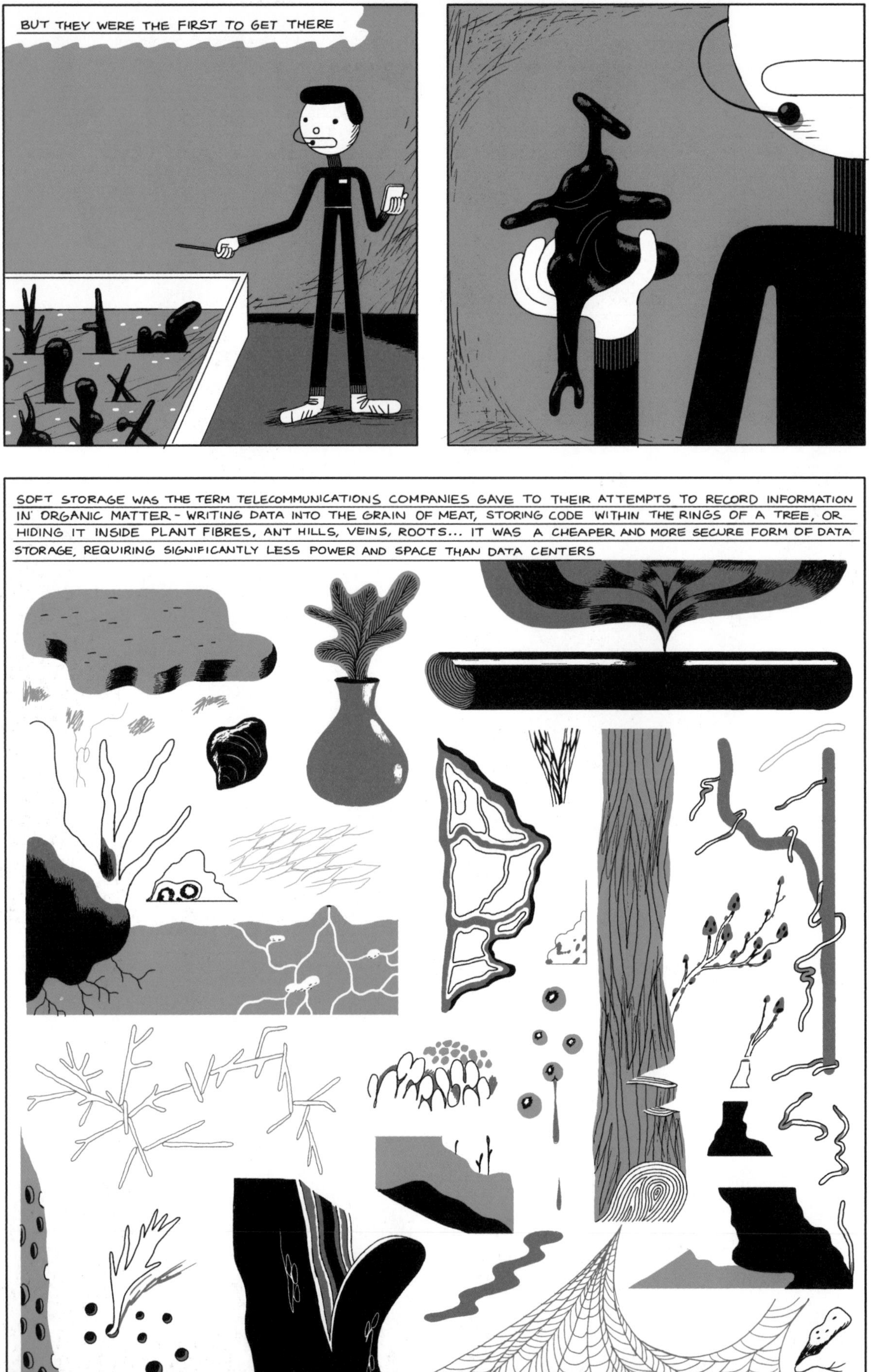
BUT THEY WERE THE FIRST TO GET THERE
SOFT STORAGE WAS THE TERM TELECOMMUNICATIONS COMPANIES GAVE TO THEIR ATTEMPTS TO RECORD INFORMATION IN ORGANIC MATTER - WRITING DATA INTO THE GRAIN OF MEAT, STORING CODE WITHIN THE RINGS OF A TREE, OR HIDING IT INSIDE PLANT FIBRES, ANT HILLS, VEINS, ROOTS... IT WAS A CHEAPER AND MORE SECURE FORM OF DATA STORAGE, REQUIRING SIGNIFICANTLY LESS POWER AND SPACE THAN DATA CENTERS

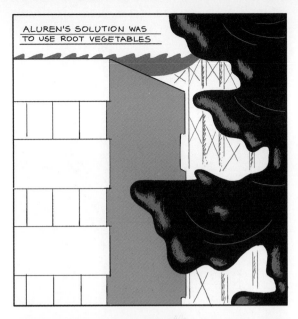

ALUREN'S SOLUTION WAS
TO USE ROOT VEGETABLES

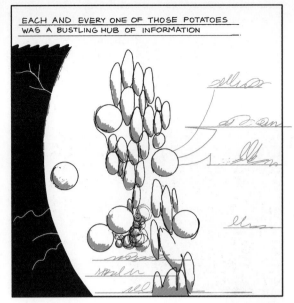

EACH AND EVERY ONE OF THOSE POTATOES
WAS A BUSTLING HUB OF INFORMATION

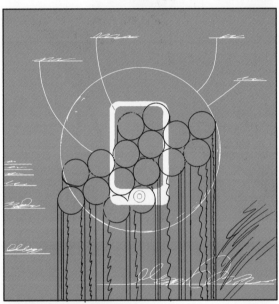

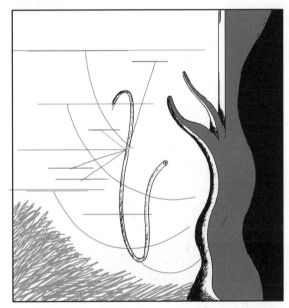

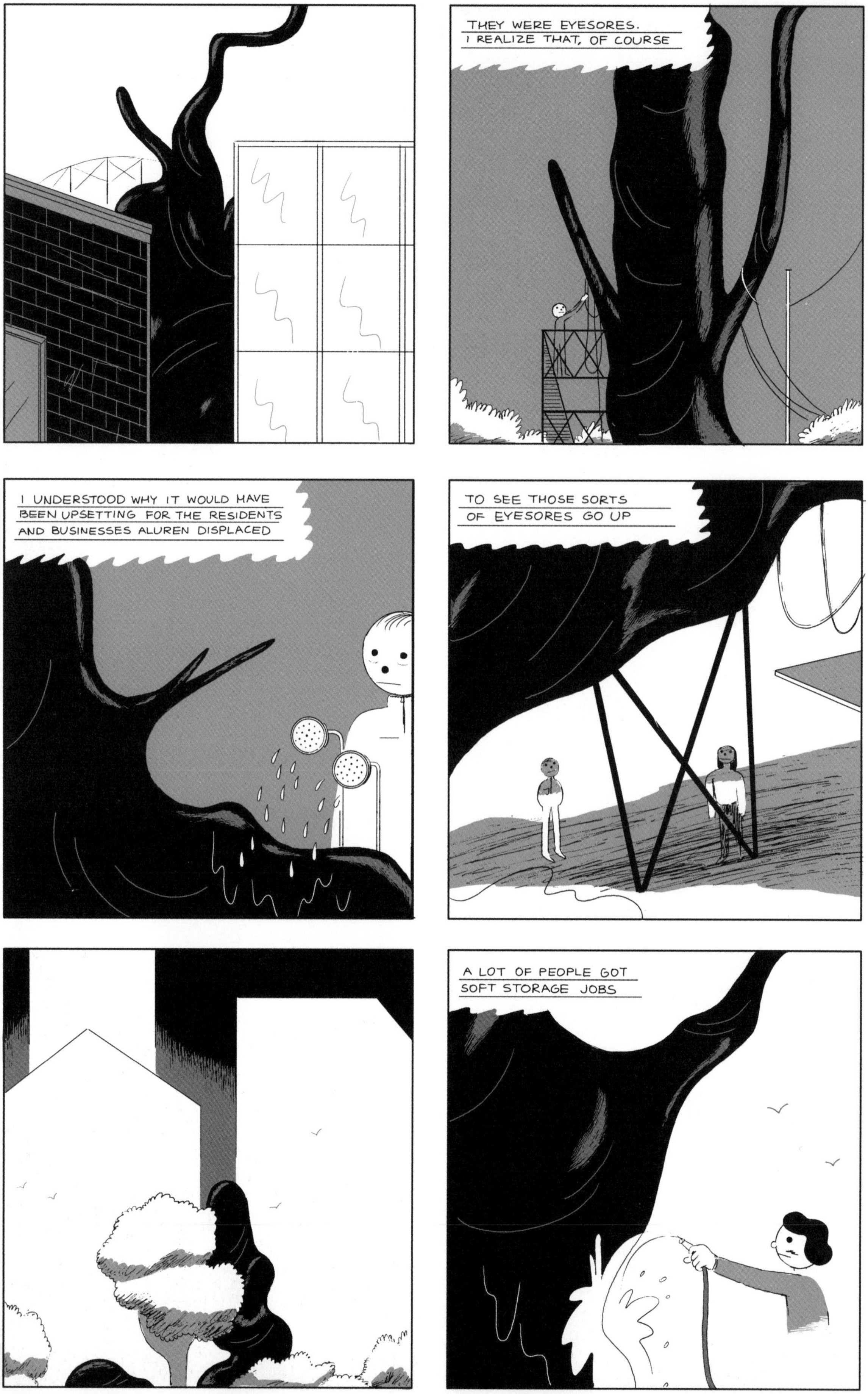
THEY WERE EYESORES.
I REALIZE THAT, OF COURSE
I UNDERSTOOD WHY IT WOULD HAVE BEEN UPSETTING FOR THE RESIDENTS AND BUSINESSES ALUREN DISPLACED
TO SEE THOSE SORTS OF EYESORES GO UP
A LOT OF PEOPLE GOT SOFT STORAGE JOBS

THE VEGETABLES NEEDED A LOT OF MAINTENANCE. WATERING, MASSAGES

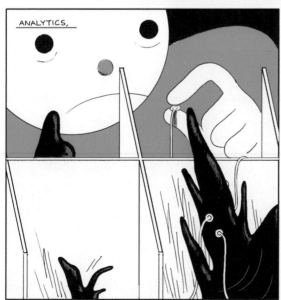

ANALYTICS,

THE WORK WASN'T EVERYONE'S CUP OF TEA, BUT BEGGARS CAN'T BE CHOOSERS

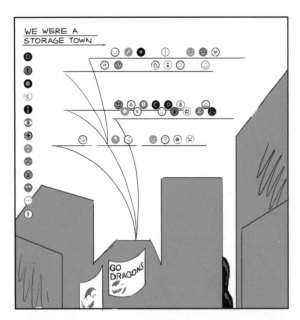

WE WERE A
STORAGE TOWN

GO DRAGONS

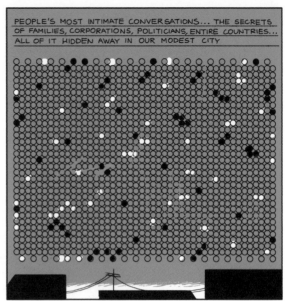

PEOPLE'S MOST INTIMATE CONVERSATIONS... THE SECRETS OF FAMILIES, CORPORATIONS, POLITICIANS, ENTIRE COUNTRIES... ALL OF IT HIDDEN AWAY IN OUR MODEST CITY

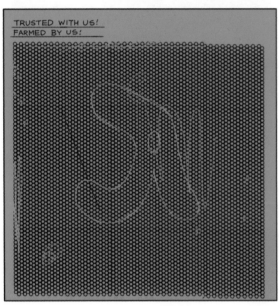

TRUSTED WITH US!
FARMED BY US!

HALL
A

GO! HUB · PE

HOWEVER,

THINGS TOOK A TURN WHEN THE COUNTRY ENTERED OUR CURRENT CRISIS

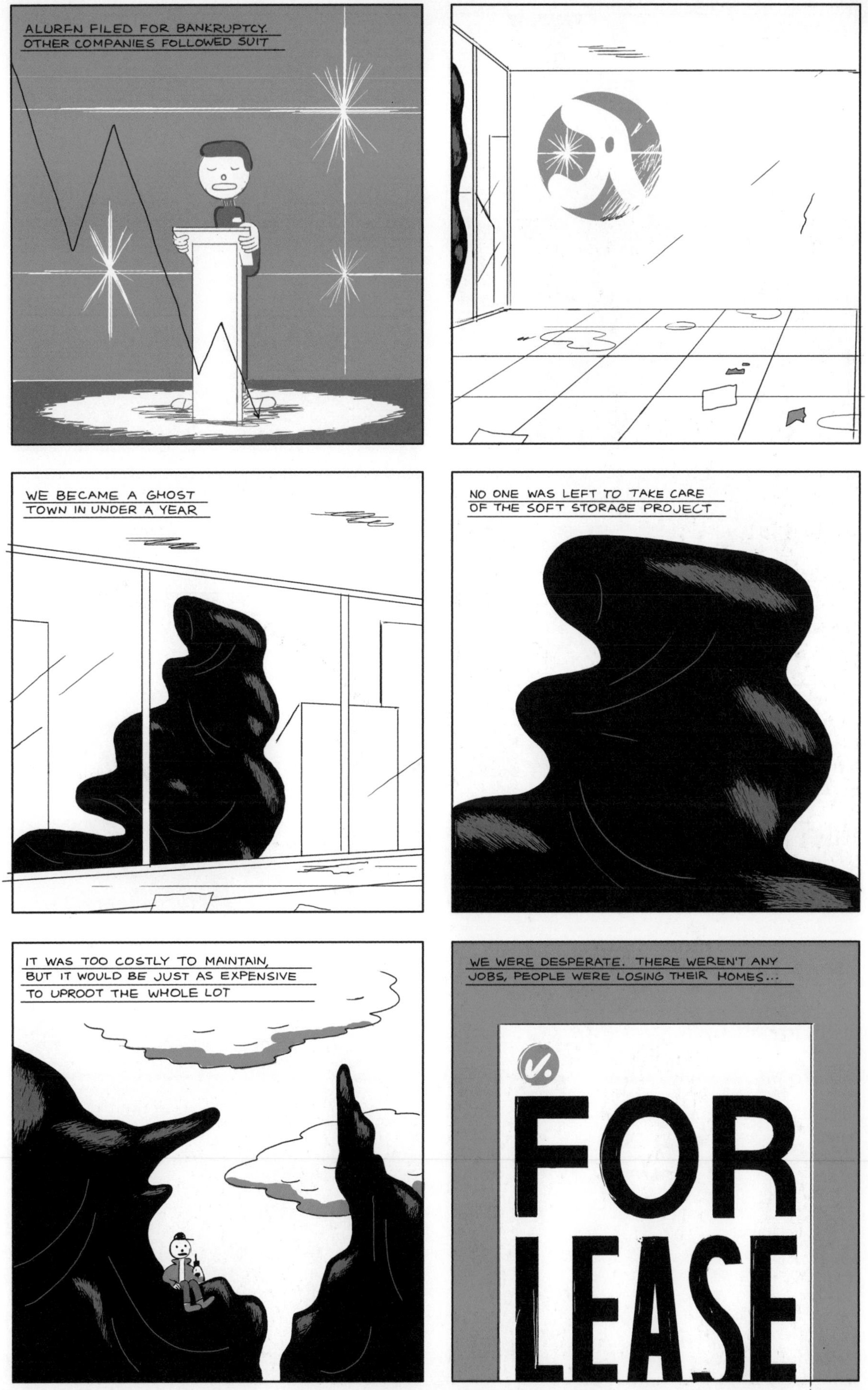
ALURFN FILED FOR BANKRUPTCY. OTHER COMPANIES FOLLOWED SUIT
WE BECAME A GHOST TOWN IN UNDER A YEAR
NO ONE WAS LEFT TO TAKE CARE OF THE SOFT STORAGE PROJECT
IT WAS TOO COSTLY TO MAINTAIN, BUT IT WOULD BE JUST AS EXPENSIVE TO UPROOT THE WHOLE LOT
WE WERE DESPERATE. THERE WEREN'T ANY JOBS, PEOPLE WERE LOSING THEIR HOMES...
FOR LEASE

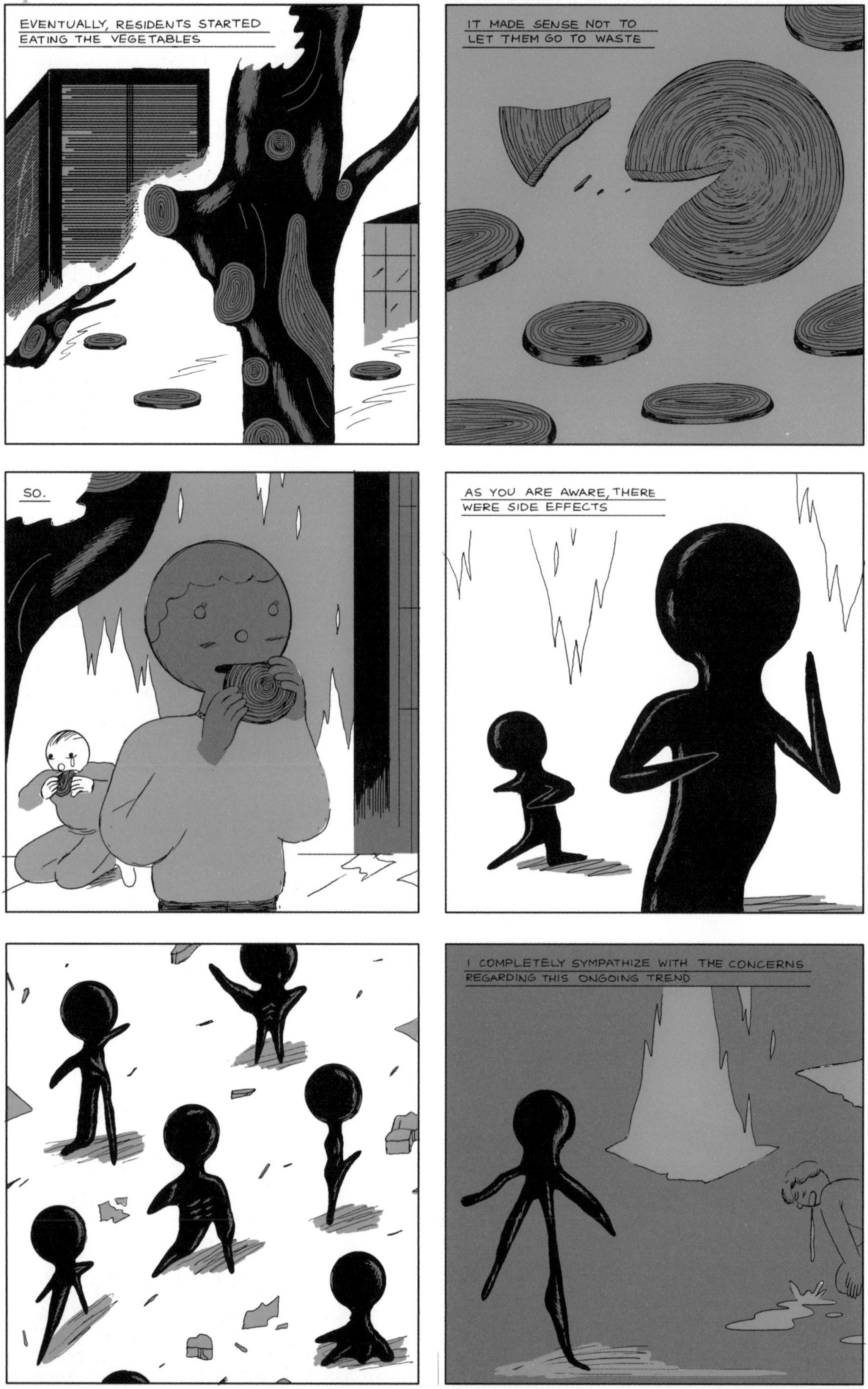
EVENTUALLY, RESIDENTS STARTED EATING THE VEGETABLES
IT MADE SENSE NOT TO LET THEM GO TO WASTE
SO.
AS YOU ARE AWARE, THERE WERE SIDE EFFECTS
I COMPLETELY SYMPATHIZE WITH THE CONCERNS REGARDING THIS ONGOING TREND

BUT CHANGE IS A PART OF ANY CITY

FACTORIES OPEN, FACTORIES CLOSE. PEOPLE COME AND GO. SHOPS GO OUT OF BUSINESS

ETC.

I HAVE LIVED HERE MY ENTIRE LIFE

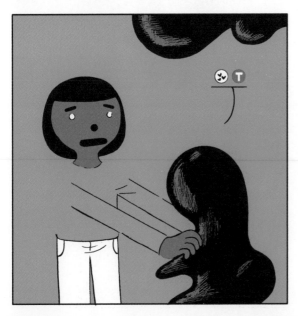

I DON'T KNOW IF THINGS ARE GOING TO STAY THIS WAY. I'D LIKE THEM TO, BUT I DON'T KNOW

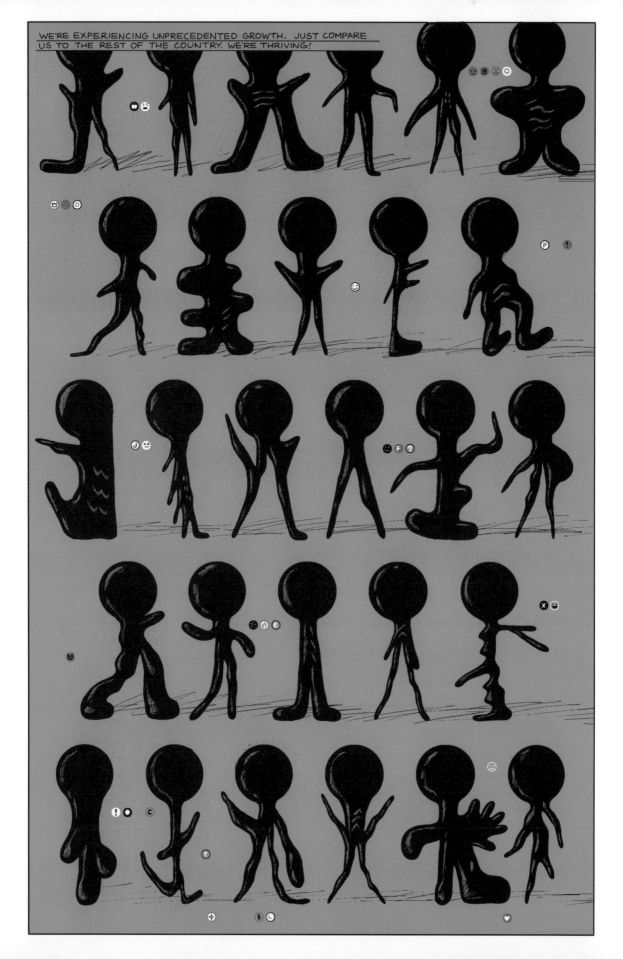

WE'RE EXPERIENCING UNPRECEDENTED GROWTH. JUST COMPARE
US TO THE REST OF THE COUNTRY. WE'RE THRIVING!

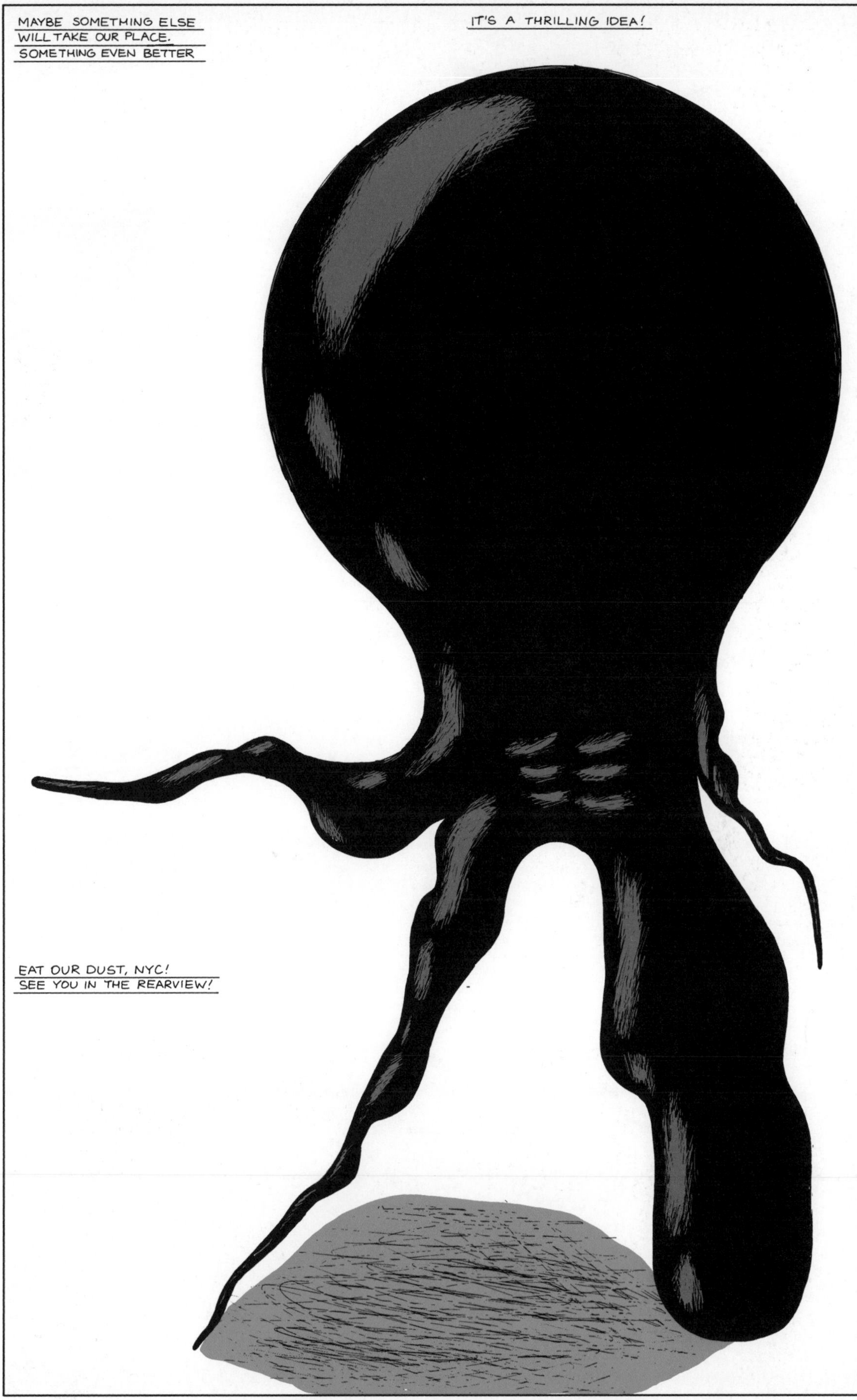
MAYBE SOMETHING ELSE
WILL TAKE OUR PLACE.
SOMETHING EVEN BETTER
IT'S A THRILLING IDEA!
EAT OUR DUST, NYC!
SEE YOU IN THE REARVIEW!

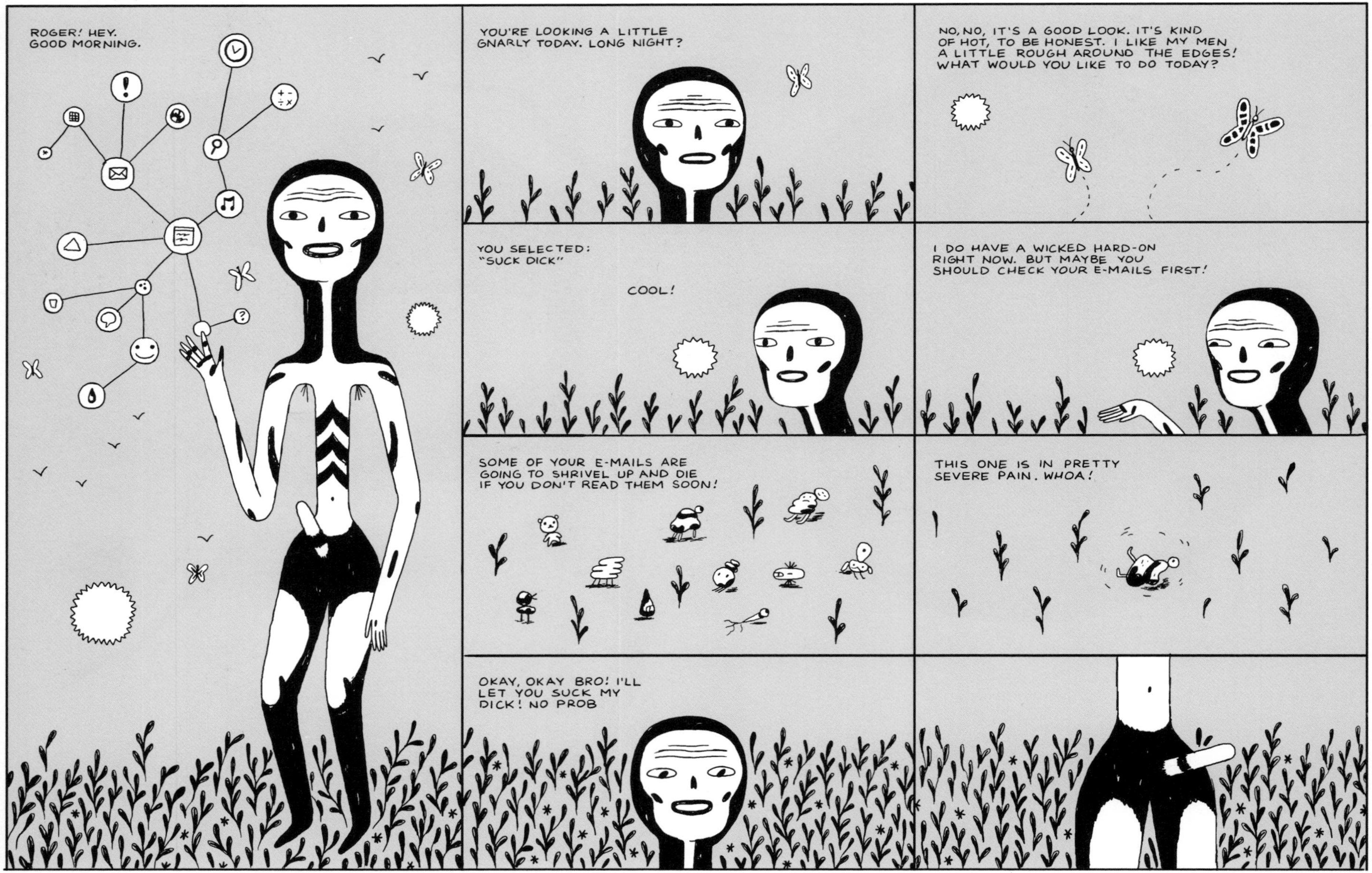
ROGER! HEY. GOOD MORNING.
YOU'RE LOOKING A LITTLE GNARLY TODAY. LONG NIGHT?
NO, NO, IT'S A GOOD LOOK. IT'S KIND OF HOT, TO BE HONEST. I LIKE MY MEN A LITTLE ROUGH AROUND THE EDGES! WHAT WOULD YOU LIKE TO DO TODAY?
YOU SELECTED: "SUCK DICK"
COOL!
I DO HAVE A WICKED HARD-ON RIGHT NOW. BUT MAYBE YOU SHOULD CHECK YOUR E-MAILS FIRST!
SOME OF YOUR E-MAILS ARE GOING TO SHRIVEL UP AND DIE IF YOU DON'T READ THEM SOON!
THIS ONE IS IN PRETTY SEVERE PAIN. WHOA!
OKAY, OKAY BRO! I'LL LET YOU SUCK MY DICK! NO PROB

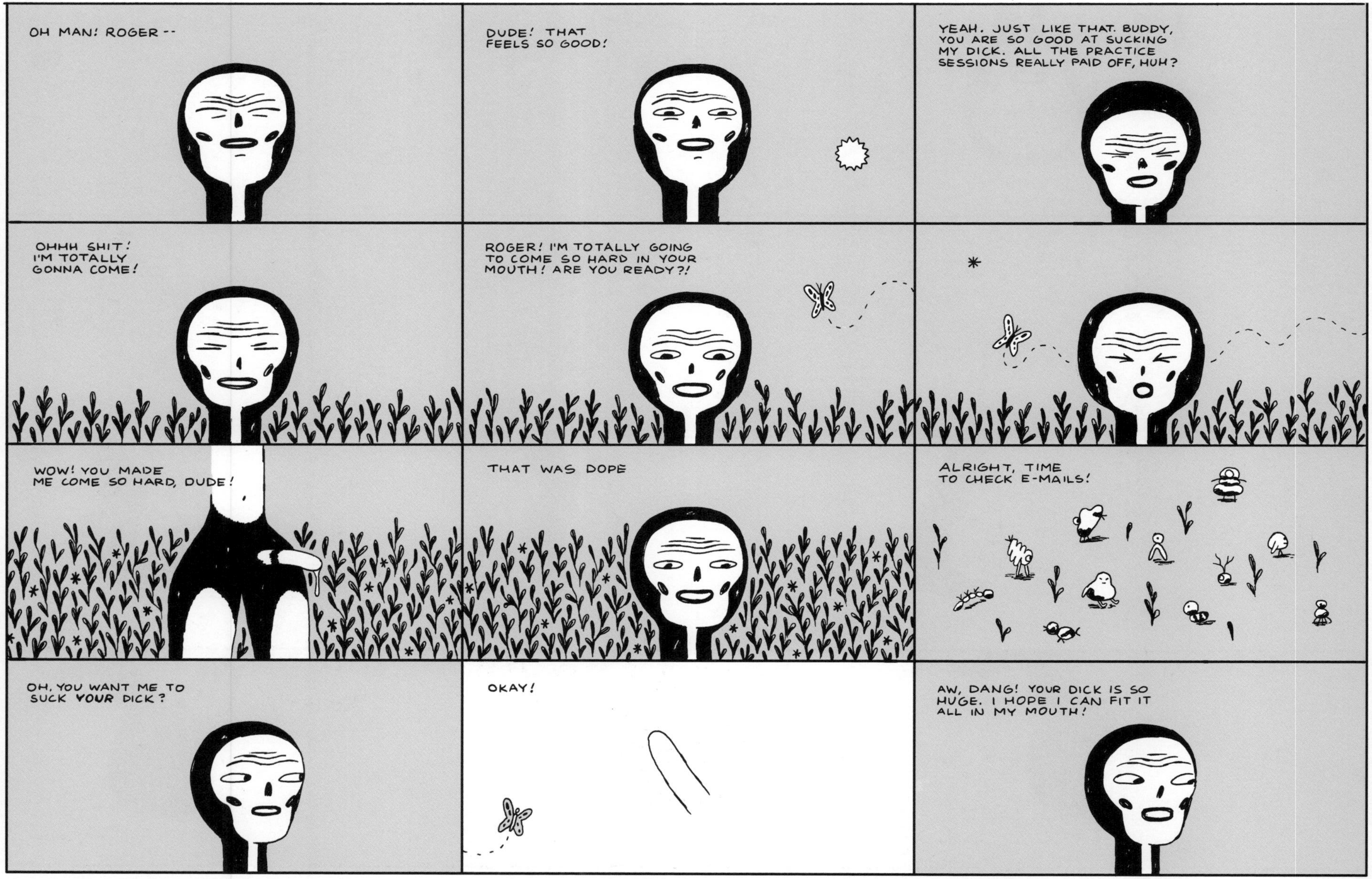
OH MAN! ROGER --
DUDE! THAT FEELS SO GOOD!
YEAH. JUST LIKE THAT. BUDDY, YOU ARE SO GOOD AT SUCKING MY DICK. ALL THE PRACTICE SESSIONS REALLY PAID OFF, HUH?
OHHH SHIT! I'M TOTALLY GONNA COME!
ROGER! I'M TOTALLY GOING TO COME SO HARD IN YOUR MOUTH! ARE YOU READY?!
WOW! YOU MADE ME COME SO HARD, DUDE!
THAT WAS DOPE
ALRIGHT, TIME TO CHECK E-MAILS!
OH, YOU WANT ME TO SUCK **YOUR** DICK?
OKAY!
AW, DANG! YOUR DICK IS SO HUGE. I HOPE I CAN FIT IT ALL IN MY MOUTH!

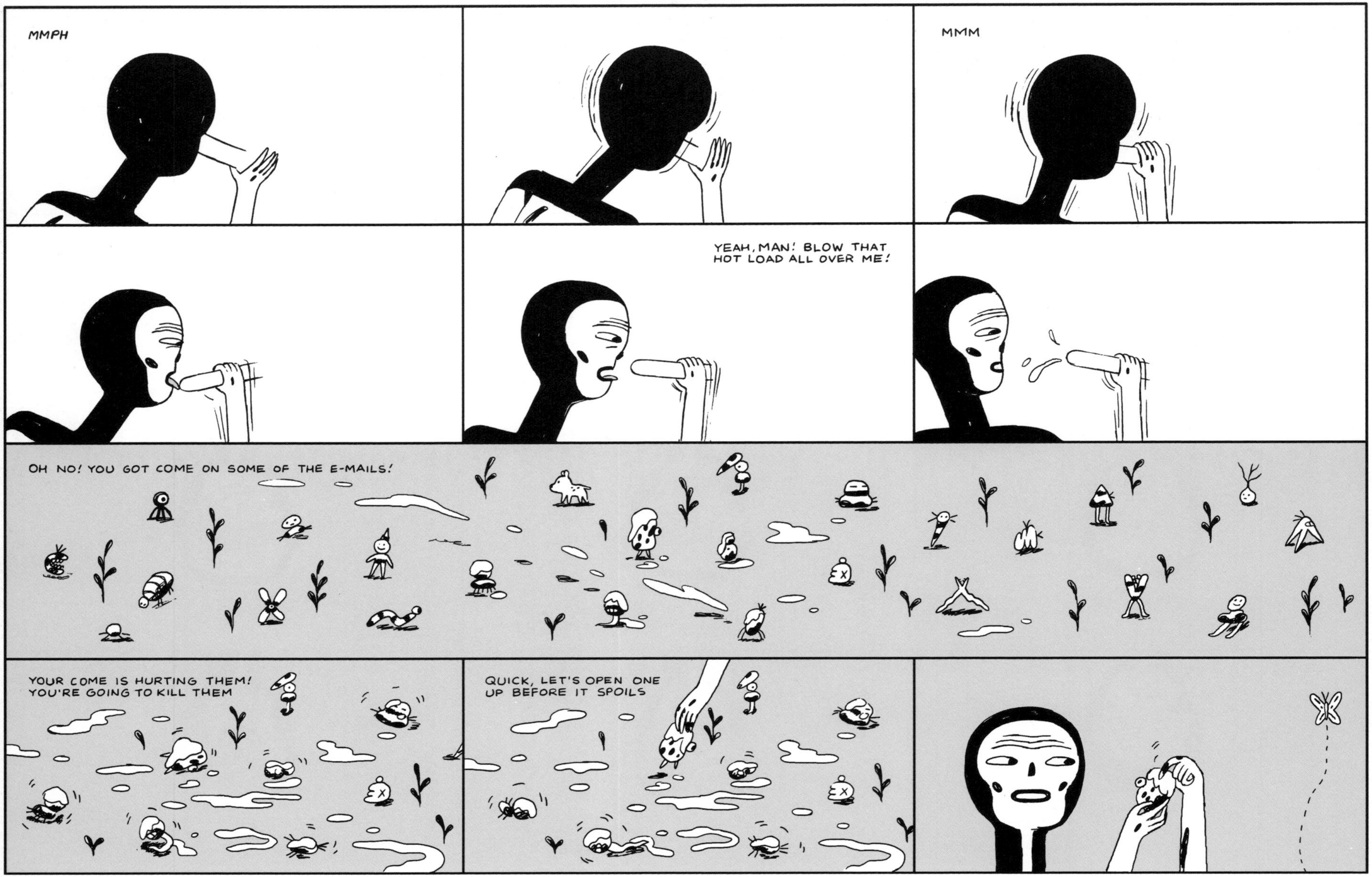
MMPH
MMM
YEAH, MAN! BLOW THAT HOT LOAD ALL OVER ME!
OH NO! YOU GOT COME ON SOME OF THE E-MAILS!
YOUR COME IS HURTING THEM! YOU'RE GOING TO KILL THEM
QUICK, LET'S OPEN ONE UP BEFORE IT SPOILS

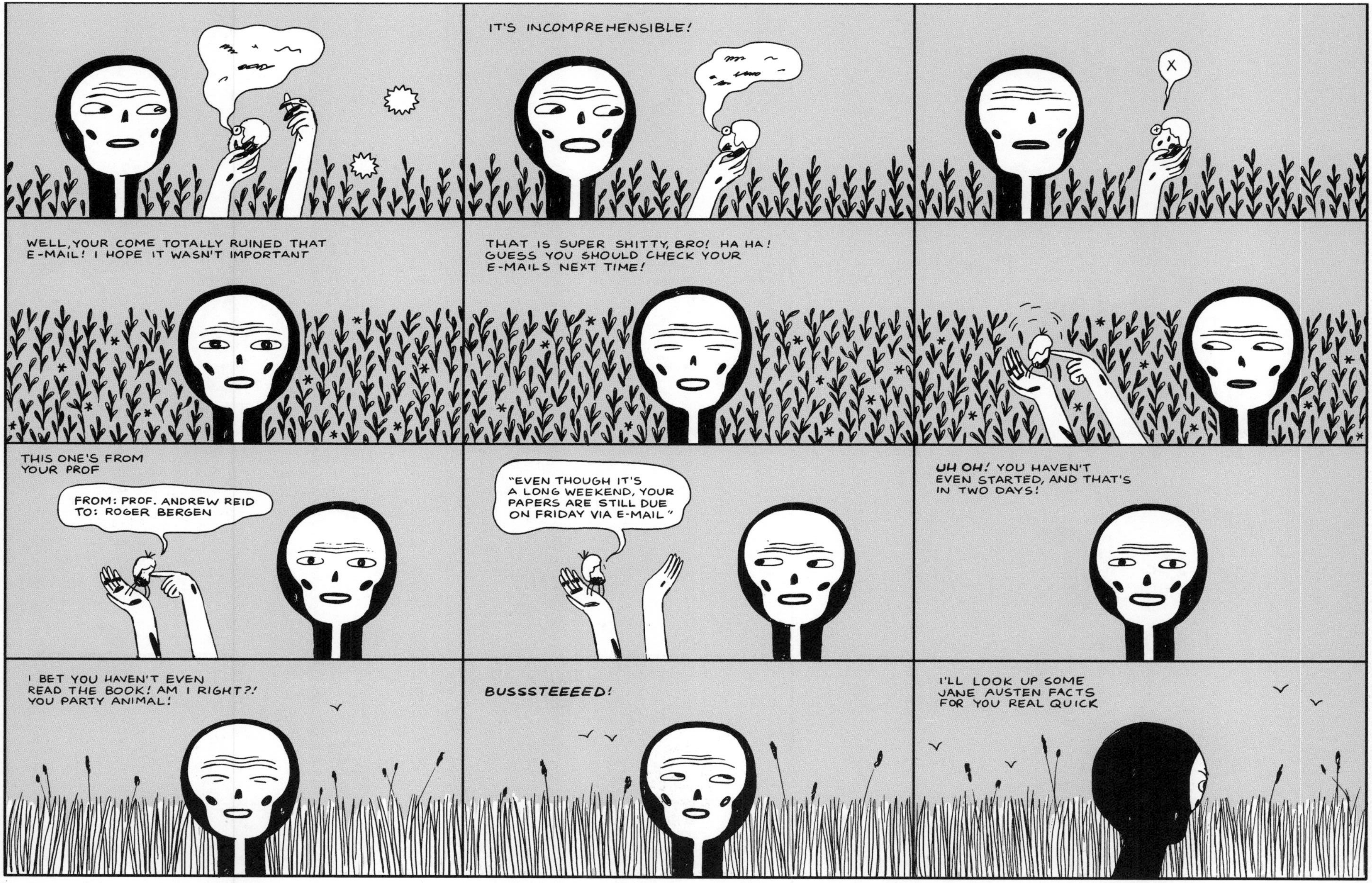
IT'S INCOMPREHENSIBLE!
X
WELL, YOUR COME TOTALLY RUINED THAT E-MAIL! I HOPE IT WASN'T IMPORTANT
THAT IS SUPER SHITTY, BRO! HA HA! GUESS YOU SHOULD CHECK YOUR E-MAILS NEXT TIME!
THIS ONE'S FROM YOUR PROF
FROM: PROF. ANDREW REID
TO: ROGER BERGEN
"EVEN THOUGH IT'S A LONG WEEKEND, YOUR PAPERS ARE STILL DUE ON FRIDAY VIA E-MAIL"
UH OH! YOU HAVEN'T EVEN STARTED, AND THAT'S IN TWO DAYS!
I BET YOU HAVEN'T EVEN READ THE BOOK! AM I RIGHT?! YOU PARTY ANIMAL!
BUSSSTEEEED!
I'LL LOOK UP SOME JANE AUSTEN FACTS FOR YOU REAL QUICK

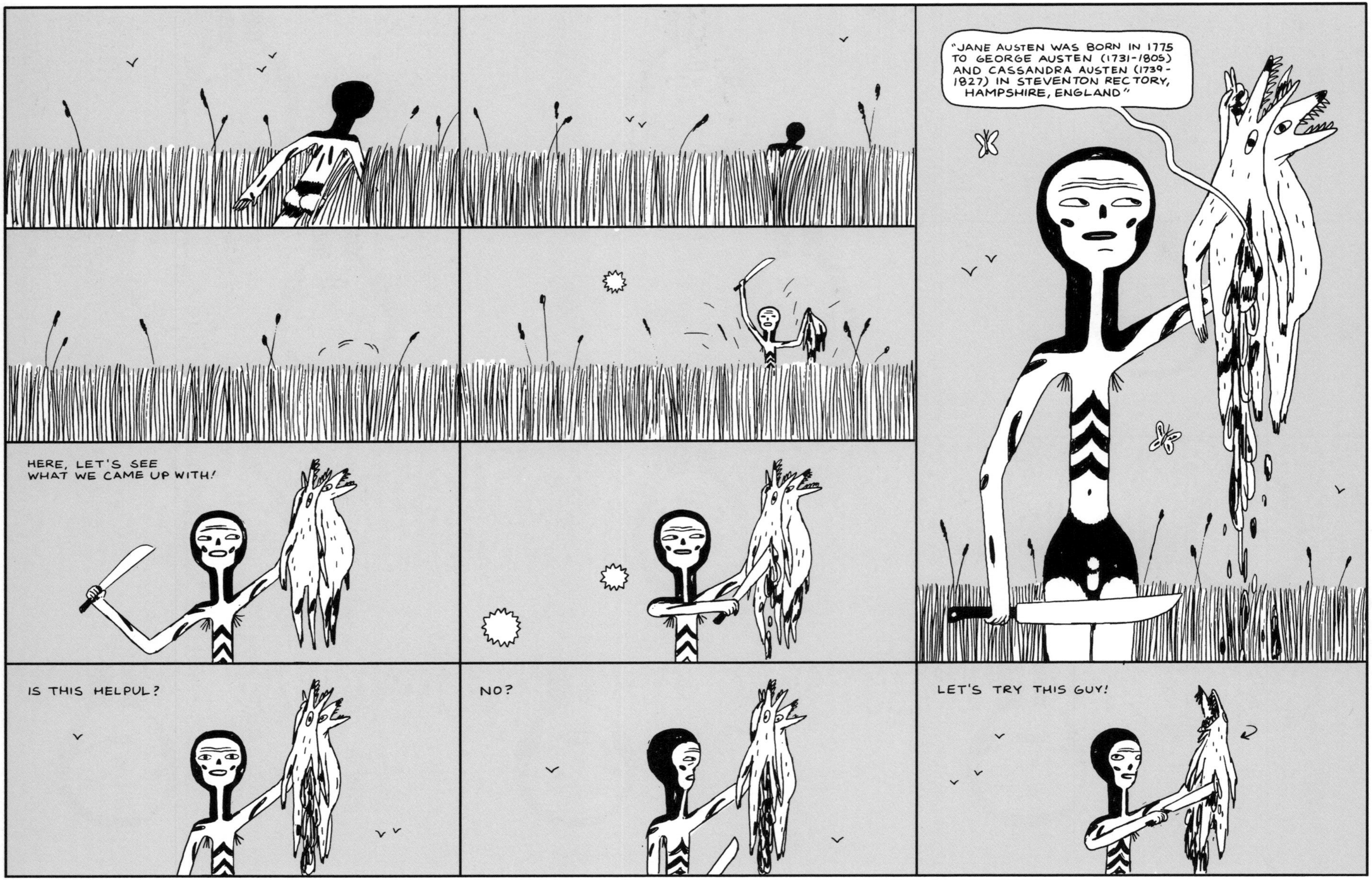

HERE, LET'S SEE WHAT WE CAME UP WITH!
"JANE AUSTEN WAS BORN IN 1775 TO GEORGE AUSTEN (1731-1805) AND CASSANDRA AUSTEN (1739-1827) IN STEVENTON RECTORY, HAMPSHIRE, ENGLAND"
IS THIS HELPUL?
NO?
LET'S TRY THIS GUY!

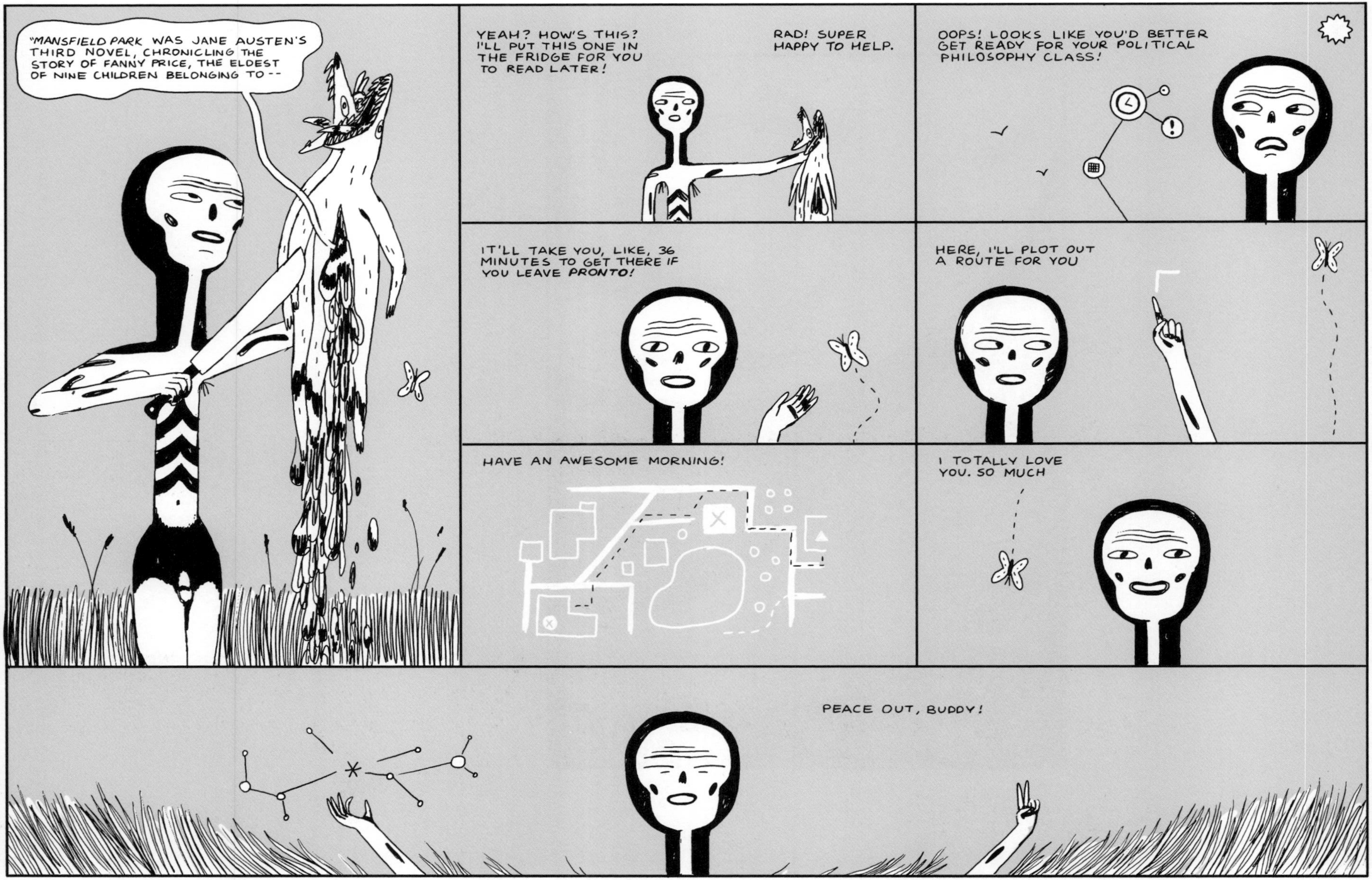
"MANSFIELD PARK WAS JANE AUSTEN'S THIRD NOVEL, CHRONICLING THE STORY OF FANNY PRICE, THE ELDEST OF NINE CHILDREN BELONGING TO--
YEAH? HOW'S THIS? I'LL PUT THIS ONE IN THE FRIDGE FOR YOU TO READ LATER!
RAD! SUPER HAPPY TO HELP.
OOPS! LOOKS LIKE YOU'D BETTER GET READY FOR YOUR POLITICAL PHILOSOPHY CLASS!
IT'LL TAKE YOU, LIKE, 36 MINUTES TO GET THERE IF YOU LEAVE *PRONTO!*
HERE, I'LL PLOT OUT A ROUTE FOR YOU
HAVE AN AWESOME MORNING!
I TOTALLY LOVE YOU. SO MUCH
PEACE OUT, BUDDY!

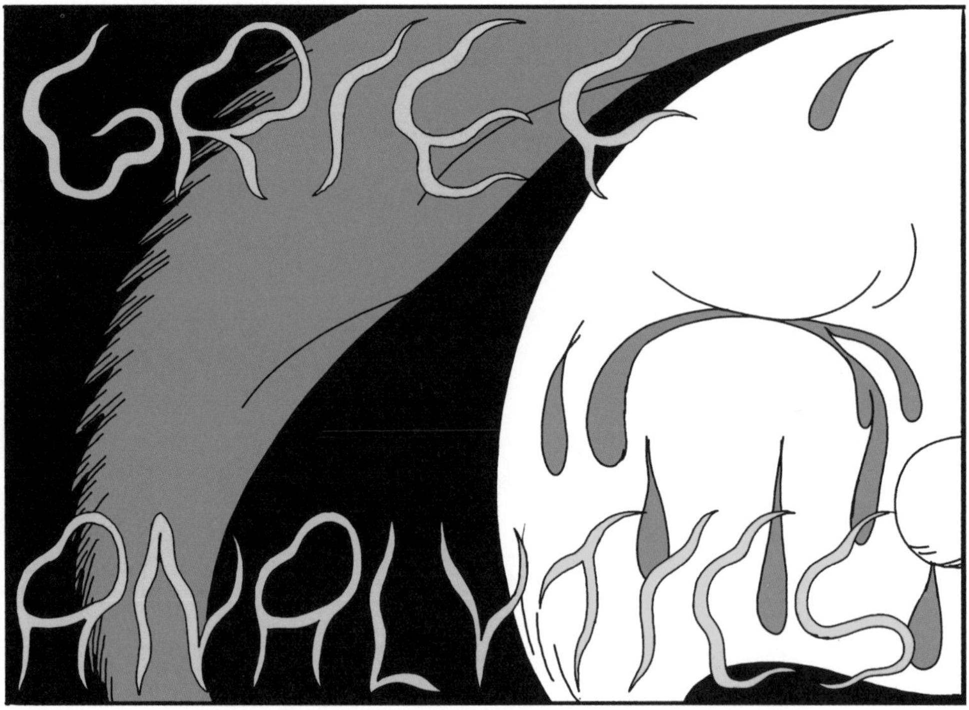
GRIEF
ANALYTICS

FOR YEARS, OUR COMPUTERS AND PHONES HAVE BEEN RECORDING US CRYING.
THE DATA THEY COLLECT IS THEN STORED, SORTED AND ORGANIZED

MICROPHONES MEASURE THE LENGTH OF EACH OF YOUR SOBS AND THE INTERVALS BETWEEN THEM, THE PITCH AND TIMBRE OF YOUR WHIMPERING, YOUR SNIVEL RATE

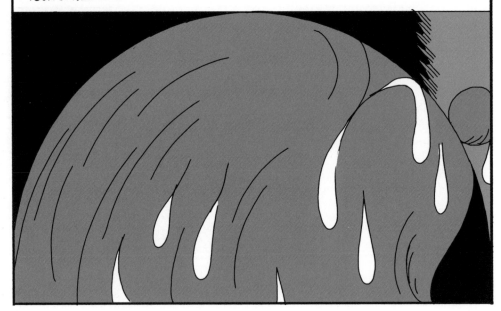

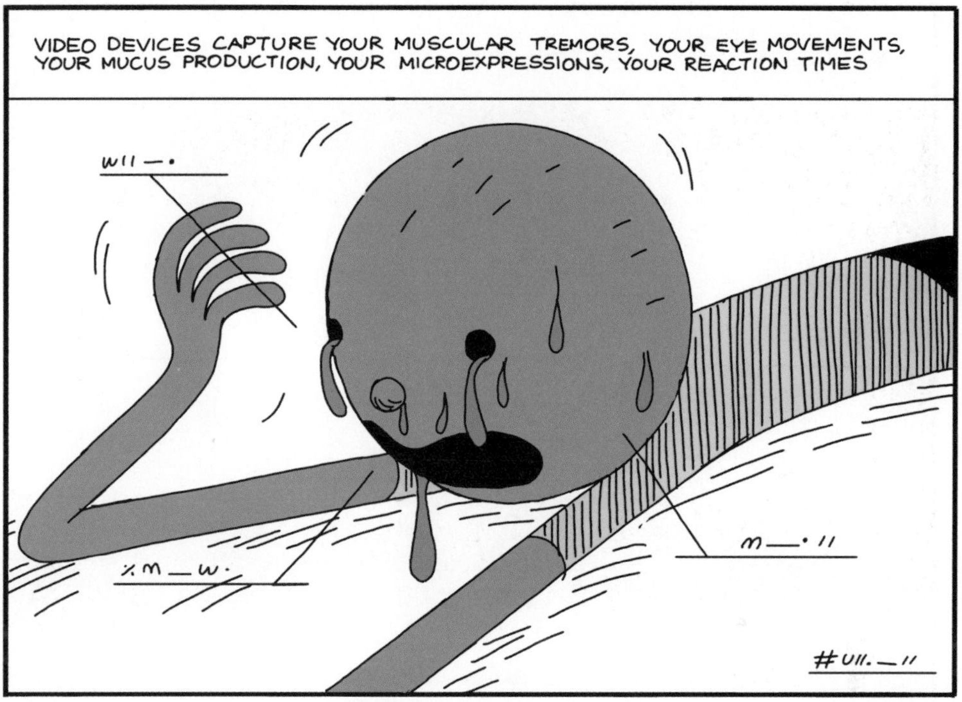
VIDEO DEVICES CAPTURE YOUR MUSCULAR TREMORS, YOUR EYE MOVEMENTS, YOUR MUCUS PRODUCTION, YOUR MICROEXPRESSIONS, YOUR REACTION TIMES

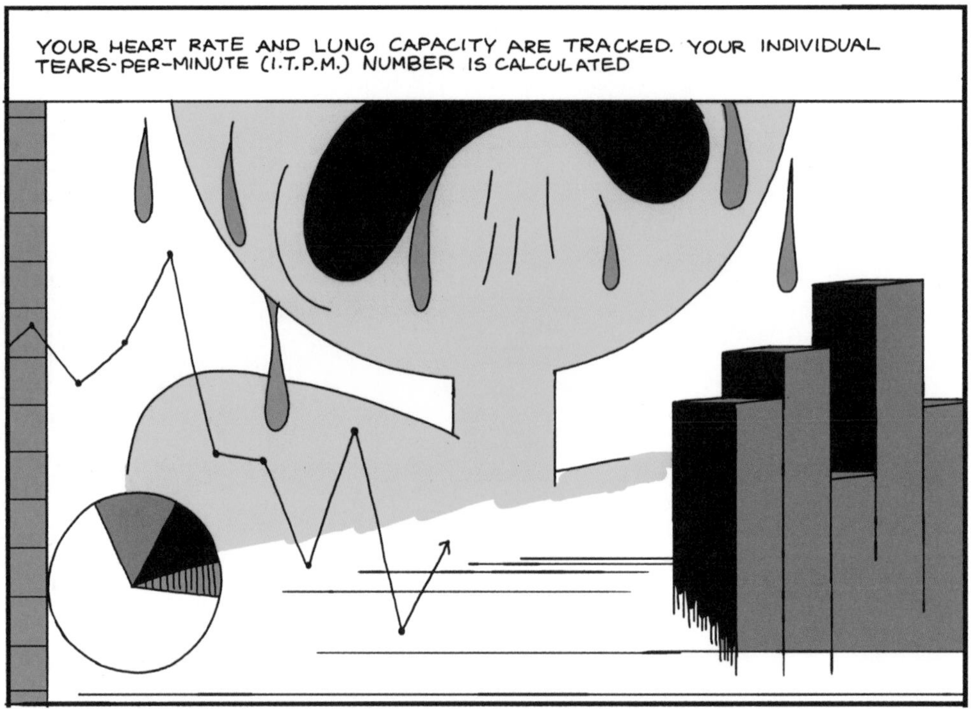
YOUR HEART RATE AND LUNG CAPACITY ARE TRACKED. YOUR INDIVIDUAL TEARS-PER-MINUTE (I.T.P.M.) NUMBER IS CALCULATED

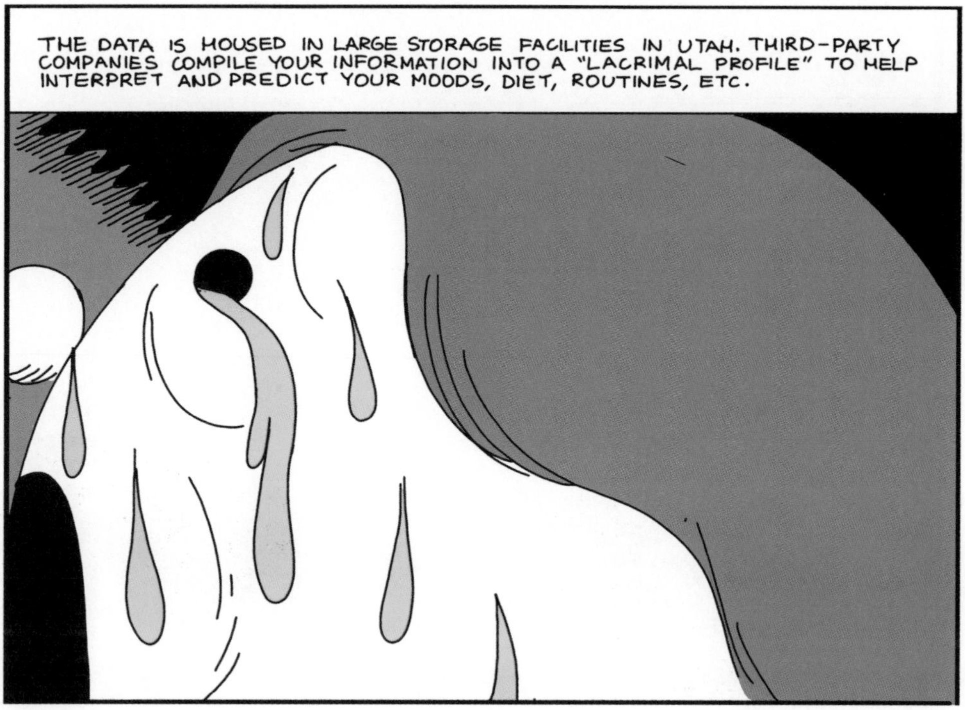
THE DATA IS HOUSED IN LARGE STORAGE FACILITIES IN UTAH. THIRD-PARTY COMPANIES COMPILE YOUR INFORMATION INTO A "LACRIMAL PROFILE" TO HELP INTERPRET AND PREDICT YOUR MOODS, DIET, ROUTINES, ETC.

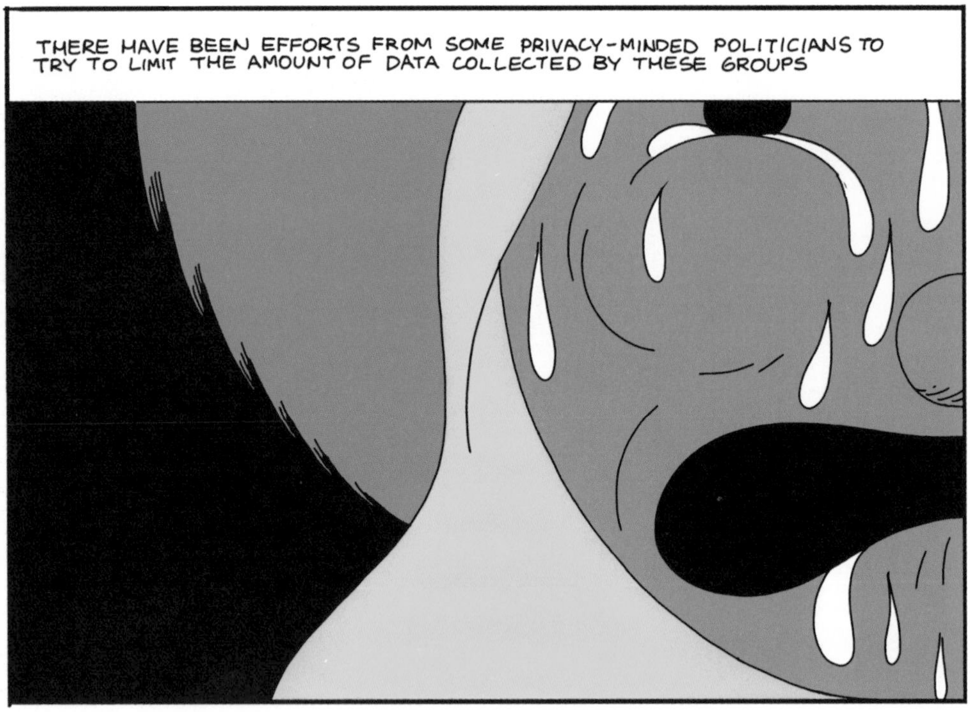
THERE HAVE BEEN EFFORTS FROM SOME PRIVACY-MINDED POLITICIANS TO TRY TO LIMIT THE AMOUNT OF DATA COLLECTED BY THESE GROUPS

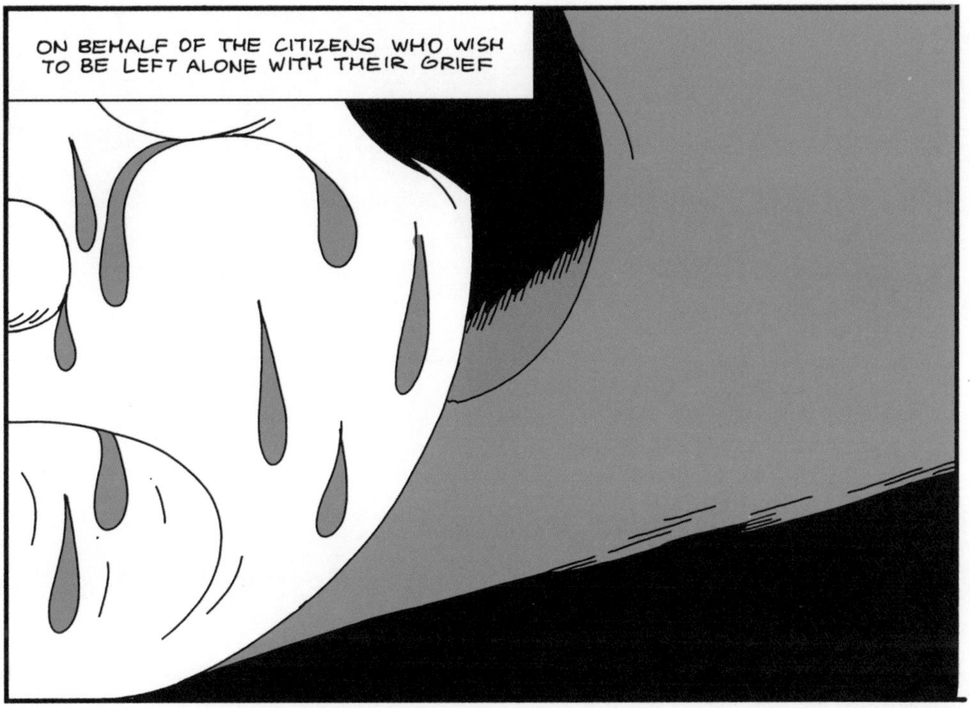
ON BEHALF OF THE CITIZENS WHO WISH TO BE LEFT ALONE WITH THEIR GRIEF

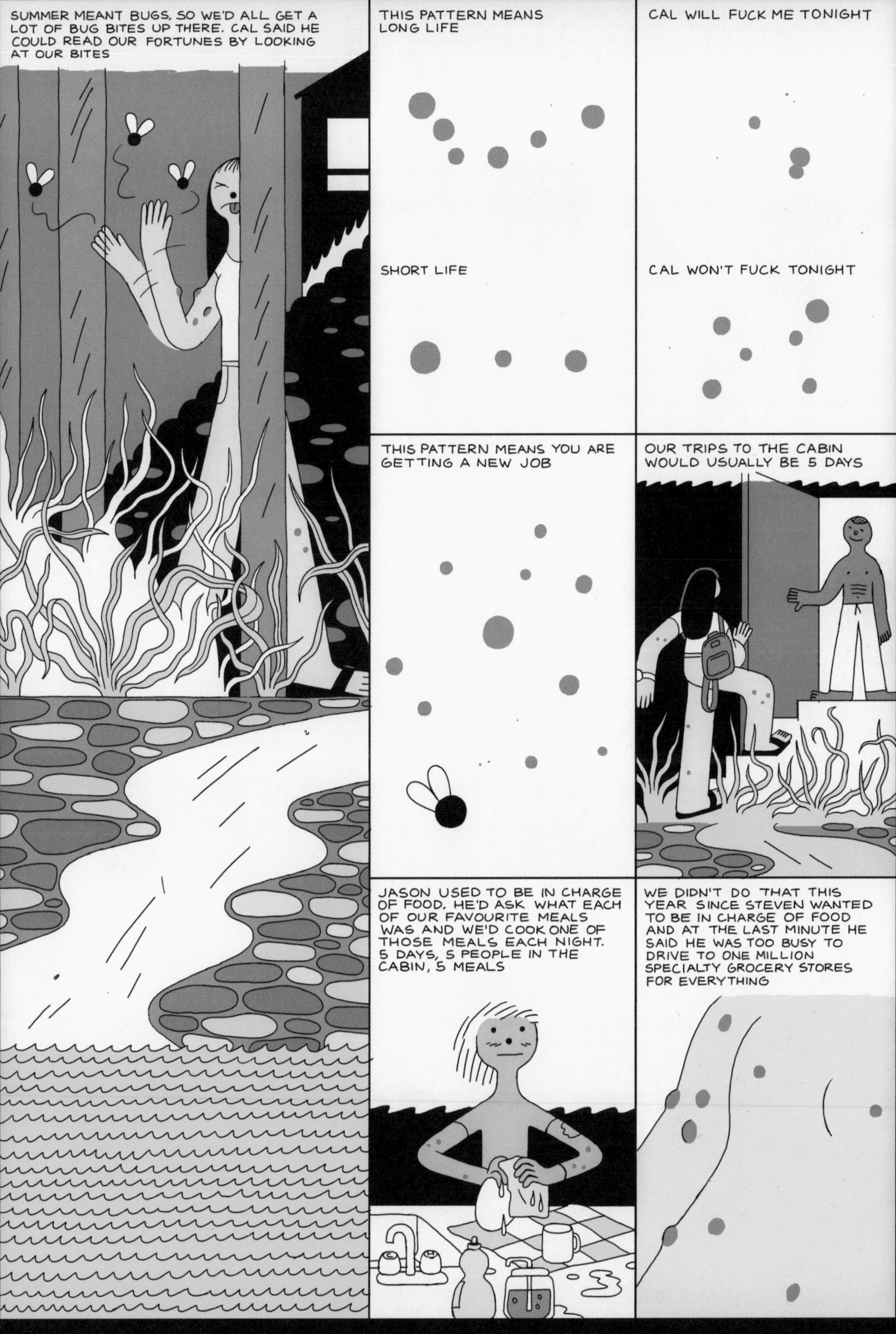
SUMMER MEANT BUGS, SO WE'D ALL GET A LOT OF BUG BITES UP THERE. CAL SAID HE COULD READ OUR FORTUNES BY LOOKING AT OUR BITES
THIS PATTERN MEANS LONG LIFE
CAL WILL FUCK ME TONIGHT
SHORT LIFE
CAL WON'T FUCK TONIGHT
THIS PATTERN MEANS YOU ARE GETTING A NEW JOB
OUR TRIPS TO THE CABIN WOULD USUALLY BE 5 DAYS
JASON USED TO BE IN CHARGE OF FOOD. HE'D ASK WHAT EACH OF OUR FAVOURITE MEALS WAS AND WE'D COOK ONE OF THOSE MEALS EACH NIGHT. 5 DAYS, 5 PEOPLE IN THE CABIN, 5 MEALS
WE DIDN'T DO THAT THIS YEAR SINCE STEVEN WANTED TO BE IN CHARGE OF FOOD AND AT THE LAST MINUTE HE SAID HE WAS TOO BUSY TO DRIVE TO ONE MILLION SPECIALTY GROCERY STORES FOR EVERYTHING

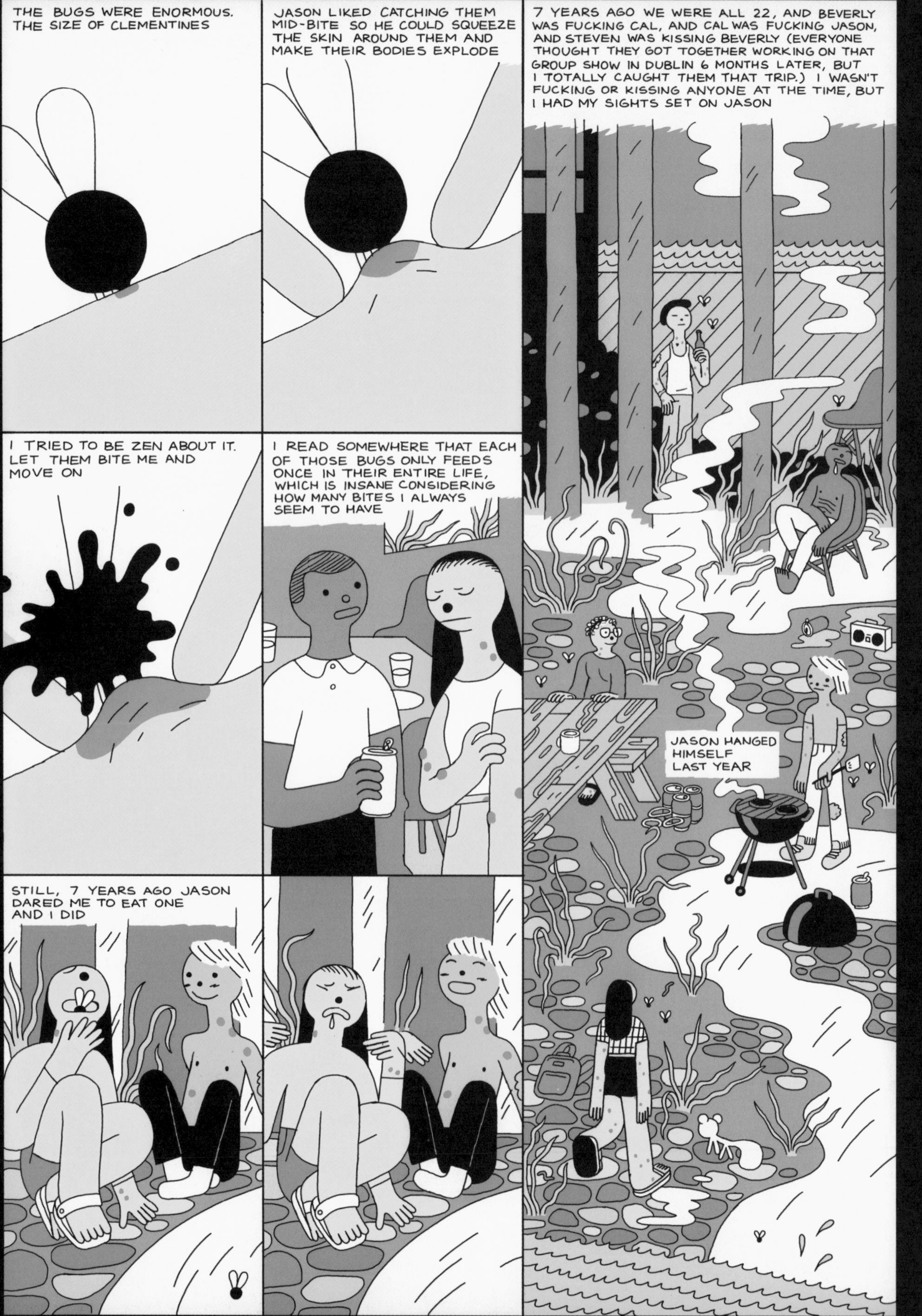
THE BUGS WERE ENORMOUS. THE SIZE OF CLEMENTINES
JASON LIKED CATCHING THEM MID-BITE SO HE COULD SQUEEZE THE SKIN AROUND THEM AND MAKE THEIR BODIES EXPLODE
I TRIED TO BE ZEN ABOUT IT. LET THEM BITE ME AND MOVE ON
I READ SOMEWHERE THAT EACH OF THOSE BUGS ONLY FEEDS ONCE IN THEIR ENTIRE LIFE, WHICH IS INSANE CONSIDERING HOW MANY BITES I ALWAYS SEEM TO HAVE
STILL, 7 YEARS AGO JASON DARED ME TO EAT ONE AND I DID
7 YEARS AGO WE WERE ALL 22, AND BEVERLY WAS FUCKING CAL, AND CAL WAS FUCKING JASON, AND STEVEN WAS KISSING BEVERLY (EVERYONE THOUGHT THEY GOT TOGETHER WORKING ON THAT GROUP SHOW IN DUBLIN 6 MONTHS LATER, BUT I TOTALLY CAUGHT THEM THAT TRIP.) I WASN'T FUCKING OR KISSING ANYONE AT THE TIME, BUT I HAD MY SIGHTS SET ON JASON
JASON HANGED HIMSELF LAST YEAR

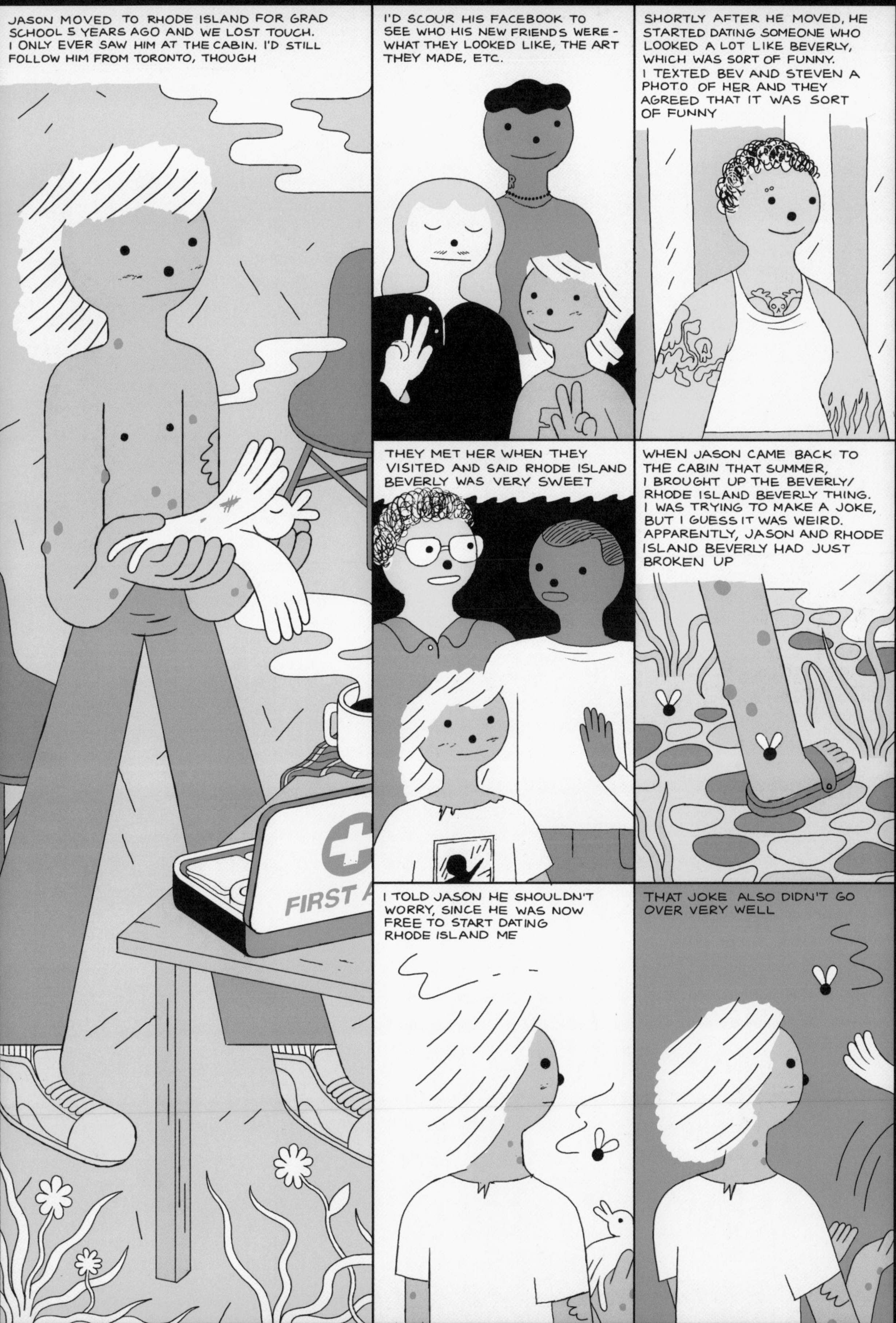
JASON MOVED TO RHODE ISLAND FOR GRAD SCHOOL 5 YEARS AGO AND WE LOST TOUCH. I ONLY EVER SAW HIM AT THE CABIN. I'D STILL FOLLOW HIM FROM TORONTO, THOUGH
FIRST A
I'D SCOUR HIS FACEBOOK TO SEE WHO HIS NEW FRIENDS WERE - WHAT THEY LOOKED LIKE, THE ART THEY MADE, ETC.
SHORTLY AFTER HE MOVED, HE STARTED DATING SOMEONE WHO LOOKED A LOT LIKE BEVERLY, WHICH WAS SORT OF FUNNY. I TEXTED BEV AND STEVEN A PHOTO OF HER AND THEY AGREED THAT IT WAS SORT OF FUNNY
THEY MET HER WHEN THEY VISITED AND SAID RHODE ISLAND BEVERLY WAS VERY SWEET
WHEN JASON CAME BACK TO THE CABIN THAT SUMMER, I BROUGHT UP THE BEVERLY/ RHODE ISLAND BEVERLY THING. I WAS TRYING TO MAKE A JOKE, BUT I GUESS IT WAS WEIRD. APPARENTLY, JASON AND RHODE ISLAND BEVERLY HAD JUST BROKEN UP
I TOLD JASON HE SHOULDN'T WORRY, SINCE HE WAS NOW FREE TO START DATING RHODE ISLAND ME
THAT JOKE ALSO DIDN'T GO OVER VERY WELL

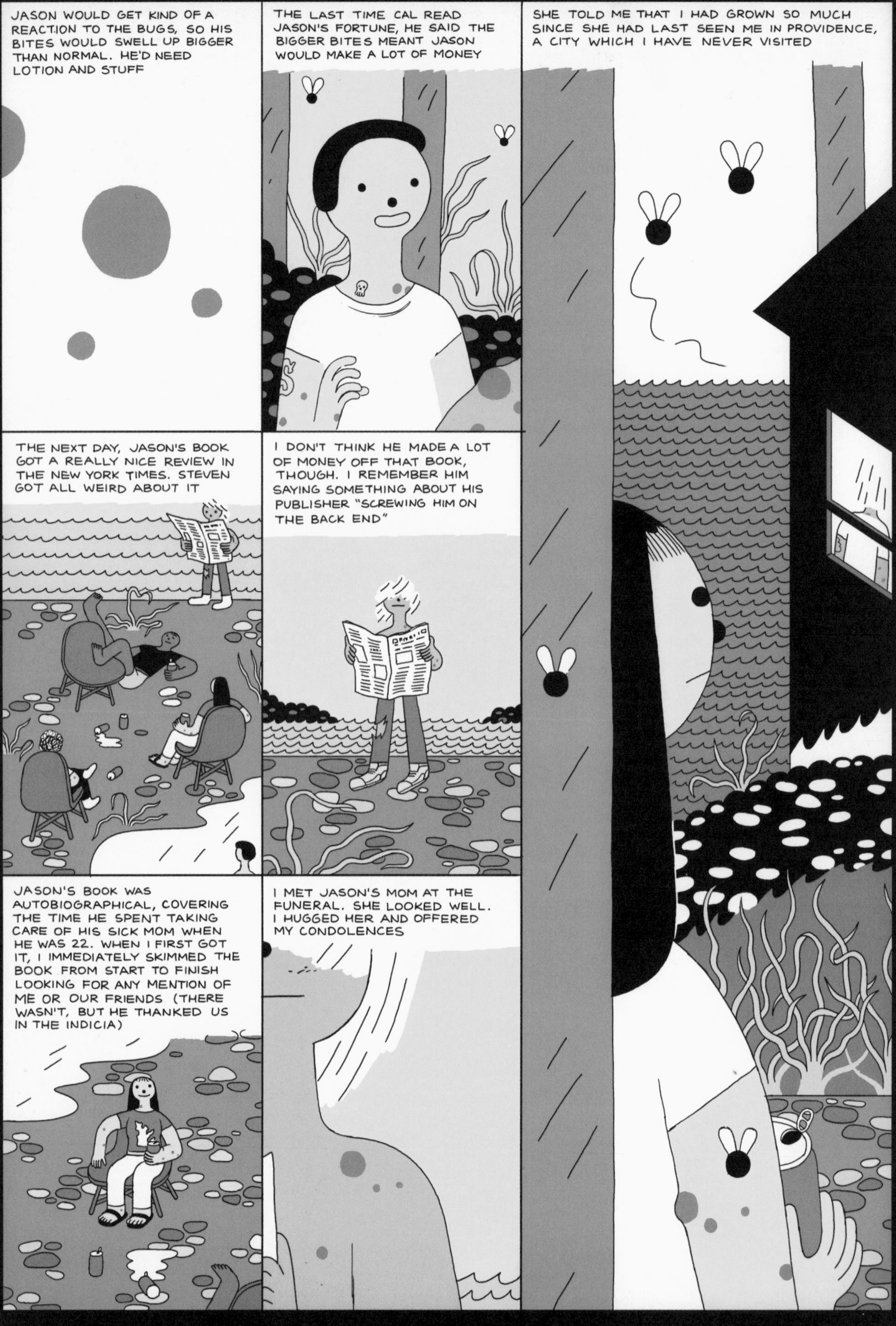
JASON WOULD GET KIND OF A REACTION TO THE BUGS, SO HIS BITES WOULD SWELL UP BIGGER THAN NORMAL. HE'D NEED LOTION AND STUFF
THE LAST TIME CAL READ JASON'S FORTUNE, HE SAID THE BIGGER BITES MEANT JASON WOULD MAKE A LOT OF MONEY
SHE TOLD ME THAT I HAD GROWN SO MUCH SINCE SHE HAD LAST SEEN ME IN PROVIDENCE, A CITY WHICH I HAVE NEVER VISITED
THE NEXT DAY, JASON'S BOOK GOT A REALLY NICE REVIEW IN THE NEW YORK TIMES. STEVEN GOT ALL WEIRD ABOUT IT
I DON'T THINK HE MADE A LOT OF MONEY OFF THAT BOOK, THOUGH. I REMEMBER HIM SAYING SOMETHING ABOUT HIS PUBLISHER "SCREWING HIM ON THE BACK END"
JASON'S BOOK WAS AUTOBIOGRAPHICAL, COVERING THE TIME HE SPENT TAKING CARE OF HIS SICK MOM WHEN HE WAS 22. WHEN I FIRST GOT IT, I IMMEDIATELY SKIMMED THE BOOK FROM START TO FINISH LOOKING FOR ANY MENTION OF ME OR OUR FRIENDS (THERE WASN'T, BUT HE THANKED US IN THE INDICIA)
I MET JASON'S MOM AT THE FUNERAL. SHE LOOKED WELL. I HUGGED HER AND OFFERED MY CONDOLENCES

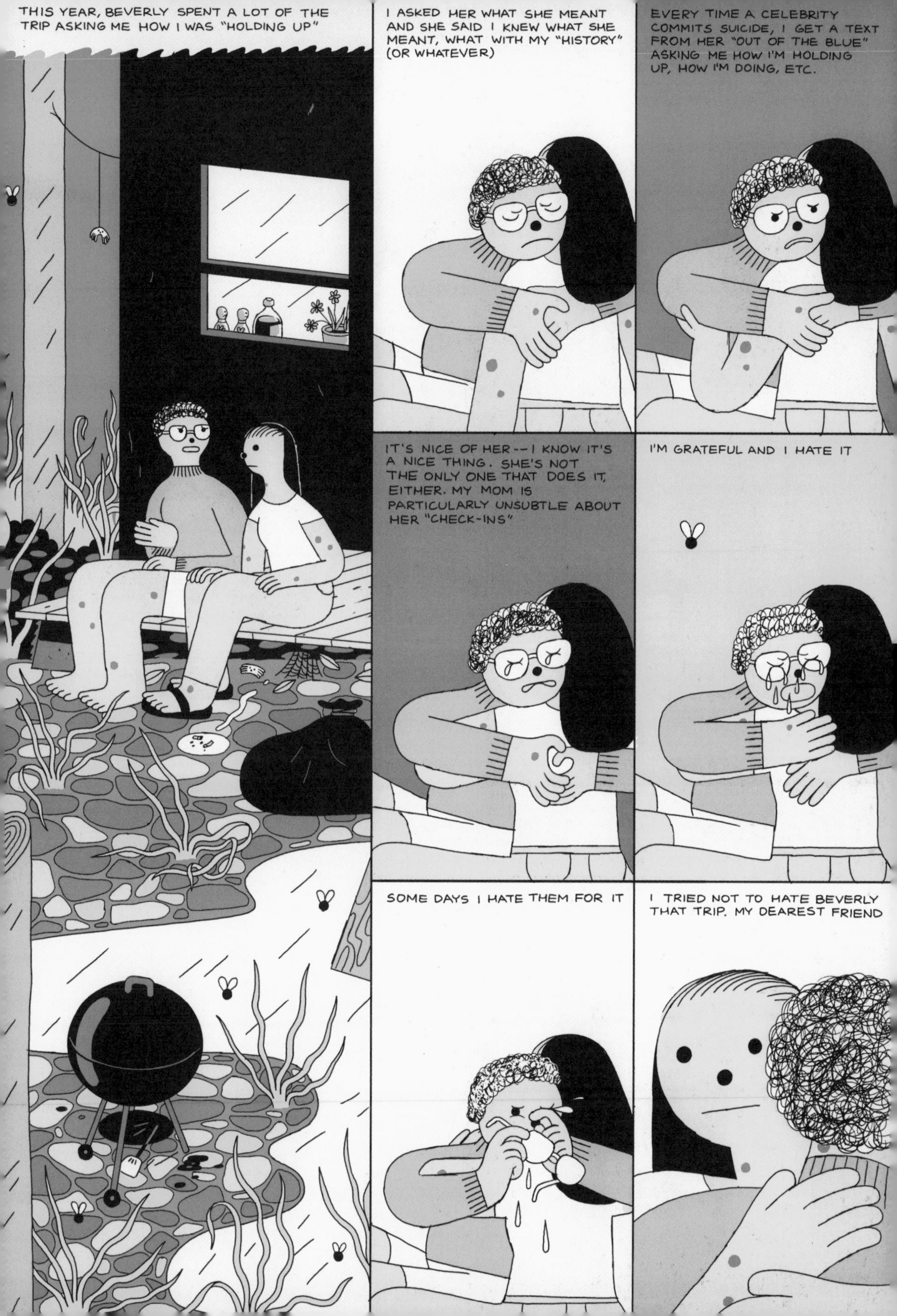
THIS YEAR, BEVERLY SPENT A LOT OF THE TRIP ASKING ME HOW I WAS "HOLDING UP"
I ASKED HER WHAT SHE MEANT AND SHE SAID I KNEW WHAT SHE MEANT, WHAT WITH MY "HISTORY" (OR WHATEVER)
EVERY TIME A CELEBRITY COMMITS SUICIDE, I GET A TEXT FROM HER "OUT OF THE BLUE" ASKING ME HOW I'M HOLDING UP, HOW I'M DOING, ETC.
IT'S NICE OF HER--I KNOW IT'S A NICE THING. SHE'S NOT THE ONLY ONE THAT DOES IT, EITHER. MY MOM IS PARTICULARLY UNSUBTLE ABOUT HER "CHECK-INS"
I'M GRATEFUL AND I HATE IT
SOME DAYS I HATE THEM FOR IT
I TRIED NOT TO HATE BEVERLY THAT TRIP. MY DEAREST FRIEND

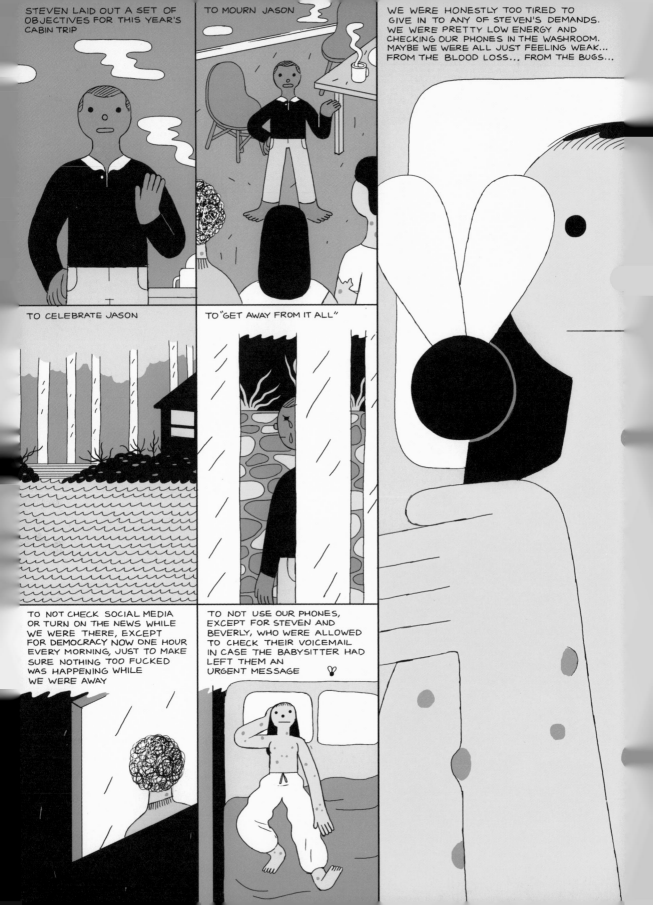

STEVEN LAID OUT A SET OF OBJECTIVES FOR THIS YEAR'S CABIN TRIP

TO MOURN JASON

WE WERE HONESTLY TOO TIRED TO GIVE IN TO ANY OF STEVEN'S DEMANDS. WE WERE PRETTY LOW ENERGY AND CHECKING OUR PHONES IN THE WASHROOM. MAYBE WE WERE ALL JUST FEELING WEAK... FROM THE BLOOD LOSS... FROM THE BUGS...

TO CELEBRATE JASON

TO "GET AWAY FROM IT ALL"

TO NOT CHECK SOCIAL MEDIA OR TURN ON THE NEWS WHILE WE WERE THERE, EXCEPT FOR DEMOCRACY NOW ONE HOUR EVERY MORNING, JUST TO MAKE SURE NOTHING TOO FUCKED WAS HAPPENING WHILE WE WERE AWAY

TO NOT USE OUR PHONES, EXCEPT FOR STEVEN AND BEVERLY, WHO WERE ALLOWED TO CHECK THEIR VOICEMAIL IN CASE THE BABYSITTER HAD LEFT THEM AN URGENT MESSAGE

ON THE PENULTIMATE NIGHT, I SAW A BUG ON MY ARM. I SQUEEZED MY SKIN AND WATCHED IT BLOW

WE ALL STARTED DOING IT. IT WAS FUN

WE PAINTED THE WALLS RED!

WEEKS LATER, WE'D FIND OUT THAT WE ACTUALLY KILLED SO MANY BUGS THAT NIGHT THAT WE SCREWED UP THE LAKE'S ECOSYSTEM FOR THE REST OF THE SUMMER

OTHER ANIMALS DIDN'T HAVE ENOUGH TO EAT WHAT WITH ALL THE MISSING BUGS FROM THE FOOD CHAIN. A LOCAL SPECIES OF FROG WENT EXTINCT

KINDA CRAZY

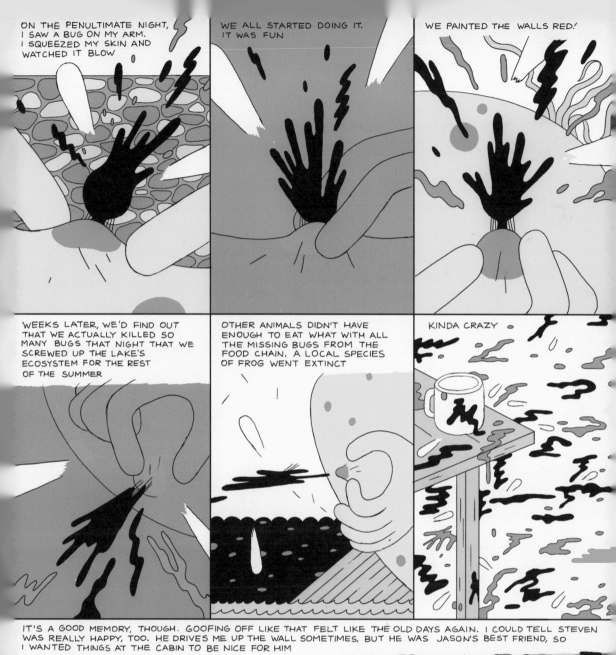

IT'S A GOOD MEMORY, THOUGH. GOOFING OFF LIKE THAT FELT LIKE THE OLD DAYS AGAIN. I COULD TELL STEVEN WAS REALLY HAPPY, TOO. HE DRIVES ME UP THE WALL SOMETIMES, BUT HE WAS JASON'S BEST FRIEND, SO I WANTED THINGS AT THE CABIN TO BE NICE FOR HIM

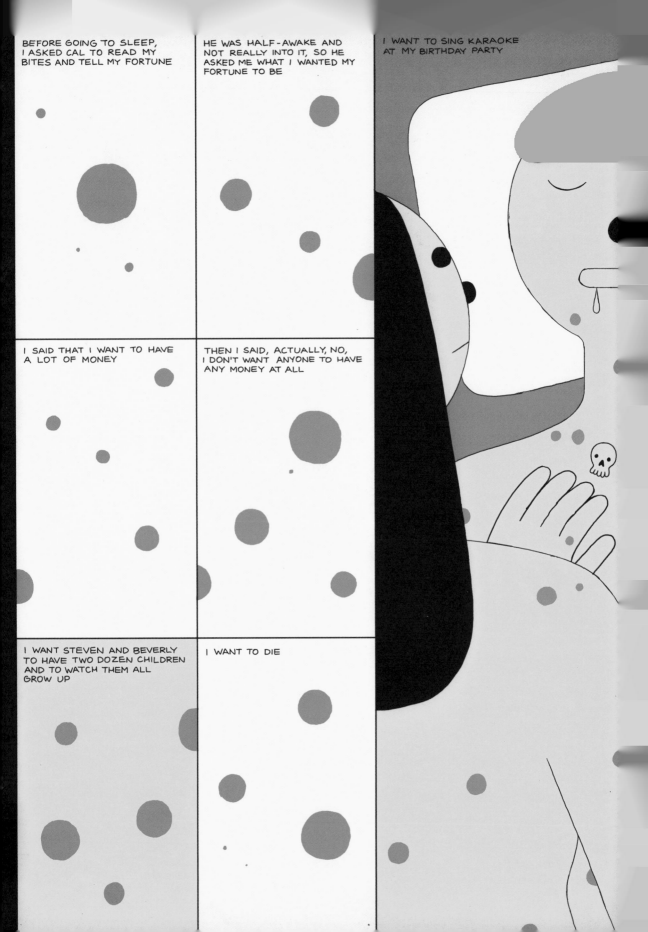

BEFORE GOING TO SLEEP,
I ASKED CAL TO READ MY
BITES AND TELL MY FORTUNE

HE WAS HALF-AWAKE AND
NOT REALLY INTO IT, SO HE
ASKED ME WHAT I WANTED MY
FORTUNE TO BE

I WANT TO SING KARAOKE
AT MY BIRTHDAY PARTY

I SAID THAT I WANT TO HAVE
A LOT OF MONEY

THEN I SAID, ACTUALLY, NO,
I DON'T WANT ANYONE TO HAVE
ANY MONEY AT ALL

I WANT STEVEN AND BEVERLY
TO HAVE TWO DOZEN CHILDREN
AND TO WATCH THEM ALL
GROW UP

I WANT TO DIE

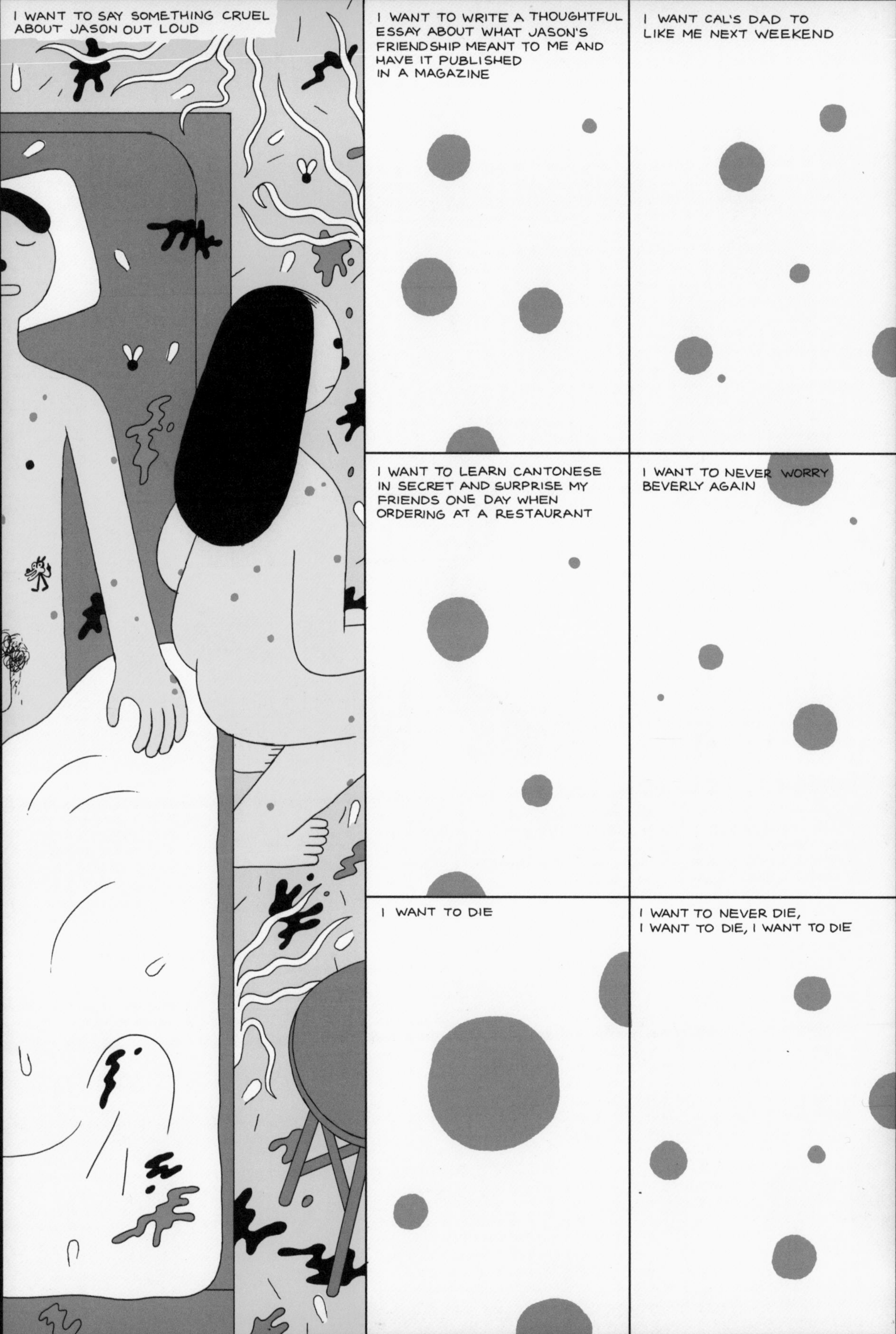
I WANT TO SAY SOMETHING CRUEL ABOUT JASON OUT LOUD
I WANT TO WRITE A THOUGHTFUL ESSAY ABOUT WHAT JASON'S FRIENDSHIP MEANT TO ME AND HAVE IT PUBLISHED IN A MAGAZINE
I WANT CAL'S DAD TO LIKE ME NEXT WEEKEND
I WANT TO LEARN CANTONESE IN SECRET AND SURPRISE MY FRIENDS ONE DAY WHEN ORDERING AT A RESTAURANT
I WANT TO NEVER WORRY BEVERLY AGAIN
I WANT TO DIE
I WANT TO NEVER DIE, I WANT TO DIE, I WANT TO DIE

THANK YOU ANNE, RYAN, PATRICK, JILLIAN, GINETTE, SADIE, ROBIN, MICKEY, HANNAH, S.T., THE BEGUILING AND MY FAMILY

SEVERAL OF THESE STORIES WERE ORIGINALLY PRINTED IN ISSUES OF *LOSE* AND *ON TOPICS*, PUBLISHED BY KOYAMA PRESS AND BREAKDOWN PRESS RESPECTIVELY. "COMPUTER" WAS ORIGINALLY PRINTED IN *KRAMERS ERGOT* #9 AND "MOSTLY SATURN" IN *ISLAND* #10.